# Regional Economic Performance within the European Union

# Regional Economic Performance within the European Union

Kenneth Button

*Professor of Public Policy, George Mason University, USA*

Eric Pentecost

*Reader in Economics, Loughborough University, UK*

Edward Elgar

Cheltenham, UK • Northampton, MA, USA

Published by
Edward Elgar Publishing Limited
Glensanda House
Montpellier Parade
Cheltenham
Glos GL50 1UA
UK

Edward Elgar Publishing, Inc.
136 West Street
Suite 202
Northampton
Massachusetts 01060
USA

A catalogue record for this book
is available from the British Library

**Library of Congress Cataloguing in Publication Data**

Regional economic performance within the European Union / edited by
Kenneth Button and Eric Pentecost .
Includes index.
1. European Union countries—Economic conditions—Regional disparities. 2. European Union countries—Economic policy. 3. Regional planning—European Union countries. 4. European Union countries—Economic integration. 5. Convergence (Economics) — European Union countries. I. Button, Kenneth. II. Pentecost, Eric.
HC240.R339 1999
338.94—dc21 99–21831
CIP

ISBN 1 85898 064 X

Printed and bound in Great Britain by Bookcraft (Bath) Ltd.

# Contents

# List of Figures

# List of Tables

# Preface

This book is concerned with examining whether the economic performance of the geographical regions of the European Union are converging or diverging. This question is not trivial given the gradual enlargement of the Union that is taking place and the deepening of the institutional structures within it. In particular, as there is a move towards major currency reforms within the EU, such as the introduction of the Single Currency, so issues of appropriate regional economic policies become more important to assist those areas losing the potential stimulus that currency variations can afford.

The work also appears at a time when there have been a number of important advances in both the theory of economic development and the ways in which it may be explored empirically. Economic growth theory has undergone important changes in recent years and techniques such as mean reversion procedures have enriched the econometricians 'tool kit. The book explores the importance of modern growth theory in explaining the relative performance of different regions. It also offers a number of empirical studies of overall regional economic development and of individual sectors. Some specific policy instruments are also examined.

The work has benefited for a variety of financial assistance over the years as its component parts have been brought together, notably a grant from the Economic and Social Research Council. It has also been considerably improved as the result of the comments of numerous people as various versions of the constituent chapters have been presented at different conferences and workshops around the world. We are particularly grateful to Lynne Evans, Scott Leitham, Ron McQuaid and Pet Reitveld who have been involved in co-authoring work that forms the basis for various fragments of this book.

KENNETH BUTTON
ERIC PENTECOST

# 1. Introduction

## 1.1 BACKGROUND

While the post-Second World period has seen economies in western Europe grown on average at between 2 and 2.5 per cent a year the growth has neither been steady[1] nor evenly spread. The study of trade cycles and temporal variations in economic growth has traditionally been a major interest of economists. The spatial distribution of economic performance has also been an important pre-occupation. It manifested itself initially in the study of international trade, and with issues involving the economic needs Third World countries, but concern with issues at a more meso level soon followed.[2] The growth of interest in federalism was one motivating factor in this but concern about social and political cohesion within nations was a more general driving force.

While there has been considerable interest amongst urban researchers into reasons why some cities' economies perform better than others, much of this interest has been at the intra-national level and has involved looking at the disparities that exist in regional income, migration and employment. The reasons for this can in part be expressed in terms of political self-interest on the part of central governments to ensure that no large element of their constituents diverge excessively from the national norm. In these cases a government may be willing to accept a slower national economic growth rate for a more equal distribution of income and welfare.

Concern with the spatial distribution of growth may also be related to matters of environmental externalities. Region's often specialise in particular types of production and some of these can be environmentally damaging. Maximising the output of the latter (e.g. the extractive industries) may lead to higher levels of GDP, but equally, if the full

1 For example the growth of western European economies averaged about 5 per cent throughout the 1950s and 1960s but fell to around 22.5 per cent in the 1970s. In the 1980s they grew a little faster but between 1991 and 1996 economic growth fell to 1.5 per cent a year. The last few years of the millennium has seen growth recover to nearer 2.5 per cent.

2 The term meso-economics is sometimes used to describe economic analysis of industrial sectors (somewhere between industrial and macro-economics). Here it is used with reference to regional and urban economics.

environmental costs were internalised, may not maximise the overall welfare of the country.

Interest in regional economic performance can also often reflect a view that divergent economic performance may be wasteful of national resources in a narrower sense. Regions with high levels of under- or unused labour are, in this scenario, seen not to be fully contributing to a nation realising its full economic potential. There are also concerns in a world of national wage agreements that an excessive focus on economic expansion in a small number of regions can, in some instances, fuel inflationary tendencies in the economy as a whole.

It is against this often conflicting background of equity and efficiency considerations that regional policies have to be formulated. In the past European states have been concerned with their own domestic regional disparities and with their individual rates of economic growth. The creation of larger economic units, and in particular, the emergence of the European Union (EU) has changed this focus to a considerable extent. European states can no longer pursue entirely separate regional policies but must for practical reasons take cognisance of what other Members are doing on account of regional externalities, as well as conforming to EU-wide regional policy initiatives.

## 1.2 ECONOMIC CONVERGENCE

Governments have always attempted in various ways to influence the spatial distribution of economic activities. Regional policies seldom have a single objective but represent a compromise across a range of different objectives. As suggested above, in terms of growth and equity there may be conflict between objectives, although equally in some cases objectives may be complementary. Here our concern is with one particular aspect of regional policy, that concerned with regional economic convergence.

Economic convergence is a topic that has long been discussed in the political science, human geography and economic literature but normally only in very broad terms. There was a particular interest in the topic in the 1950s and 1960s in the context of Third World development and the late 1990s has seen a strong resurgence of work in the field, mainly to do with the industrialised countries and with sub-national regions.

From a political perspective, if the growth rates of regions deviate significantly this, it is feared, can generate instabilities. Those in the poorer regions feel resentment at the prosperity of others. From an economic perspective, divergent growth not only has implications for the relative affluence of different groups, but may also reflect an overall pattern of development which is not efficient because some areas are not as productive as they could be. Equally, however, differential growth may be seen, in a more dynamic sense, to offer important demonstration effects and, as such, to provide a stimulus for regions where economic performance is initially lagging behind.

The topic of economic convergence is also one with a long intellectual pedigree. Traditional trade theory and the notion of comparative advantage implicitly assumes that trade will allow greater prosperity for all but says little about the relative scale of the benefits. Neo-classical economics essentially ignored the issue arguing that perfect factor mobility, ubiquitous information and fully competitive markets would lead to convergence.

The Keynesian Revolution brought with it fresh ideas regarding regional development and, in particular, the notion that the effects of cumulative and circular causation would produce divergent regional growth patterns. More recently the ideas of economies of scale that underlay the circular causation arguments have given way to the New Growth Theories that again focus on potentially divergent growth but explain it largely in terms of information concentrations.

Linked to these new theories of economic growth is a fresh analysis of the usefulness of some of the instruments of regional economic policy. While there are a number of issues, one of the key areas of recent interest has been the role of infrastructure in the economic growth process. In the past, Keynesian macroeconomists have favoured infrastructure projects as an important component of public works programs – the economic stimulation coming from the injection of resources into the economic system and from the resultant set of multiplier impacts. More recently, the interest has switched to examining the ways in which public infrastructure can of itself assist in the development of regional economies. It is, in this case, treated more as an input to the production function than as a component of demand-management.

## 1.3 THE EUROPEAN UNION DIMENSION[3]

The late twentieth century is often seen as being characterised by globalisation and internationalism, but within this general framework has been the emergence of macro-regionalism. In the past there have been integrated economic units exhibiting varying degrees of economic cohesion but in the main these have been in the form of empires. The new macro-regionalism has brought together groups of, usually, contiguous independent states that perceive a mutual benefit in co-ordination of some of

3 The term European Union (or EU) is used throughout this book as short hand for the various phases of European economic integration (e.g. European Economic Community or European Community) while recognising that it is strictly a relatively recent innovation. In practice, there is also a widely used short-hand whereby the European Union is used for the political grouping and the Economic Community for the legal body.

the economic and political activities. The EU is one, relatively mature, manifestation of this but one can also point to the North American Free Trade Agreement (NAFTA) and other looser structures.

The European economic integration process, that seriously got under way with the creation of the European Coal and Steel Community in the early 1950s, has always implicitly embraced objectives involving economic convergence as well as European economic expansion.

The enhanced level of integration that now exists within Europe as the EU has both broadened and deepened its powers, as well as embracing a larger geographical area, has brought with it new challenges. While the embracing of the Single European Market concept in the early 1990s represented a major challenge in this process, the prospect of a Single European Currency (the euro) and the possibility of enlargement of the EU to include some of the former communist states of central and eastern Europe are inevitably going to pose even more difficult problems for policy makers.

The EU now embraces a much more diverse range of economic regions together with a more divergent set of national governments with varying aspirations. The economic disparities between many of the regions is considerable and the challenges facing policy makers are large.[4] On the other hand the EU institutions are beginning to mature. The statistics upon which policy decisions often rest are now more comprehensive, consistent and up-to-date than previously. The legal framework in which the EU institutions operate is now more experienced and a substantial case history of important guidelines has been developed.

EU regional policy is also not new and there are now a growing number of cases representing both successes and failures that can potentially guide future policy initiatives. To-date, however, analysis has been rather limited.

Coupled with this, the research community within Europe has become better integrated and communications channels are now more comprehensive, all of which improve our understanding of how regional economies function and how various policy instruments impact on objectives. New thinking on regional economics has also emerged from outside of the EU and its relevance for future Union policies has not been ignored.

Nevertheless, despite these very important advances, our understanding of the forces that have shaped the existing pattern of regional economic development in Europe is far from complete and our appreciation of exactly how every policy tool functions is still inadequate. One aim of this book is

4 As an example, and to slightly pre-empt later chapters, the gross domestic product (measured in terms of purchasing power standards) of the southern periphery of the EU, from Greece through Southern Italy to southern and western Spain and Portugal, is typically half to two-thirds the Union's average.

to look in detail at some of the areas where uncertainty and controversy remains.

## 1.4 THE STRUCTURE OF THE BOOK

Since the book is not intended as a comprehensive compendium of information on EU regional policy, nor to provide a detailed history of its evolution.[5] its structure is designed to reflect its focus on some of the more analytical issues thrown up by regional policy developments in the European Union. Again the coverage makes no claim to be comprehensive and many analytical matters are not dealt with or, if so, only in a cursory way.

Initially, in Chapter 2, the book, provides details of the main economic characteristics of the regions of the Union and this is followed in Chapter 3 by an account of the development of EU policies with a bearing on regional development. This discussion not only embraces the direct regional initiatives of the Union, such as the European Regional Development Fund, but also covers other measures with important regional implications, such as the Common Agricultural Policy.

The fourth chapter provides an overview of the alternative theories of regional economic growth. The aim here is both to provide background to the policy debates which have taken place in the EU and to set out the framework of the rather more technical modelling and estimation found later in the book within its broader analytical context. A particular focus is placed on the new growth theories of people such as Lucas and Romer that put emphasis on potential spatial divergences in economic development.

The main analytical findings are set out in a number of chapters. Chapter 5 is concerned with the broader analysis of the real economic convergence which has occurred across the EU regions. In particular he quantitative analysis deploy techniques developed by Barro, Sala-i-Martin and others to explore why some slower regions within EU countries are catching up with the pace setters, while others are not. Chapter 6 particularly examines the convergence that is taking place in the UK economy as a whole and makes use of pooled data methods.

Chapter 7 is concerned with convergence in labour markets. It looks in particular at the labour markets in Germany and the UK. It also offers a case study examination of spatial developments in the UK service sector using time-varying parameter techniques. The importance of service sector activities is growing and policies are continually being sought to explore ways of using this as an instrument in regional policy formulation.

5 This has been well explored several times before (for instance, see Armstrong, 1978; 1992).

More detailed analysis is presented on the impact of infrastructure investment, and in particular transport networks, on regional economic growth in Chapter 8. This follows in particular from debates in the late 1980s stimulated by Aschauer and others, about the role government should play in providing social overhead capital as a means of attaining faster economic growth.

The final chapter, although entitled 'Conclusions', really offers some concluding thoughts on the issues the EU will be confronted with in the future and their implications for regional economic policy.

# 2. The Regions of the European Union

## 2.1 INTRODUCTION

The European Union is not a static entity. The spatial composition of the European Union has changed considerably since its early days in the late 1950s. The six original members of the European Economic Community (EEC) (France, West Germany, Italy, The Netherlands, Belgium and Luxembourg) that signed the Treaty of Rome in 1957 were joined in 1973 by the UK, Ireland and Denmark, in 1981 by Greece, in 1986 by Spain and Portugal and by Finland, Austria and Sweden in 1995. The Union also incrementally lost Greenland, which exercised its right to remain linked to Denmark but to withdraw from the Union, but gained the former German Democratic Republic when German reunification occurred in 1989.

Within Member States important economic changes also take place at the meso and micro levels as regions and industries fluctuate in their economic performance. Important institutional changes also take place as regions are given more or less autonomy in the management of their own affairs – the recent moves towards Scottish devolution being but one example of this.

Not surprisingly, given its diversity of membership, the European Union is not a homogeneous economic space. Physically, it represents a large geographical area embracing a wide diversity of natural resources, distinctive terrain and ethnic groupings. There are numerous languages spoken and its inhabitants come from a broad range of cultural backgrounds. There are differences in regional and in political preferences.

Not withstanding this, the long historical development of its composite national states has resulted in planning regions with quite distinct political and economic features. Indeed, one of the main challenges of formulating EU policy has always been to seek out common features and to find compromises amongst the diversities which remain. The result is that not only are there very wide disparities in the regional economies of the EU but in many cases these disparities have been long-lived. Many regions which have traditionally been prosperous tend to remain so while numerous others which have suffered from poor economic growth rates remain relatively poor. The objective of this chapter is to provide a description of some of the key distinguishing features associated with the regions within the EU.

## 2.2 ECONOMIC DIVERSITY

Issues of regional convergence centre around the question of diversity. As societies or economies converge so there is less divergence. A major problem is that of defining exactly what is meant by divergence and how the key parameters may be quantified to see if diversity is expanding or shrinking. Even if positive indicators are found, however, the issue still remains concerning normative judgements on the desirability of convergence or, more weakly, on the optimum degree of convergence.

While there is usually an intuitive understanding of its meaning, exactly what is meant by economic diversity is seldom made explicit at the institutional level. In terms of the European Union there was, for example, a tendency in the 1960s for policy makers when seeking quantifiable parameters to think in terms of industrial, semi-industrial and agricultural regions and in the 1970s to treat diversity in terms of per capita income levels, unemployment rates and the extent of out-migration from an area.[1] As the institutions of the Union have evolved and as membership has expanded so rather more types of delineation have come to the fore as policies have developed.

The need for a more refined set of criteria has become important as the objectives of policy have changed. The initial emphasis of the Union was on economic development in a narrow sense with a particular emphasis on improving agricultural efficiency and developing markets for industrial products. Greater concern with issues of political integration has led to diversity being seen more directly in terms of the economic flexibility of regions to respond to changing economic conditions. Additional factors, especially with regard to the environment, have led to diversity being reviewed in the context of levels of pollution and contamination.

At the regional economic level there has been a move away from broad numerical parameters to thinking of diversity in terms of economic composition, e.g. degradation in urban areas or regions with declining industrial bases. In some instances the aim has been to be proactive in the sense of looking at divergent growth paths rather than taking a snapshot of the situation at a moment in time.

There are now also efforts to create a wider index of 'quality of life' that takes into account factors such as life expectancy, pollution and congestion as well as the more conventional economic indicators such as GDP and sparcity of population (Commission of the European Communities, 1998).[2] These wider indicators are not the focus of the analysis deployed here.

1 For more details see Despicht and Flockton (1970).

2 These types of indicators are intended to form part of a European System of integrated economic and environmental Indices (ESI).

Defining diversity at the operational level is, therefore, important from the perspective of formulating and implementing regional policy. Whether divergence exercises a positive or negative effect is much less certain. Cultural diversity is often seen as important for sociological reasons and certainly without it many industries, and in particular tourism, would not succeed. In economic terms diversity in performance can be seen as a stimulus for enhanced effort as well as providing a hedge against the risk of excessive concentration on one sector or region. Running counter to this, diversity can mean dispersions in welfare that are considered unacceptable.

## 2.3 SPATIAL VARIATIONS

The EU has expanded its membership over time and now it is comprised of fifteen essentially industrialised economies (see Figure 2.1). Each state, however, has its own regional geography and legacy. Table 2.1 offers some basic geographical information.

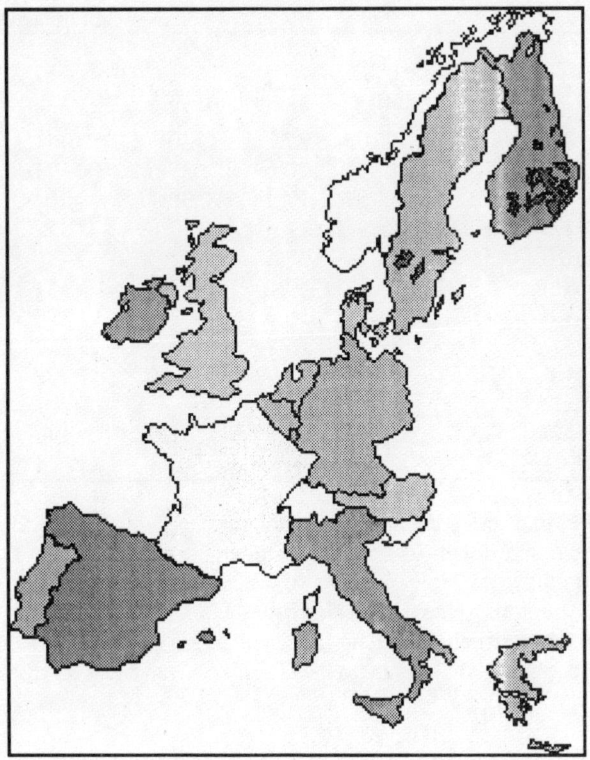

Figure 2.1 *The countries of the European Union*

France, for instance, is a large, relatively sparsely populated nation but with a considerable concentration of inhabitants in one area around Paris, with other parts, notably the agricultural regions of the west and south-west, underpopulated.[3] The UK is largely an island economy isolated by sea from the Continent while Greece is physically separated from the rest of the EU Members by intervening non-member nations. Germany was divided for an extended period after the Second World War and has been going through a process of political, social and economic reunification. Italy has for a long period been a dual economy with important divisions in terms of economic structure and economic performance between the north and the south (the Mezzogiorno). Belgium has distinct cultural differences between the Walloon and Flemish regions of the country.

Table 2.1. *EU Member surface areas and population densities*

| Country | Area km$^2$ | Population '000 | Densely (%) | Intermediate (%) | Thinly (%) | Population density inhab/km$^2$ |
|---|---|---|---|---|---|---|
| Belgium | 30.5 | 10.1 | 53.6 | 42.7 | 3.7 | 331 |
| Germany | 356.7 | 80.6 | 49.3 | 32.3 | 18.4 | 226 |
| Denmark | 43.1 | 5.2 | 32.6 | 27.2 | 40.3 | 121 |
| Spain | 505.8 | 38.7 | 49.9 | 20.6 | 29.6 | 77 |
| France | 544.0 | 56.3 | 43.6 | 17.3 | 39.1 | 104 |
| Greece | 131.6 | 10.2 | 65.9 | 11.5 | 22.6 | 78 |
| Italy | 301.0 | 56.4 | 45.4 | 37.5 | 17.0 | 187 |
| Ireland | 68.9 | 3.5 | 37.7 | 0.0 | 62.3 | 51 |
| Netherlands | 41.0 | 15.2 | 59.8 | 36.5 | 3.7 | 370 |
| Portugal | 91.9 | 9.8 | 53.4 | 26.8 | 19.8 | 107 |
| UK | 241.8 | 57.5 | 60.6 | 28.0 | 11.4 | 238 |
| EU (11) | 2,355.6 | 343.7 | 50.5 | 28.0 | 21.5 | 146 |

Much of the time series economic and social data available for the EU are still at the national level. For regional statistical purposes, the EU is divided into a number of Nomenclature of Territorial Units of Statistics (NUTS). Level 1 regions, which are effectively the regions employed by the Member States for normal, domestic data collection and policy-making purposes, are, in turn subdivided in to NUTS level 2 and level 3 regions.

3 About 19 per cent of the population of France live on 2 per cent of the land in the Paris area.

Most complete EU data series relate to the highest level of aggregation (NUTS 1 and 2) although some useful series are available at NUTS level 3.

In narrower economic terms, the degree of industrialisation and levels of specialisation differ considerably between and within the Member States. Although there are various ways in which one can measure the nature and performance of economies, it is clear from the indicators in Tables 2.2 and 2.3 that regional and national economic diversity has been extensive across a wide range of alternative indicators.[4]

Table 2.2. *Unemployment in EU Member States, 1987–97*

| Member State | 1987 | 1989 | 1991 | 1993 | 1995 | 1997 |
|---|---|---|---|---|---|---|
| Spain | 20.8 | 17.4 | 16.0 | 22.3 | 23.1 | 21.1 |
| Finland | 5.2 | 3.8 | 7.0 | 17.9 | 16.9 | 14.8 |
| Italy | 10.2 | 10.0 | 8.7 | 10.3 | 11.9 | 12.3 |
| France | 10.3 | 9.3 | 9.0 | 11.2 | 11.3 | 12.0 |
| Sweden | 2.5 | 1.9 | 2.7 | 8.6 | 8.7 | 10,4 |
| Ireland | 18.1 | 14.9 | 14.6 | 15.7 | 12.2 | 10.1 |
| Denmark | 6.3 | 5.7 | 5.3 | 7.6 | 8.2 | 9.8 |
| Greece | 7.4 | 6.7 | 6.9 | 8.6 | 9.1 | 9.6 |
| Belgium | 11.0 | 7.2 | 6.1 | 8.1 | 9.4 | 8.9 |
| UK | 11.0 | 7.4 | 8.6 | 10.5 | 8.7 | 7.1 |
| Portugal | 7.0 | 4.8 | 3.6 | 5.3 | 7.3 | 6.7 |
| Denmark | 5.8 | 7.6 | 8.5 | 10.9 | 7.4 | 5.7 |
| Netherlands | 9.9 | 8.5 | 5.7 | 6.3 | 7.0 | 5.2 |
| Austria | – | – | 3.8 | 4.0 | 3.9 | 4.4 |
| Luxembourg | 2.5 | 1.7 | 1.5 | 2.3 | 2.8 | 2.5 |

In more detail, one sees that in terms of differences between the rich and the poor countries, Germany's real gross domestic product is 14 per cent above the EU average whereas Portugal and Spain are some 46 per cent below the average. In terms of the diversity between the regions in a country, Italy has a GDP per capita range of 70 compared to Greece which has a range of just 10. With respect to unemployment, the UK has the largest range between regions of high and low unemployment.

The peripheral regions of the EU are generally considered, because of their distance from the core growth areas, as in need of particular economic support (Table 2.4). They also joined the Union some time after its inception and, therefore, missed the early dynamic phase of industrial

4 International comparisons also reflect wider diversities than in federal systems such as the US (Organisation for Economic Cooperation and Development, 1989) and Australia (Armstrong and King, 1994).

growth. These regions, however, are not homogeneous and their individual economic performances have also varied quite considerably over time.

Table 2.3. *Regional economic variations across the EU (NUTS 1 level of aggregation)*

| Country | GDP per capita (EU=100) (Average 1986–8) | | | Unemployed (%) 1990 | | | Participation rate (%) 1988 | | |
|---|---|---|---|---|---|---|---|---|---|
| | Nat. average | Reg. max | Reg. min | Nat. average | Reg. max. | Reg. min. | Nat. average | Reg. max. | Reg. min. |
| Belgium | 100.7 | 154.2 | 83.4 | 7.6 | 10.8 | 5.5 | 39.7 | 40.7 | 37.0 |
| Denmark | 112.5 | 132.6 | 94.7 | 7.9 | 9.1 | 6.8 | 65.3 | – | – |
| Germany | 113.6 | 182.7 | 97.8 | 5.2 | 10.4 | 3.0 | 47.8 | 51.7 | 42.1 |
| Greece | 54.8 | 58.5 | 48.5 | 7.5 | 9.7 | 4.2 | 40.7 | 43.6 | 37.6 |
| Spain | 73.6 | 86.6 | 58.5 | 16.1 | 24.1 | 12.4 | 37.8 | 39,9 | 35.3 |
| France | 109.3 | 165.6 | 87.8 | 8.7 | 11.8 | 6.4 | 44.6 | 49.9 | 39.5 |
| Irelands | 64.5 | – | – | 16.4 | – | – | 38.0 | – | – |
| Italy | 103.5 | 137.3 | 66.9 | 10.2 | 21.7 | 3.4 | 41.9 | 46.3 | 37.4 |
| Luxembourg | 121.7 | – | – | 1.5 | – | – | 42.5 | – | – |
| Netherlands | 104.2 | 123.6 | 86.6 | 8.0 | 9.4 | 7.5 | 45.4 | 46.7 | 42.0 |
| Portugal | 52.6 | 59.7 | 41.9 | 5.1 | 12.4 | 2.8 | 46.3 | 47.4 | 38.0 |
| UK | 106.5 | 128.3 | 80.6 | 3.3 | 15.7 | 3.9 | 50.2 | 52.3 | 43.1 |

*Source*: Commission of the European Communities (1991)

Table 2.4. *Average annual growth rates of EU's peripheral economies*

| | GDP per annum (average %) | | | | | | GDP per capita (EU12=100) |
|---|---|---|---|---|---|---|---|
| | 1957–72 | 1973–79 | 1979–85 | 1982–85 | 1986–95 | 1973–95 | 1995 |
| Spain | 6.9 | 1.4 | 0.5 | 1.8 | 2.9 | 2.6 | 76 |
| Greece | 7.4 | 3.3 | 1.7 | 1.6 | 1.4 | 2.3 | 48 |
| Portugal | 6.8 | 4.1 | 1.2 | 0.9 | 3.2 | 2.7 | 58 |
| Ireland | 4.5 | 2.8 | 2.7 | 2.4 | 8.0 | 4.3 | 86 |

Ireland, in particular, has enjoyed quite steady economic growth since the 1950s whereas Greece has tended, after economic expansion up until the mid-1980s, to grow rather more slowly. Spain has experienced a rather erratic economic growth path with periods of severe recession followed by quite dramatic growth as it has restructured in the post-Franco era. Of the more recent members, both Sweden and Finland have enjoyed steady economic growth in the post-war period although their short-term economic performances suffered in the mid-1990s and restructuring took place.[5]

Further, at the sectoral level, there are quite major variations in the significance of agricultural and primary production sectors across Members (Table 2.5).[6] There are very considerable differences between the economic performance of regional economies in Europe irrespective of the unit of analysis adopted. Indeed, the variations between national incomes and other national economic indicators often exceeds those between regions within individual Members States.

Table 2.5. *Employment (per cent) by sector in the EU, 1990*

| Country | Agriculture | Industry | Services |
|---|---|---|---|
| Belgium | 2.7 | 30.5 | 66.8 |
| Denmark | 5.7 | 27.6 | 66.7 |
| France | 6.0 | 30.0 | 63.9 |
| Germany | 4.2 | 40.3 | 55.5 |
| Greece | 22.2 | 25.7 | 52.1 |
| Ireland | 14.0 | 29.0 | 57.0 |
| Italy | 8.5 | 32.2 | 59.3 |
| Luxembourg | 3.5 | 28.9 | 67.6 |
| Netherlands | 4.4 | 25.6 | 70.1 |
| Portugal | 17.4 | 34.0 | 48.6 |
| Spain | 10.9 | 33.0 | 56.1 |
| UK | 2.3 | 31.2 | 66.5 |

*Source*: Statistical Office of the European Communities

There are, of course, many reasons why historically such differences have arisen. The more important issue for current policy, as we argue later, is the degree to which the economic performance of regions is converging or diverging. Without a clear indication of this it is both difficult to successfully conduct *ex ante* studies of the effectiveness of policy portfolios in the past or to design improved strategies for the future.

Even within each of these broad production categories, however, there are major differences in the nature of the goods produced and the efficiency with which they are produced. Overall, agriculture is of considerable

5 In particular the sparsely populated northern regions of these countries have suffered as the traditional collective bargaining structure has virtually collapsed as industrial restructuring has been carried through. The situation since 1997 has improved somewhat.

6 Leonardi (1993) contains useful case studies of various regional issues in the EU.

importance in Greece, Portugal, Ireland and Spain (all have in excess of 10 per cent of their employment in that sector) compared to Belgium and the UK where it represents less than 3 per cent of total employment. The UK, Netherlands, Belgium and Denmark have their employment dominated by service sector activities, while Germany, despite having a very large service sector, retains a significant amount of manufacturing employment.

There are also important variations in levels of productivity and in productivity growth between the Member States. In recent years the EU has achieved economic growth largely by raising output per worker rather than through extra employment. Between 1985 and 1995 of the 2.3 per cent annual growth in real GDP, about 80 per cent of this can be attributed to higher productivity[7]. Productivity does differ, however, between regions of the Union.

In terms of industrial production, countries such as Germany, France and the Benelux states are considerably more productive than are most of the peripheral members.[8] Belgium and Germany, for example, are the most productive countries in the world in terms of labour hours worked. Equally, in term of agricultural production, countries such as the UK and Netherlands are extremely cost effective.

While there is often an understandable tendency in the literature when reviewing regional differences in Europe to focus on problem areas, such as regions with declining heavy or extractive industries, there are also important growth sectors. In recent years, for example, the service sector has grown significantly in all EU states and, while not reaching the 70 per cent of gross domestic product it accounts for in the US, is still the largest

7 In aggregate terms, employment in the EU increased from 135.5 million in 1985 to 142.5 million in 1995 – an increase of 7 million jobs. The job creation in the Union, however, compares poorly with that in the US where 65 per cent of its growth in GDP over the same period was attributable to increased employment.

8 There are also important cross effects between the population density and the industrial composition of the regions of the EU. The table below indicates the more even spread of manufacturing and construction across the EU – EU (12 minus Luxembourg) – regions whereas agriculture and mining tend to be concentrated in the thinly populated areas.

| Sector | % of employed persons Population density classes | | |
|---|---|---|---|
| | Dense | Intermediate | Thin |
| Agriculture and Mining | 1.7 | 5.9 | 15.1 |
| Manufacturing and Construction | 26.6 | 32.6 | 29.8 |
| Electricity and Transport | 7.7 | 6.2 | 5.8 |
| Finance and Real Estate | 13.2 | 9.1 | 5.8 |
| Non-market services | 24.8 | 22.0 | 20.9 |
| Trade, Hotels, Restaurants and other Services | 26.0 | 24.2 | 22.6 |

single sector in all Members. In 1995 services accounted for 66.1 per cent of EU employment. Between 1985 and 1995, for example, an additional 11.9 million jobs were created in market services and another 1.4 million in non-market services. The main concentrations of services industries are around the northern capital cities but include the Côte d''Azur.

This is not entirely a new situation and, indeed, by the early 1980s, Keeble *et al.* (1981), reported that, 'service industries are by far the most important source of regional growth within the Community'. Even so, within the EU there are significant variations between Member States and regions as to the importance of the service sector in their economies. In terms of growth, the indications are that during the 1980s, Portugal, Ireland, Luxembourg and Italy experienced the highest relative growth rates whilst the UK, Belgium and Spain recorded relatively low rates.

The economic diversity that exists among the various member countries of the EU is, however, small when compared to that between the economic regions within it. Table 2.6 provides details of unemployment rates and the per capita gross domestic product (relative to the EU average) at the level 1 regions of the Union (see also again Table 2.2).[9]

The scale of the regional economic disparities are immediately apparent.[10] Even within a country such as the Netherlands which has a high proportion of mobile and flexible service sector employment, there are significant differences in regional unemployment rates.[11] Equally, there are wide variations in the gross domestic product per capita between the countries different regions. In other countries such as Italy, which is characterised by the dual nature of its economy (which extends beyond the simple north/south division to embrace agricultural/industrial divisions and geographical divisions in the productivity of both agriculture and industry – Graziani, 1978), the differences are even more pronounced.[12]

9 Unemployment also tends to vary with population density. It tends to be higher in the more densely populated regions (e.g. 11.9% in the dense regions and 9.0% in the regions that have intermediate levels of population density – Commission of the European Communities, 1998). The pattern extends to long-term employment whether measured in terms of per cent of the unemployed or of the total labour force. There are also strong links between the number of young people in a region and the local unemployment rate with people under 25 being nearly 2.5 times more likely to be out of work than older workers. (Germany is an exception to this because of its apprenticeship system.)

10 The ten worst-affected regions of the EU regarding unemployment in 1995 had an average rate of 27.7 per cent which was nearly eight times the rate for the ten least-affected regions.

11 Overall, the EU Commission has estimated that about 50 per cent of unemployment in the Union in 1997 is structural unemployment.

12 The situation has improved slightly from that in the late 1960s when over the entire Mezzogiorno per capita income was less than two-thirds of the

Table 2.6. *Unemployment rates and gross domestic product (relative to the EU average)*

| Country | Region | Unemployment (%) | | | Gross Domestic Product | | |
|---|---|---|---|---|---|---|---|
| | | 1975 | 1981 | 1990 | 1975 | 1981 | 1990 |
| Belgium | *Vlaams Gewest* | 5.3 | 10.7 | 5.3 | 107 | 105 | 106 |
| | *Bruxelloise* | 5.3 | 10.7 | 9.3 | 167 | 170 | 166 |
| | *Wallonne* | 6.5 | 12.8 | 10.3 | 93 | 87 | 85 |
| Denmark | *Denmark* | 7.0 | 10.1 | 8.0 | 119 | 110 | 107 |
| France | *Ile de France* | 4.3 | 5.7 | 7.2 | 195 | 156 | 166 |
| | *Paris Basin* | 3.9 | 7.1 | 9.1 | 104 | 105 | 102 |
| | *Pas-de-Calais* | 5.0 | 8.9 | 11.8 | 99 | 97 | 91 |
| | *Est* | 2.7 | 5.6 | 6.6 | 103 | 108 | 105 |
| | *Quest* | 4.2 | 6.4 | 9.1 | 78 | 92 | 94 |
| | *Sud-Ouest* | 4.9 | 7.4 | 9.1 | 80 | 93 | 95 |
| | *Centre-Est* | 4.3 | 6.2 | 7.7 | 111 | 106 | 106 |
| | *Mediterranee* | 6.0 | 8.5 | 11.3 | 85 | 97 | 96 |
| Germany | *Baden-Wurtt* | 2.0 | 2.2 | 2.7 | 122 | 119 | 124 |
| | *Bayern* | 2.7 | 2.3 | 3.1 | 109 | 109 | 120 |
| | *Berlin (West)* | 4.1 | 4.7 | | 135 | 131 | |
| | *Bremen* | 3.6 | 4.1 | 9.8 | 152 | 149 | 148 |
| | *Hamburg* | 3.0 | 2.6 | 7.5 | 182 | 193 | 184 |
| | *Hessen* | 1.8 | 2.3 | 3.9 | 120 | 125 | 136 |
| | *Niedersachsen* | 3.2 | 3.8 | 6.4 | 101 | 99 | 101 |
| | *Nordrhein-Pf* | 3.4 | 3.0 | 6.4 | 118 | 112 | 112 |
| | *Rheinland-Pf* | 3.2 | 3.2 | 4.2 | 104 | 102 | 104 |
| | *Saarland* | 3.5 | 5.1 | 7.0 | 107 | 105 | 109 |
| | *Schleswig-Hst* | 4.0 | 2.9 | 5.9 | 99 | 99 | 99 |
| Greece | *Voreia* | | 2.9 | 6.9 | | 50 | 46 |
| | *Kentriki* | | 4.1 | 6.0 | | 60 | 45 |
| | *Attiki* | | | 8.8 | | | 50 |
| | *Nisia* | | | 3.4 | | | 45 |
| Ireland | *Ireland* | 9.2 | 10.5 | 14.2 | 61 | 64 | 68 |
| Italy | *Nord-Ovest* | 3.3 | 4.5 | 6.4 | 94 | 110 | 119 |
| | *Lombardia* | 2.0 | 2.9 | 3.3 | 97 | 117 | 135 |
| | *Nord-Est* | 2.2 | 3.4 | 4.0 | 78 | 95 | 118 |
| | *Emilia-Romag* | 2.4 | 4.1 | 4.1 | 88 | 113 | 127 |
| | *Centro* | 3.5 | 4.6 | 7.1 | 72 | 96 | 107 |
| | *Lazio* | 7.8 | 7.2 | 10.6 | 75 | 91 | 115 |
| | *Campania* | 6.4 | 10.6 | 19.2 | 49 | 61 | 70 |
| | *Abruzzi-Moli* | 5.7 | 6.7 | 10.3 | 53 | 70 | 87 |
| | *Sud* | 7.6 | 8.2 | 17.1 | 49 | 60 | 69 |
| | *Sicilia* | 7.2 | 7.6 | 21.0 | 52 | 61 | 66 |
| | *Sardegna* | 8.6 | 11.4 | 18.4 | 55 | 64 | 74 |
| Luxembourg | *Luxembourg* | 1.1 | 3.0 | 1.6 | 116 | 115 | 124 |
| Netherlands | *Noord-Ne'land* | 4.1 | 6.5 | 10.2 | 111 | 142 | 102 |
| | *Oost-Ne'land* | 3.4 | 5.2 | 7.5 | 92 | 87 | 85 |
| | *West-Ne'land* | 2.5 | 4.3 | 7.0 | 117 | 111 | 110 |
| | *Zuid-Ne'land* | 4.6 | 7.2 | 6.8 | 98 | 89 | 95 |
| United Kingdom | *North* | 6.2 | 10.8 | 10.1 | 86 | 89 | 87 |
| | *Yorks & Humb* | 4.2 | 7.9 | 8.0 | 87 | 84 | 92 |
| | *East Midlands* | 3.8 | 6.9 | 5.9 | 90 | 87 | 97 |
| | *East Anglia* | 4.5 | 6.5 | 4.2 | 80 | 86 | 102 |
| | *South East* | 3.8 | 5.3 | 4.7 | 105 | 107 | 121 |
| | *South West* | 4.0 | 5.3 | 4.9 | 85 | 87 | 96 |
| | *West Midlands* | 4.5 | 11.0 | 6.9 | 90 | 81 | 92 |
| | *North West* | 5.4 | 10.0 | 9.1 | 92 | 89 | 91 |
| | *Wales* | 4.8 | 10.4 | 7.6 | 82 | 85 | 84 |
| | *Scotland* | 6.5 | 10.3 | 10.1 | 92 | 93 | 93 |
| | *N. Ireland* | 8.5 | 13.6 | 17.1 | 77 | 72 | 74 |

national average and in three provinces – Basilicata, Molise and Calabria – it was respectively 57 per cent, 54 per cent and 49 per cent of the national average.

Variation in the regional mix of economic activity also extends well beyond the range exhibited by the national economies of the EU. Taking agricultural employment in 1988 as an illustration, the percentage employed in the sector ranged from 45.9 per cent in the Kentriki Ellada region of Greece down to 0.2 per cent in the Brussels Gewest region of Belgium and to 0.3 per cent in the Bremen region of Germany. These structural differences make it particularly difficult to develop a common regional policy because of the divergent needs of the various geographical areas involved.

There is an increasing mobility of population within Europe. The different countries of Europe, however, exhibit variations in terms of population density within an overall pattern of urbanisation (Table 2.7). Much of the move to cities has involved development of suburban areas rather than a growth in the cores. The pattern is long-established in northern European countries but is newer in the southern Member states. This trend within countries poses a variety of issues concerning congestion and environmental protection as well as being important in terms of labour markets *per se*. At a more macro level there has been a general drift Southwards of population within Europe, in part a reflection of the wider international trend towards sun-belt living. This is a pattern that exists both within many EU countries[13] and between countries.

Table 2.7. *Distribution of annual population change by land area, 1980–90 (data at the NUTS3 regional level)*

| Country | <–1.0% | –1<–>0% | 0<–>0.5% | 0.5<–>1.5% | >1.5% |
|---|---|---|---|---|---|
| Germany | 0.0 | 9.8 | 38.9 | 50.9 | 0.4 |
| Greece | 1.4 | 16.6 | 40.5 | 41.5 | 0.0 |
| Netherlands | 1.9 | 16.6 | 40.5 | 41.5 | 0.0 |
| UK | 0.0 | 15.6 | 35.7 | 48.7 | 0.0 |

While data at the regional level are not available, the Commission has also highlighted, in its *Fifth Periodic Report on the Social and Economic Situation in the Regions*, important spatial differences in research and technology development. At the national level, countries such as the UK (4.6 per cent), France (5.1), Germany (3.8), Ireland (5.0) and Denmark (5.9) have large numbers of research workers and engineers compared to Greece (1.4 per cent), Portugal (1.1) and Spain (2.2). Similar differences exist in

13 For example, to the South-West and East Anglia in the UK, to the Alrgave in Portugal and to the Mezzogiorno in Italy. This trend has also been accompanied by a population shift to coastal areas.

terms of total expenditure on research and technological development. This is felt to be relevant for the longer-term development of the more backward regions which, within Member States, are thought to be even more under represented in this context.[14]

The regions of the EU are also part of the much larger global market and, as such, their economic performance is affected by wider market shifts. In particular, the productive underpinnings of a regional economy can be influenced not simply by factor mobility within the Union but also by inflows from outside.[15] Foreign direct investment can play an important role in job creation, for instance, and may generate important sectoral multiplier effects.[16] Direct investment has grown significantly in the EU but at a rate considerably below the USA. The amount of foreign direct investment flowing into regions varies and much of the data are at the national level. It is also not always important for a depressed region that the investment is physically within its boundaries if there are significant positive spillover effects from adjacent areas where the resources have been placed.

The aggregate amount of foreign direct investment coming into EU Members in 1986–95 was ECU 227 billion with the majority of it coming into France and the UK.[17] (In comparison, although there are problems in the data making direct assessments difficult, the US received about ECU 470 billion over the same period and Japan about ECU 5.2 billion.). The peripheral states of the EU, that have some of the most severe regional problems received considerably less (Table 2.8). The overall implications of this for regional convergence as a whole across the EU is, therefore, rather uncertain.

## 2.4 SOME BASIC EVIDENCE ON ECONOMIC CONVERGENCE AT THE EU REGIONAL LEVEL

We now turn to examine, in a very preliminary way, the extent to which economic convergence has occurred across the regions of the European Union over the past two decades and to discuss the extent to which this has been influenced by market forces and the degree to which policy initiatives,

14 It is particularly important if the New Growth Theories discussed later in the book have validity.

15 Measuring flows in foreign direct investment poses a variety of statistical problems, see Commission of the European Communities (1994).

16 Although there is the longer-term problem that investment in branch plants may not create significant longer-term value added effects or add to the labour skill base.

17 Over the same period the outflow from the EU was about ECU 280 billion, 56 per cent of which went to the US.

such as the adoption of the European Monetary System (EMS) and the Exchange Rate Mechanism (ERM) have been important. A much more rigorous econometric analysis follows in subsequent chapters.

Table 2.8. *Shares of foreign direct investment flows from non-members going to EU states (%)*

| Country | 1986–95 | 1986–90 | 1991–95 |
|---|---|---|---|
| Belgium/ Luxembourg | 6.83 | 5.15 | 8.27 |
| Denmark | 2.25 | 1.86 | 2.28 |
| Germany | 6.50 | 3.79 | 7.21 |
| Spain | 8.01 | 8.95 | 7.21 |
| France | 14.71 | 10.32 | 18.45 |
| Greece | 0.38 | 0.51 | 0.28 |
| Ireland | 1.77 | 1.80 | 1.76 |
| Italy | 5.35 | 7.38 | 3.63 |
| Netherlands | 8.74 | 7.98 | 9.41 |
| Austria | 0.68 | 0.58 | 0.77 |
| Portugal | 1.27 | 1.26 | 1.27 |
| Finland | 0.84 | 1.21 | 0.52 |
| Sweden | 6.68 | 2.97 | 9.84 |
| United Kingdom | 35.98 | 46,28 | 27.23 |

*Note*: From 1984 to 1991 the data refer to the EU (12) and from 1992 to 1996 to the EU (15). For all countries, except Austria, the figures relate to the sum of equity and other capital (excluding reinvested earnings). For Austria the data relate to equity capital and for France from 1994 include short term credits. Data for Ireland and Greece are estimates or based on partner country declarations.

Initially we briefly explain the statistical measurement techniques adopted and set them in the context of some other empirical studies looking at different aspects of convergence in the EU.

In practice, economic convergence can be viewed in a number of different ways. In economic terms there are two aspects of convergence: nominal convergence (such as Hall *et al.*, 1992) and real convergence (such as Durlauf and Johnson, 1992; Ardeni 1992). The former, in the Union context, is generally seen to concern such things as convergence in exchange rates, interest rates and inflation rates.

The Maastricht Treaty of 1992 set out specific, quantitative convergence criteria for these nominal variables, that we now know have been satisfied by the majority of EU Member States. It is convergence in the real economy which is of interest here and this ties in with issues like that of wealth creation, unemployment and productivity growth. We now turn, therefore, to examine the extent to which convergence in real economic terms has occurred across the regions of the European Union over the past two decades, and to discuss the extent to which this has been influenced by market forces and the degree to which policy initiatives, such as the adoption of the European Monetary System, have been important.

The EU Commission has been engaged in a number of exercises seeking to discover if spatial economic convergence has been taking place. In particular, the Commission of the European Communities (1991) found by examining base data that there was a trend towards the reduction of inequality among the 12 members that could be traced back to the mid-1960s but that this had been reversed in the mid-1970s although further marginal reductions in inequalities were found from 1986 to 1990.[18]

There are in practice a variety of simple technical methods available for examining convergence include using such indicators as changes in the coefficient of variation of the dispersion of regional performance over time or intertemporal variations in Theil's 'U-statistic'.[19] The analysis favoured in this study employs coefficients of variation and similar measures although there are also a number of more rigorous techniques available.[20]

18 Cardoso (1993) amongst others has offered a critique of this analysis pointing in particular to the inadequate treatment of migration factors. In particular, it is argued that due to out migration the convergent periods observed by the Commission simply reflected a movement down a decreasing marginal product of labour curve. Allowance for this indicates that convergence between 1984 and 1988 was considerably less than the Commission's estimates. This was also a view taken by Cuadrado Roura and Suárez-Villa (1992) who maintained that, 'Over half of this [convergence] trend can be explained by the national economic performances, which drove regional growth, and the remainder by out migration from the poorer regions towards the more advanced ones within the EEC and, in some cases, within nations.'

19 Molle (1990b) calculated Theil indices of gross regional product per head for the period from 1950 to 1985 (see table below). This reveals that regional disparities decreased up to the late 1970s (the a/b ratio falls) but increased after the oil crises of the 1970s to be followed by a further convergence. The calculations set out are in terms of exchange rate parities, using purchasing power parities thatsomewhat reduce the effect but the overall pattern remains the same. Similar techniques have also be employed by Emerson *et al.* (1992) when assessing the spatial implications of a single European currency.

| | 1950 | 1960 | 1970 | 1980 | 1985 |
|---|---|---|---|---|---|
| (a) Disparities among regions | 0.124 | 0.102 | 0.078 | 0.098 | 0.071 |
| (b) Disparities among countries | 0.095 | 0.081 | 0.061 | 0.082 | 0.056 |
| (a/b) | 0.76 | 0.79 | 0.79 | 0.84 | 0.79 |

20 See Barro and Sala-i-Martin (1992b) for a general discussion of alternative econometric techniques. Button and Pentecost (1993b) provide an illustration of

While these techniques have a number of statistical limitations, they are good at pin-pointing general trends and are relatively straightforward to interpret.

The available data make it possible to carry out rather more complete assessments using these basic measures at only a relatively high level of spatial aggregation. Table 2.9, for example, provides coefficients of variation for regional household GDP (at level 1 regional aggregation) within the European Union for the period 1977 to 1990 and the ratios of top to bottom deciles.

Table 2.9. *Coefficients of variation and ratios of top to bottom deciles of regional GDP at level 1 aggregation*†

| | 1977 | 1978 | 1979 | 1980 | 1981 | 1982 | 1983 | 1984 | 1985 | 1986 | 1987 | 1988 | 1989 | 1990* |
|---|---|---|---|---|---|---|---|---|---|---|---|---|---|---|
| Coefficients of variation | | | | | | | | | | | | | | |
| $V_9$ | 0.23 | 0.23 | 0.23 | 0.24 | 0.25 | 0.24 | 0.24 | 0.24 | 0.24 | 0.24 | 0.23 | 0.23 | 0.23 | 0.23 |
| $V_{10}$ | | | | | 0.26 | 0.25 | 0.25 | 0.25 | 0.26 | 0.25 | 0.24 | 0.24 | 0.24 | 0.24 |
| $V_{12}$ | | | | | | | | | | 0.30 | 0.30 | 0.30 | 0.29 | 0.25 |
| Ratios of top to bottom deciles | | | | | | | | | | | | | | |
| $D_9$ | 1.84 | 1.83 | 1.82 | 0.86 | 1.91 | 1.88 | 1.84 | 1.86 | 1.88 | 1.85 | 1.81 | 1.83 | 1.83 | 1.84 |
| $D_{10}$ | | | | | 2.00 | 1.96 | 1.93 | 1.95 | 1.97 | 1.93 | 1.90 | 1.91 | 1.91 | 1.84 |
| $D_{12}$ | | | | | | | | | | 2.60 | 2.57 | 2.57 | 2.54 | 2.06 |

*Notes*:
The subscript 9 indicates data relating to the regions of France, Germany, Italy, Luxembourg, Belgium, Netherlands, Eire, UK, Denmark; 10 includes Greece and 12 includes Spain and Portugal.
† Based upon NUTS level 1 data.
* Data for Greek regions not available.
*Source*: Base data taken from Eurostat, *REGIO Regional Data Base*, Luxembourg, EC, 1991.

Table 2.10 offers some indication (coefficients of variation) of trends in economic performance for the more disaggregate level 2 regions although the lack of full data series for a substantial number of Member States make these calculations less satisfying. The calculations are done separately for the set of Members in 1977 (covering 1977 to 1990), for the ten Members after Greece joined (for the period 1981 to 1990) and for the full twelve Members from 1986.

a more rigorous approach to EU regional convergence, employing mean reversion methods, and reassuringly it yields very similar results to the basic statistical methods.

The changing coefficients seen in these tables, both in terms of the coefficients of variation and the decile ratios, provide general guidelines. For example, they can be seen as relating to the implications for regional income disparities of successive enlargements as these have brought more peripheral regions into the Union (Keeble *et al.*, 1988). The picture is one of long-term convergence for the original members of the Union with some short-term fluctuations (for example at the time of the oil crises in the mid-1970s and early 1980s).

Table 2.10. *Coefficients of variation (level 2 regions)* †

| | 1977 | 1978 | 1979 | 1980 | 1981 | 1982 | 1983 | 1984 | 1985 | 1986 | 1987 | 1988 | 1989 | 1990* |
|---|---|---|---|---|---|---|---|---|---|---|---|---|---|---|
| $V_9$ | 0.20 | 0.20 | 0.18 | 0.19 | 0.21 | 0.23 | 0.20 | 0.20 | 0.25 | 0.19 | 0.17 | 0.17 | 0.17 | 0.17 |
| $V_{10}$ | | | | | 0.23 | 0.26 | 0.24 | 0.2 | 0.28 | 0.23 | 0.20 | 0.20 | 0.20 | 0.17 |
| $V_{12}$ | | | | | | | | | | 0.30 | 0.29 | 0.30 | 0.29 | 0.29 |

*Notes*:
* Data for Greek regions not available
† Data limitations mean that there are missing observations from some years

The addition of new, peripheral regions adds to the overall degree of dispersion in performance but does not impact on the converging pattern seen for the original states.[21] Further, the economic performance of the regions of each new Members' own economic performance improves through time after their joining – the coefficient of variation declines for both the Ten and Twelve over time. The picture is much the same irrespective of the level of spatial aggregation and is found when employing the alternative decile ratio measure, although the trend is less pronounced.

Table 2.11 shows the coefficients of variation for regional GDP per capita across the larger countries individually from 1975.[22] This demonstrates that the dispersion in income per head is very different across the EU members and has changed somewhat over the sample period. For example, although in 1975 the Netherlands had the lowest dispersion of real income per head in the EU, by 1988 not only has income become more dispersed than in 1975, but also France, the United Kingdom and Italy have a lower level of dispersion. Spain clearly demonstrates substantial regional income convergence, although, given its initial high level of regional

21 This is reflected in the coefficient of variation being higher for the Ten after Greece's accession in 1981 than for the Nine and, again, after it rises with the admission of Portugal and Spain.

22 Cardoso (1993) provides a similar type of analysis but over a much shorter time period which tends to hide some of the longer–term trends.

income differentiation, it still had the greatest dispersion of income per capita within in the Union in 1988.

Table 2.11. *Convergence/divergence in regional gross domestic product by EU country, 1975–90 (selected years)*

| | | 1975 | 1977 | 1979 | 1981 | 1983 | 1986 | 1988 | 1990 | Mean |
|---|---|---|---|---|---|---|---|---|---|---|
| Belgium | (3) | 0.10 | 0.13 | 0.14 | 0.13 | 0.13 | 0.14 | 0.13 | 0.16 | 0.13 |
| Netherlands | (4) | 0.01 | 0.01 | 0.06 | 0.03 | 0.04 | 0.10 | 0.07 | 0.08 | 0.05 |
| France | (8) | 0.05 | 0.07 | 0.05 | 0.03 | 0.11 | 0.08 | 0.03 | 0.01 | 0.06 |
| West Germany | (11) | 0.16 | 0.12 | 0.03 | 0.06 | 0.11 | 0.08 | 0.14 | 0.09 | 0.11 |
| Italy | (11) | 0.11 | 0.08 | 0.06 | 0.03 | 0.11 | 0.07 | 0.05 | 0.02 | 0.05 |
| UK | (11) | 0.04 | 0.13 | 0.02 | 0.03 | 0.01 | 0.04 | 0.04 | 0.02 | 0.04 |
| Spain | (8) | – | – | – | – | 0.42 | 0.15 | 0.21 | 0.21 | 0.26 |

*Note* Figures in parentheses denote the number of regions used to compute the coefficient of variation.

In contrast to the income per head tables, Table 2.12 shows the dispersion of unemployment rates across the EU over the sample period and at the level 1 degree of aggregation. The pattern for the nine countries which were Members in 1975 seems to show increasing dispersion of unemployment rates over the period from 1983, giving rise to a much greater dispersion in unemployment rates in 1989 than in 1975 and 1977 partly due to the oil price shocks of the mid-1970s.

Table 2.12. *Coefficients of variation for unemployment rates, 1975–89 (selected years)*

| | 1975 | 1977 | 1979 | 1981 | 1983 | 1985 | 1987 | 1989 |
|---|---|---|---|---|---|---|---|---|
| $V_9$ | 0.33 | 0.33 | 0.10 | 0.17 | 0.26 | 0.35 | 0.47 | 0.68 |
| $V_{10}$ | – | – | – | – | 0.80 | 0.59 | 0.65 | 0.51 |
| $V_{12}$ | – | – | – | – | – | – | 0.64 | 0.64 |

*Notes:* as for Table 2.8

The inclusion of Spain and Portugal in the sample, from 1987, has the effect of actually reducing the coefficients of variation in years 1987 and 1989. This is largely because the dispersion of rates of unemployment in the nine core countries increased during the 1980s, reversing the trend of the 1970s.[23]

This analysis raises another interesting issue. GDP per capita seems to show clear signs of convergence in the longer term while at the same time unemployment shows little sign of converging over the full sample period. This suggests that income convergence is not related to unemployment convergence or, if it is, not in any simple manner. The reason for this is unclear, although several hypotheses could be put forward.

Explaining the differing pictures which emerge regarding convergence of regional unemployment and output in Europe is not easy from aggregate data. One explanation may be simply that the quality of data differs between the two indicators. In one case allocating output to regional economies is notoriously difficult while in the other, varying levels of underemployment between regions can seriously distort unemployment measures. But the differences may also reflect the changes in the nature of employment which have occurred over the period as de-industrialisation has taken place (Wabe, 1986). Essentially the pattern of unemployment has changed little but relative labour productivity has changed as industry and technology have altered.

Migration effects may also have played a role. The empirical evidence from US regional studies tends to suggest that migration at any one time is too small to seriously influence the short-term economic performances of regions – for example, Barro and Sala-i-Martin (1991). Migration within Europe has also been on a relatively small scale, particularly between countries.[24] The evidence from Europe seems to be that migration may be influenced by economic conditions although, because of the nature of the available data, it is difficult to paint a transparent picture in the short term and, for example, the importance of cultural factors in the pattern of migration may also be important.

While there were clear centripetal movements to the more prosperous core regions in the mid-1980s, not all international movements were from the wealthier regions of the Union and there are numerous examples of labour leaving high-income areas (Molle, 1990a). Interestingly, however a general pattern does emerge regarding internal migration and the degree of convergence in regional GDP. For example, as seen in Table 2.6, the performances of the regions of the Netherlands, France and Belgium diverged between 1975 and 1988 but this was in the context of migration being to their poorer areas (Cardoso, 1993).

23 The extent to which this type of trend may have been associated with a decline in regional policy during the 1980s is discussed in Wise and Chalkley (1990).

24 For example there were only 628,547 inter-regional moves by males within France between 1975 and 1982 (Eurostat, 1990) and moves between countries tend to be much smaller in number than those within a country even in the EU.

In contrast, Italy and West Germany exhibited convergence at a time when migration was to their wealthier regions. The flows are, however, small and there is little detail about the type of people who are migrating (in terms of skills, education, etc.) and the nature of the resources they are taking with them to their destinations. These latter factors may be as important as the level of overall movement.

Regional economic policy questions have grown in importance in recent years both because of the enlargements which have taken place and the bringing in of different types of region, and because of the efforts being made at greater integration within the Union. There are, however, quite divergent views on the mechanisms that drive regional economic performance. At one end of the spectrum is the position that factor mobility and differences in factor prices will ultimately lead to convergence in real economic performances while, at the other, is the view that a variety of factors ranging from scale economies through to illusions about wage levels will produce increased divergence.

In either case, however, there may be the need for regional economic policies, either to speed up a natural convergence process or to counteract forces of divergence, although the nature of these policies may differ. The problem then is less one of whether intervention is necessary but rather one of when, how and with what intensity the regional policy should be carried through.

The main difficulty, as indicated by the plethora of theories which abound regarding European regions' economic potentials, is essentially a lack of clear analysis of the problems. This part of the book has looked at what has happened to the EU regions since the inception of the EU and examined the degree of economic convergence which has materialised. Without this type of information it is difficult to see how a meaningful regional policy can emerge for the EU.

# 3. The Development of the European Union's Regional Policy

## 3.1 INTRODUCTION

Variations in regional economic performance within the European Union are of increasing concern to European policy-makers as moves toward greater economic and political integration progress.[1] The very broad reason for this is essentially to do with a common economic problem, namely whether there is a trade-off which exists between efficiency and equity. The primary aim of European integration, in terms both of increasing international and inter-regional trade and of increasing harmonisation in policy making, is to generate aggregate gains for the Union as a whole.[2] This may, however, if some economic theories prove correct, lead to greater variations in regional well-being – an idea inherent in the concept of the two-tier Europe which is sometimes mooted.

The objective of this chapter is not to develop new theories of regional development, or even to refine existing ones, but rather to explore what has been happening in terms of developing regional policy within the EU. It also seeks to offer some initial assessment of the impacts of the policies pursued. In particular, it addresses the general question of whether over the years the performance of the regional economies of the EU have converged or diverged. This is done within the broad framework of the overall economic performance of the Union and taking account of factors such as periodic expansions in membership.

The initial aim is to provide a brief outline of EU regional policy developments, particularly in the context of their intentions to overcome what are sometimes seen as a weakening in national regional policy

1 The *Fourth Periodic Report of the European Union*, for instance, points out that '... income per head in the top ten regions of the Community was more than three times that in the bottom ten in 1988 .... Moreover, international comparison suggests that the disparities in the Community are at least twice as wide as those in the USA.'

2 For details of recent developments in the Union's regional policy, see Armstrong (1992), Armstrong and Taylor (1993), Begg (1989), Molle (1990a), Swann (1992). See also, Sutherland, 1986.

instruments as integration takes place. Some basic calculations, using standard statistical measures of dispersion, are employed to gain an initial impression of the extent and patterns of economic convergence which are emerging.

## 3.2 ECSC REGIONAL POLICY

Europe emerged from the Second World War with new political boundaries and much of its infrastructure destroyed. The war, however, had produced a degree of economic integration between the two conflicting groupings. The Axis powers brought the productive potential of occupied territories within their war efforts while the Allies, at least partially, brought transport and some productive activities within a co-ordinated structure. In the post-war effort to reduce the prospects of subsequent major military conflicts ideas of further and alternative forms of economic integration were brought to the fore as part of a wider political initiative.

The creation of the International Monetary Fund, the World Bank, the General Agreement on Tariffs and Trade and the United Nations epitomised this approach at the global level. Each of these has subsequently played an important role in formulating and implementing regional economic policies, including those for Europe, but generally at a more aggregate level than we are concerned with here.

At the European level, concerns that past disputes were frequently closely entwined with nationalism brought forth a rather more political-economic response towards integration. While there was strong motivation underlying plans for integration it encountered major practical problems. Despite numerous political statements, the reluctance of states to surrender national sovereignty presented immediate, large-scale action. Rather, the ideas of the *functional approach to unity*, embodying gradual progression towards unity, advocated by Jean Monnet and Robert Schumann were adopted.

The Council of Europe was one of the earlier initiatives stemming from ideas advanced in the French Resistance.[3] On the more practical front, the Organisation for European Economic Cooperation (which was subsequently to expand beyond Europe as the Organisation for Economic Cooperation and Development) was created in 1948 to administer Marshall Aid. This represented, amongst other things, American sponsorship of European co-operation as a bulwark against communism. The creation of the Benelux Economic Union in 1944, linking the economies of the Netherlands,

3 Efforts to create a purely European military alliance, the European Defence Community, however took this too far and were rejected.

Belgium and Luxembourg, represented a major initiative at developing a customs union as well and as an economic union.[4]

The current arrangements within Europe can be directly traced back to the creation of the European Coal and Steel Community (ECSC) in 1951. This attempt at co-ordinated restructuring was designed to improve the overall efficiency of the heavy industries of the Member States in the period immediately after the initial post-Second World War reconstruction had began.[5] It sought to bring them under the control of a European High Authority. In doing this, policy makers recognised that some regions' economies largely dependent on heavy industry and extractive activities would suffer. From the outset, therefore, policies were envisaged that would compensate such adversely affected areas.

## 3.3 THE POLICY OF THE EUROPEAN COMMUNITY AND UNION

As we highlighted earlier, the economic nature of the European Union has changed considerably over time with expansion of membership. The nature of the Union has also evolved. The move to a Single European Market (under the 1986 Single Europe Act) removed, after 1992, major institutional trade barriers between Member States and the Treaty on European Union (the 'Maastricht Treaty') will, if fully enacted, bring about closer economic and political union.

These changes have brought with them concerns not simply about fulfilling the overall economic potential of the Union, but also with the spatial distribution of 4 to 6 per cent economic growth which is anticipated to flow in the long term from the 1986 Act. The Treaty of Rome contained four explicit requirements for common policies and the two most significant of these related to transport and agriculture. Both have obvious spatial economic implications. Subsequently, the regional dimension became more transparent as Union policy began to embrace a social policy and as measures to bring about closer monetary ties between Member States brought with them the political need to create mechanisms for the spatial redistribution of resources.[6]

Strengthening the economic unity of the European Community and ensuring its harmonious development are among the main aims of the Treaty of Rome. The very choice of the name 'Community' by the founding

4 There was also a political element in the establishment of the ECSC. It was seen by France in particular as a way to rebuild Germany's heavy industry without creating a military threat to France.

5 The members being the Benelux countries together with France, Italy and West Germany.

6 See Thirwall (1974), Armstrong (1978) and Cheshire *et al.* (1991).

fathers in 1957 says much about both their desire to promote balanced prosperity in all the Member States and, more importantly, their acceptance of the need for mutual solidarity in all the areas covered by this ambitious project. The Treaty of Rome, however, contained no provisions relating to an active regional, grant-giving policy at the Union level.[7] The European Investment Bank (EIB) created under the Treaty, however, consistently devoted a large part of its resources to loans for the more economically backward regions.

It took only a few years for the Union to begin to examine the regional issue[8] and to develop a whole range of tools for reducing national and regional economic disparities: agricultural policy, structural policy, social policy, regional policy, each supported by its own financial instrument; the Guidance Section of the European Agricultural Guidance and Guarantee Fund (EAGGF), the European Social Fund, the European Regional Development Fund and the financial instruments for fisheries guidance.

The early years after the signing of the Treaty of Rome saw some improvements in the internal position of most Member States although this also coincided with a period of rapid economic expansion that required making maximum use of every region's resources. In the period 1958 to 1968 regional disparities per capita income diminished in all Member countries save Italy. [9]

In addition to Union policies, the individual Members states were very active in developing their own domestic regional policies as were the

7 Giersch (1949) and others had foreseen some of the problems that this might subsequently create.

8 For instance, both the *Birkelbach Report* of 1963 and the *Bersani Report* of 1966 touched on regional policy. In 1965 a *Memorandum on Regional Policy in the Community* was presented by the Commission setting out objectives of regional policy and how actions of Member States could be co-ordinated. A second memorandum appeared in 1969 (*Proposals for the Organisation of Means of Action in Relation to Regional Development in the Community and a Note on Regional Policy in the Community*) setting out proposals for an administrative structure for developing and overseeing regional policy.

9 For comparative purposes, the per capita income in the peripheral regions of selected Union countries is compared to the national averages for those counties in the following table.

| Country | 1958 | 1963 | 1968 |
|---|---|---|---|
| France | n.a. | 85.2 | 86.2 |
| West Germany | 89.5 | 93.1 | 93.2 |
| Italy | 73.0 | 73.1 | 71.6 |
| North Netherlands | 85.5 | 86.4 | 87.0 |

countries which joined as part of subsequent enlargements.[10] These policies, because of variations in the perceived nature of the national regional economic problems and because of differing approaches to economic intervention, were often quite diverse in their nature.

French and Dutch economic planning in the 1960s and 1970s, for instance, embraced strong land-use controls and fiscal policy elements aimed at containing economic expansion in congested regions (the Paris area and the Randstadt respectively). Fiscal instruments (grants and soft loans), while generally differing in their detail, were used in most Member States to attract investment to depressed regions. Italy was particularly active in putting public sector and nationalised industry investment into the Mezzigiorno. The sectors favoured by national regional policies varied, with the Netherlands and Germany giving more attention to the service sector, mainly because of its perceived higher labour intensity than other Members.

From the outset, the Commission of the Union had played a limited role in all of this in that it policed national regional aid policies to ensure that national policies did not violate Union policy on state aid. This picture of very limited involvement changed somewhat, however, after the Paris Summit of 1972. Here it was decided to establish a European Regional Development Fund (ERDF) which came into being in 1975. The argument underlying the need for a strong regional policy was set out in a statement issued at the Summit:[11]

> There can be no European union without economic and monetary union, and no economic and monetary union without adequate and effective regional policy backed by a fund with substantial resources...the Heads of State or of Government agreed that a high priority should be given to the aim of correcting, in the Community, the structural and regional imbalances which might affect the realisation of Economic and Monetary Union.

The result of this has been the development of an institutional structure that seeks to integrate the institutional practices of Member States with the needs of an integrated EU regional policy. The resultant institutional

10 Indeed, it was argued by the UK government in its statement on *The United Kingdom and the European Community* (Cmnd. 4715) that joining the Community in 1973 would '... not inhibit the continuation and further development of vigorous regional policies which are necessary both on economic and social grounds'

11 The normal economic arguments for enacting an effective regional policy from the point of view of maximising overall economic growth include the fact that regional economic disparities lead to higher national unemployment rates than would be the case if regional disparities were less severe; inflationary pressures increase as regional economic disparities widen; and regional economic disparities lead to a sub-optimal use of a nation's infrastructure.

setting, seen in Figure 3.1, involves several different levels of institutions (Commission of the European Communities, 1999). The basis of the structure is that markets and need to function interactively. The direct influences are the institutional arrangements within a firm that, combined with the institutional arrangements between firms, are the main direct impact on economic growth. The indirect influences are provided by public administration and social capital, comprising the habits, customs and local culture, and the national and EU institutional and policy framework.

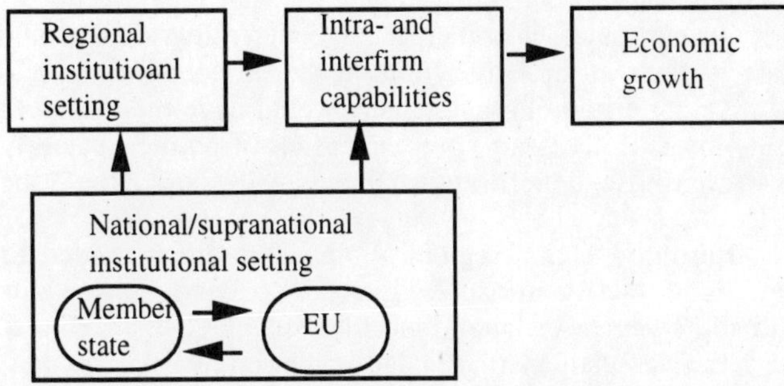


Figure 3.1 *The institutional setting for EU policy making*

The creation of the ERDF can be seen to be, in part, to fit into the indirect influences. It is the result of a need to compensate Union Members for the loss of important national discretionary powers (especially regarding exchange rate flexibility) which accompanies any form of tighter monetary integration.

This argument was buttressed somewhat by the subsequent publication of the *Thompson Report* (European Commission, 1973) which was concerned specifically with congested and overcrowded regions in the EU.[12] The claim was that strong regional policy was needed for social and environmental reasons which extended well beyond those geographical areas traditionally seen as experiencing economic difficulties:

> The physical poverty of the under-privileged regions is matched only by the mounting environmental poverty of the areas of concentration. The pressure on housing, the miseries of commuting on overloaded roads, or overcrowded trains, the pollution of the air and the water – all these developments mean that the environmental case for closing the geographical gaps is as powerful a one for those who live in the so-

12 The Report was based on the not unremarkable view that 'It cannot be said that economic activity throughout the Community has developed evenly, nor has expansion been geographically balanced.'

called prosperous areas of the Community as it is for those in the poorer regions.

The *MacDougall Report* (European Commission, 1977) was to provide a somewhat stronger empirical and intellectual basis for a Union regional policy. It reiterated the arguments concerning the imbalances which would result from closer economic integration within the Union and the liberalisation of intra-member trade which would accompany it. It also anticipated that major changes would be needed in the scale and direction of the Union budget. In particular, it argued that greater integration would increase aggregate welfare in the Union (and hence, in economic terms, meet the so-called Kaldor criteria in that gainers would have the resources to over-compensate losers if necessary) but for reasons of political stability actual transfers from those benefiting to those losing out would be necessary.

In the 1980s, European Union regional policy, therefore, tended to move away from fiscally active measures, like tax concessions, towards capital grants and some degree of labour subsidy. Jacques Delors, former President of the EU, was critical of the latter measures because they artificially reduced the cost of labour and capital in a region. They also ran counter to the competitive ethos of the EU and could have slowed the later adjustment to the Single European Market. Delors recommended measures that did not distort market forces. He suggested aid for physical infrastructure and the encouragement of local entrepreneurialism or the development of locally integrated systems of business activities. Yet he drew a false distinction between what appeared to be market and non-market forces. His position was that by distorting these prices optimal market adjustment would be achieved. In effect, he rejected one form of distortion in favour of another. The reason was that impediments to the operation of market forces would have been removed.

Between 1987 and 1993, Structural Funds doubled in real terms, after adjustments made in 1988.[13] Lagging regions (Objective 1) are defined as those whose GDP lies 25 per cent below the EU average.[14] These regions

13 The Union has six major financial instruments with which to implement its structural policies: the Regional Development Fund, the European Social Fund, the EAGGF Fund Guidance Section, the Financial Instruments for Fisheries Guidance, the Cohesion Fund, and loans from the European Investment Bank.

14 Between 1994 and 1999 the Structural Funds pursued six priority Objectives:

- Objective 1: structural adjustment of regions whose development is lagging behind;
- Objective 2: economic conversion of declining industrial areas;
- Objective 3: combating long-term unemployment, integration into working life of young people and persons exposed to exclusion from the labour market;

include the whole of Ireland, Greece and Portugal, 58 per cent of Spain, 36 per cent of Italy, 3 per cent of the UK and France and the new Länder of Germany. A total of 21 per cent of the EU's population live in lagging regions. Between 1983 and 1993, 60 per cent of funds were directed at lagging regions. Total aid was 1.2 per cent of the regions' aggregate GDP in 1989, which rose to 1.6 per cent in 1993. These EU transfers represented 3 per cent to 5 per cent of the GDP of Greece, Ireland and Portugal and about 3 per cent to 7 per cent of their fixed investment, over the same period.

The growth of the ERDF has been somewhat slower than was initially anticipated and, indeed, the Union budget as a whole was only around 1 per cent of Union gross domestic product in the early 1990s (Table 3.1). The budget also continues to be dominated by agricultural expenditures.

Table 3.1. *Scale of the European Regional Development Fund and total Structural Funds (ECU)*

| Year | ERDF Appropriations | ERDF Commitments | EAGGF Commitments | ESF Commitments | Union GDP |
|---|---|---|---|---|---|
| 1975 | 258 | | | | 1131600 |
| 1976 | 394 | | | | 1297700 |
| 1977 | 379 | | | | 1413800 |
| 1978 | 581 | | | | 1569200 |
| 1979 | 945 | | | | 1765900 |
| 1980 | 1165 | 1137.8 | 624.5 | 1014.9 | 2048857 |
| 1981 | 1540 | 1636.8 | 720.5 | 996.2 | 2279894 |
| 1982 | 1760 | 1844.8 | 756.8 | 1510.3 | 2487657 |
| 1983 | 2010 | 2127.4 | 865.9 | 1877.7 | 2680530 |
| 1984 | 2140 | 2383.2 | 796.3 | 1854.3 | 2886590 |
| 1985 | 2290 | 2496.0 | 498.2 | 2228.2 | 3094862 |
| 1986 | 3098 | 3328.1 | 853.5 | 2523.0 | 3547756 |
| 1987 | 3311 | 3662.1 | 940.5 | 3523.6 | 3736796 |
| 1988 | 3684 | 3827.0 | 1179.7 | 2870.6 | 4053121 |
| 1989 | 4495 | 4666.2 | 1461.6 | 3478.4 | 4406733 |
| 1990 | 5408 | 522.6 | 1925.7 | 3504.8 | 4738555 |
| 1991 | 5940 | 5191.6 | 2262.1 | 4017.6 | 5045198 |

*Source:* Simms (1995)

- Objective 4: adaptation of workers to industrial changes and to changes in production systems;
- Objective 5(a): adjustment of agriculture and fisheries structures;
- Objective 5(b): economic diversification of fragile rural areas;
- Objective 6 (Finland and Sweden): structural adjustment of regions with extremely low population density.

Objectives 1, 2, 5(b) and 6 are limited to designated areas while Objectives 3, 4 and 5(a) cover the entire Union.

Furthermore, the European Regional Development Fund has often been used as a balancing device in political bargains, rather than as a strict regional economic policy instrument. In a way it can be seen as being designed to appease Member States who felt that their financial contributions to the Union exceeded the transfers they were receiving in return.

National sentiment also arises in another sense. In particular, there seems to be an inherent feeling that while regional redistribution of resources to poorer regions is desirable, governments should place a priority on assisting their own depressed areas.[15] The result has been (Table 3.2) a national distribution of assistance which it would be difficult to justify on any strict regional economic criteria.

Table 3.2. *European Regional Development Fund national quotas, 1975 and 1980 (%)*

| Country | 1975 | 1980 |
|---|---|---|
| Belgium | 1.5 | 1.11 |
| Denmark | 1.3 | 1.06 |
| France | 15.0 | 13.64 |
| Ireland | 6.0 | 5.94 |
| Italy | 40.0 | 35.49 |
| Luxembourg | 0.1 | 0.07 |
| Netherlands | 1.7 | 1.24 |
| Germany | 6.4 | 4.65 |
| United Kingdom | 28.0 | 23.80 |
| Greece | | 13.00 |

*Source*: Simms (1995)

Between 1986 and 1993 unemployment rose by 1.3 per cent in the Objective 1 regions, compared to a decline of 0.3 per cent for the EU as a whole. Declining industrial regions (Objective 2 regions) are those which have a large representation of declining industrial sectors like mining, steel, textiles and shipbuilding. In 1990, total aid was approximately ECU 60 billion or about 0.24 per cent of total gross domestic production of the EU.

It is clear that with a small total EU budget for regional development purposes, and little real redistributive intent among many Member States, regional inequality will slow down the adjustment process of the Single

15 For example, witness the result of a poll conducted in the EU: 'European citizens are prepared….to help the less prosperous regions, but....people feel more solidarity with the regions of their own countries than with regions in other Community countries'.(*Bulletin of the European Community*, vol. 14, no. 7/8).

Market and undermine the Economic and Monetary Union (EMU). For most Member States, as seen below, the problem is that regional fiscal activism runs up against the constraint of the budget deficit and total public debt limits, contained in the Maastricht Treaty of 1991.

Despite these limitations, the European Union's regional policy had progressed, especially in institutional terms, by the mid-1980s. As Table 3.3 shows, by that time the policy comprised three broad components with either an explicit or an implicit regional orientation. Several of these exhibit a range of sub-institutional, usually sectoral, components.

Table 3.3. *European Union regional policy elements in the mid-1980s*

**1. European Regional Development Fund (ERDF)**

**2. Other Instruments & Policies with a Built in Regional Element**
- European Investment Bank (EIB)
- European Social Fund (ESF)
- European Coal and Steel Community (ECSC)
- European Agricultural Guidance & Guarantee Fund (EAGGF)

**3. Coordination Policies**
- Competition Policy
- Regional Impact Accessment
- Regional Development Programme
- Periodic Reports
- Regional Policy Priorities and Guidelines
- Programme Contracts
- Integrated Operations
- Transfrontier Programmes
- Regional Policy Committee

Within this framework, the criteria upon which assistance is given have been refined over time. Table 3.4 provides details of the major shifts which have taken place between 1975 and 1990 and emphasises the change in focus towards injecting resources on a spatial need, rather than on a project-based, set of criteria. In addition, the money which was being channelled through the structural funds was increasing significantly in magnitude (both in absolute terms and relative to the total EC budget) and being funnelled more explicitly towards direct regional assistance (Table 3.5).

The Single European Act has moved the position on somewhat. As an element of the bargain struck between the more developed and the less developed Member States it was agreed that, in return for the more intensive competition inherent in the internal market, compensation would be given to the poorer Members.[16] An element of this was a revision to the Rome Treaty which, while not directly calling for the creation of a Union regional policy, did state that the aim of the Union should be to reduce disparities between various regions and to reduce the backwardness of less-favoured regions.

Table 3.4. *European Regional Development Fund: rates of assistance*

| 1975 | 1985 | 1988 |
|---|---|---|
| *Projects*<br>Private productive investments – 20% of cost, up to 50% of public aid | *Projects*<br>Industry, craft and services – up to 50% of public aid | *Objective 1 Regions*<br>Up to 75% of cost and, as a general rule, at least 50% of public expenditure |
| *Infrastructure*<br>30% of public expenditure for investments less than 10 million units of account<br>10–30% of public expenditure for larger investments | *Infrastructure*<br>50% of public expenditure for investments less than 15 million ECU of account<br>50–50% of public expenditure for larger investments | *All Other Regions*<br>Up to 50% of cost, as a general rule, at least 25% of public expenditure |
| | *Community Programmes*<br>Up to 50% of all public expenditure | |
| | *National Programmes of Community Interest*<br>Up to 50% of all public expenditure (may reach 55%) | |

Table 3.5. *Structural fund expenditure, 1970–1990 (million ECU)*

| | 1970 | 1975 | 1980 | 1985 | 1990 |
|---|---|---|---|---|---|
| Regional | | 75.3 | 1,26.4 | 2,495.3 | 4,704.5 |
| Social | | 157.9 | 1,014.2 | 2,188.5 | 3,321.9 |
| Agricultural | | 158.8 | 624.7 | 852.9 | 1,449.0 |
| Total funds | 64.0 | 392.0 | 2,765.3 | 5,536.6 | 9475.4 |
| Total EC Budget | 5,44.4 | 6213.6 | 16,057.5 | 28,223.0 | 46,808.7 |

16 Explicitly, Title V, Article 130A of the Act states that, '... the Community shall aim at reducing disparities between the various regions and the backwardness of the least-favoured regions'. This should be taken in the context of forecasts of significant economic growth at the Community level (estimated at between 4.5 and 6.5 per cent by Cecchini, 1988) which would provide the prospect of pulling up lagging regions without posing a major absolute burden on the more prosperous parts of the Community. Mackay (1993) provides a discussion of this issue.

The Union budget settlement of 1988 also laid down that structural funds, such as the ERDF and the European Social Fund (ESF), should grow and that structural spending in 1993 should be twice that of 1987 (reaching ECU 14.2 billion). The additional expenditure was to be focused on the poorest regions. Further, there was to be closer co-ordination between these funds and the guidance section of the European Agricultural Guidance and Guarantee Fund (EAGGF) (Commission of the European Communities, 1989). Despite the scale of the changes implicit in the 1988 measures, they still represent a process of negotiation rather than strict, technical assessment of the best way forward (Cheshire *et al.*, 1991).

Launched on 1 November 1993, the new European Union demands a considerable strengthening of solidarity between Member States and, as a consequence, of the Union structural policies. The signing of the Treaty of Maastricht in December 1991 gave the development of the European economy a new dimension. By setting the aim of economic and monetary union (EMU) by the end of the century, the Treaty significantly altered the purpose of increased economic and social convergence. The very success of this new and decisive stage in the construction of Europe could be undermined by the persistence of excessive economic and social disparities between Member States. Furthermore, Article 2 of the Treaty explicitly makes the promotion of economic and social cohesion one of the essential conditions for the success of the Union.

The strengthening of economic and social cohesion was seen as a necessary precondition for the establishment of economic and monetary union. It also represented a challenge to the members of the Union, to the extent that effective convergence of their economic and monetary policies became vital. Above all, however, there is a challenge to those countries whose development is still lagging behind the core members.

Amongst the criteria that all Member States wishing to adopt the single currency needed to meet, the Maastricht Treaty gave prominence to the control of public deficits. This has required a determined effort from all countries, but it is the less wealthy countries that have had the most difficult job in bringing the public finances under control. These countries have been forced to impose very strict budgetary discipline, while at the same time bringing their prosperity up to the Union average swiftly, which demands continuing, and perhaps even increasing, public investment.

It is in order to help countries experiencing particular difficulties and at the same time help the Union itself to strengthen as far as possible and as quickly as possible its economic and social cohesion that the authors of the Treaty on European Union amended Article 130d of the EEC Treaty (inserted by Article 23 of the Single European Act) to provide for the creation of a Cohesion Fund before 31 December 1993.

This tool for providing assistance and ensuring solidarity is a specific type of policy instrument – unlike the other Structural Funds – in both its objectives and the way it functions. The other Structural Funds are mainly intended to deal with the problem of regional disparities, whether in regions with long-standing problems of under-development or in regions undergoing extensive industrial conversion. They aim to help reduce and, if possible, eliminate these pockets of under-development through structural programmes and individual structural projects.

The purpose of the Cohesion Fund is entirely different even if, indirectly, the assistance it provides contributes to promoting regional development and assistance is co-ordinated with the operations of the other Community solidarity instruments. The purpose of the Fund is to enable all Member States to join the final phase of the economic and monetary union as rapidly as possible, by helping those with the greatest number of handicaps to overcome them.

The Protocol on economic and social cohesion annexed to the Maastricht Treaty lays down that 'Community financial contributions will be made to the Member States of the Union' with a per capita GNP of less than 90 per cent of the Community average that have a program leading to the fulfilment of the conditions of economic convergence as set out in Article 104c of the Treaty.

In accordance with these two criteria, four Member States – Spain, Portugal, Greece and Ireland, with a total population of almost 63 million or nearly one-fifth of the population of the EU – receive assistance from the Cohesion Fund.

Article 130d lays down that the Cohesion Fund provides 'a financial contribution to projects in the fields of environment and trans-European networks in the area of transport infrastructure' – in other words, projects in areas where any reduction in public investment because of strict budgetary discipline would be extremely damaging. Countries receiving assistance, therefore, have had to give an undertaking not to reduce their own investments in transport infrastructure and environmental protection.

In addition to the direct benefits they bring to the inhabitants of assisted areas, and the fauna and the flora of the area, environmental projects are generally an important source of economic activity and long-term employment. Without undermining the principle that the polluter should pay, the Cohesion Fund provides funding for projects involving costs deemed disproportionate to the public finances of the country concerned.

With regards to transport infrastructure, it is seen important that these countries be connected as effectively as possible to the main centres of activity in the Union and in neighbouring countries. Projects supported by the Cohesion Fund must make a contribution to the trans-European communications (TENs) networks.[17]

17 These networks have gradually been developed by the EU to improve exting transport and communications links and to fill-in missing links (Commission of the European Communities, 1992).

All the projects financed by the Cohesion Fund in the fields of environment and transport must contribute to the overall economic development of the Member State concerned, thereby strengthening the economic and social cohesion of the Union. Projects must be of a sufficient scale to have a significant impact in the field of environmental protection or in the improvement of trans-European transport infrastructure networks.[18]

The granting of assistance from the Fund is also conditional on the beneficiary Member State making a real effort not to run up an excessive public deficit. If a country refuses to bring its public finances under control within the time limit set by the Council, assistance from the Fund may be suspended.

Finally, for the same reasons, the Regulation establishing the Fund stipulates that there will be a thorough prior appraisal of all projects, usually in co-operation with the European Investment bank (EIB), to guarantee that the 'medium-term economic and social benefits [are] commensurate with the resources deployed.' The European Commission and the beneficiary countries must also ensure that the implementation of the projects for which assistance is provided is closely monitored to guarantee that the objectives pursued by the Cohesion Fund are adhered to and that projects are carried out efficiently.

At the Edinburgh Summit in 1992, the European Council decided that ECU 15 billion (at 1992 prices) would be made available to the Cohesion Fund over the period 1993–99, rising from ECU 1.5 billion in 1993 to more than ECU 2.6 billion in 1999. This made the Fund a force for economic development since, although projects receiving financing from the Cohesion Fund cannot at the same time receive assistance form the Structural Funds, such projects are intended to be complementary with other projects supported from the EU's budget, particularly those concerning the trans-European networks.

The impact of Cohesion Fund measures may be all the greater in that the level of assistance varies between 80 and 85 per cent of the public expenditure on a project. This is a higher level of financing than provided by the Structural Funds (Table 3.6).[19] Preparatory studies and technical support for the preparation of a project can receive 100 per cent financing, particularly if they are undertaken at the EU Commission's initiative. On the other hand, where a project generates net revenue for the promoters, be it an infrastructure the use of which involves fees borne directly by users or productive investments in the environment sector, the assistance provided from the Cohesion Fund is adjusted accordingly.

18 The total cost of a project or group of projects is not normally be less than ECU 10 million.

19 The Commission approved 225 programmes under the Structural Fund in 1994, 508 in 1995 and 173 in 1996, amounting to ECU 14.4 billion, 17.2 billion and 22.4 billion respectively.

Table 3.6. *Cohesion Fund and the Structural Funds*

| | Cohesion Fund | Structural Funds |
|---|---|---|
| Aims | To reduce economic disparities between member states | To reduce regional disparities |
| Parties involved | Projects are agreed between the Commission and the Member State concerned | While the Member State bears the main responsibility, the regional authorities and the promoters play a prominent role in the management of programmes |
| Conditions | Strict conditions: compliance with the convergence programmes is a condition of funding | No conditions |
| Geographical coverage | Four Member States limits for the other | Objective 1, 2 and 5b regions. No regional objectives |
| Areas | Environment and transport infrastructures only | In principle, no sector is excluded |
| Procedures | Funding is granted on a project-by-project basis | Most of the funding is granted for programmes |
| Funding available | ECU 16 223 million between 1993 and 1999 | ECU 172 506 million between 1993 and 1999 |

The Regulation establishing the Cohesion Fund laid down an indicative allocation of the resources available between the four beneficiary countries (Table 3.7).[20] The Regulation also lays down that a suitable balance be struck between financing for transport infrastructure projects and financing for environmental projects. This more pragmatic approach is justified by the needs, possibilities, availability and feasibility of projects that impose choices that vary from country to country.

It is difficult to assess the overall effectiveness of any regional policy, let alone to evaluate the component instruments that comprise it. Developing a meaningful counterfactual is perhaps the most difficult of these problems. What one can say, however, is that by the mid-1990s the

20 Initially, Spain, 52–58 per cent; Greece, 16–20 per cent; Portugal, 16–20 per cent; and Ireland, 7–10 per cent.

economic indicators were not showing a dramatic improvement in terms of the performance of most of the targeted types of region, especially in terms of reducing unemployment (Table 3.8).[21]

Table 3.7. *Assistance from the Cohesion Fund in 1993 (ECU)*

| Member State | Total | Environment | Transport |
|---|---|---|---|
| Spain | 858 450 703 (54.9%) | 252 083 242 (29%) | 606 367 461 (71%) |
| Portugal | 283 568 700 (18.1%) | 122 794 100 (43%) | 160 774 600 (57%) |
| Greece | 280 364 000 (17.9%) | 175 222 400 (62%) | 105 141 600 (38%) |
| Ireland | 41 887 100 (9.1%) | 55 917 250 (39%) | 85 969 850 (61%) |
| Technical Assistance | 374 125 | | |
| Total | 1 564 644 628 (100%) | 606 016 992 (38.7%) | 958 253 511 (61.3%) |

On July 1997, the European Commission presented a communication entitled Agenda 2000 describing the outlook for the European Union for the early years of the next century. The communication refers to economic and social cohesion in a chapter on the Structural Funds and the Cohesion Fund. For the period 2000–06, the European Commission proposes a budget for economic and social cohesion policy (aid for less-prosperous regions and less-favoured social groups) of 0.46 per cent of the Union's gross national product (GNP). This is the percentage decided by the European Council in Edinburgh for the end of the period 1993–9. On this basis, ECU 257 billion (at 1997 prices) would be available for operations under the Structural Funds and the Cohesion Fund between 2000 and 2006, as compared with ECU 200 billion (at 1997 prices) for 1993–9. ECU 45 billion of this amount would be earmarked for the new Member States. As a rule, total transfers from the Structural Funds and the Cohesion Fund to a current or future Member State should not exceed 4 per cent of its GNP.

[21] There is some evidence that the Cohesion Fund countries (Spain, Ireland, Greece and Portugal) in aggregate have improved their relative positions within the EU, at least in terms of their GDP per capita (Commission of the European Communities, 1999).

Table 3.8. *Economic indicators for assisted EU regions, 1989–96*

| Regional Group | % unemployment | | | GDP per capita (% of EU) | | |
|---|---|---|---|---|---|---|
| | 1989 | 1993 | 1997 | 1998 | 1993 | 1995 |
| Objective 1 | 14.6 | 16.1 | 17.4 | 63.9 | 66.2 | 67.5 |
| Objective 2 | 11.0 | 12.3 | 11.9 | 94.8 | 96.0 | 96.2 |
| Objective 5b | 6.5 | 7.0 | 7.8 | 81.7 | 85.3 | 85.7 |
| Objective 6 | – | 18.9 | 19.8 | 88.1 | 77.2 | 81.6 |
| Others | 6.5 | 8.2 | 8.1 | 113.8 | 116.3 | 116.7 |
| EU (15) | 8.8 | 10.5 | 10.7 | 100 | 100 | 100 |

*Note*: Definitions of the Objective Regions are contained in footnote 13.

The Commission proposed that the current seven priority 'Objectives' be reduced to three: two regional Objectives, and a horizontal Objective for human resources. It is planned that the percentage of the Union population covered by Objectives 1 and 2 be reduced from the present 51 per cent to 35–40 per cent by 2006. The total amount allocated to the Objective 1 regions, including those receiving transitional (phasing-out) support, should cover about two-thirds of the Structural Funds available for the 15 Member States, a share comparable to the average for the current programming period.[22]

For the Structural Funds, the Commission proposed co-financing a single multi-annual programme for each region. The number of Community Initiatives would be limited to three (cross-border, trans-national and inter-regional co-operation; rural development; human resources) and their share of Structural Fund resources would be reduced to 5 per cent. Where possible, more room for manoeuvre would be left to the committees managing the implementation of the funds.

Greater efficiency would be sought by more systematic use of financial instruments other than grants (such as low-interest loans, loan guarantees and equity participation), and a reserve of at least 10 per cent of the funds would be set aside to be allocated not earlier than mid-term to regions with good performance in terms of effective use of European aid already distributed.

[22] For the programming perod 1194 to 1999, Objective 1 regions were allocated 68 per cent of funds; Objective 2 regions, 11 per cent; Objective 5b regions, 4 per cent and Objective 6 regions, 0.5 per cent. Some 55 per cent of resources goes to 16 per cent of the EU population in four countries – Greece, Ireland, Spain and Portugal..

After 1999, the Commission proposed the strict application of the criterion by which only regions whose per capita GDP is less than 75 per cent of the Union average would be eligible for assistance under Objective 1. Aid intensities would reflect the size of the population, the gap between regional wealth and the Union average and national wealth. Additional support would be granted to regions with very high unemployment.

For those lagging regions then eligible under Objective 1 that come out above the 75 per cent threshold, a phasing-out mechanism would be defined. Regions with very low population density which were eligible for Objective 6 would have special arrangements. The particular situation of very remote regions should be dealt with within Objective 1 between 2000 and 2006.

For all the regions confronted with major economic and social restructuring needs, the Commission proposes a new Objective 2. This would include areas affected by change in the industrial services or fisheries sectors, rural areas in serious economic decline, and urban districts in difficulty. For this Objective, the Commission proposed a geographical concentration on the worst affected areas and a coverage as consistent as possible with the areas assisted by the Member.

Similar to Objective 1, Union intervention under the new Objective 2 areas would combine all forms of structural support, including measures linked to human resources. Areas eligible for Objectives 2 and 5(b) – rural areas – no longer eligible under the new selection criteria continue to benefit during a transitional period from limited financial support.

A new Objective 3 would be introduced for regions not covered by Objectives 1 and 2. It would help them adapt and modernise their systems of education, training and employment. A determined effort is being made to modernise labour markets in accordance with the multi-annual plans for employment and the new chapter on employment introduced in the Treaty of Amsterdam.

The Commission proposed that the Cohesion Fund be kept in its present form after 1999. The Fund would pursue its co-financing of trans-European transport networks (TENs) and projects in the environmental field in Member States with a per capita GNP of less than 90 per cent of the Union average. Financing from this Fund would continue to depend on convergence efforts made by the countries concerned (conditionality principle).

For those countries eligible for Cohesion Fund assistance that adopt the single currency (i.e., those taking part in the third phase of EMU), this would mean observing the terms of the Pact for Stability and Growth. As regards the GNP criterion, the Commission proposed a mid-term review in 2003. The annual financial endowment of the Cohesion Fund for the current Member States would be of the order of ECU 3 billion per annum at the beginning of the 2000–6 period.

As the applicant countries need time to adapt to the workings of the Structural Funds, the Commission is proposing the introduction of pre-accession aid from 2000. From accession onwards, Structural Fund programmes and Cohesion Fund projects would replace pre-accession aid, taking account of the absorptive capacity of credits in each country.

In concrete, financial terms, the Commission proposed allocating ECU 38 billion to the new Member States preceded by ECU 7 billion for pre-accession during the period 2000–06 for the Structural Funds and Cohesion Fund. At the end of this period, structural aid for enlargement would represent almost 30 per cent of total Union structural funding.

Taking a wider view, the EU has never been fixed but has continued to expand over time. This has implications both for potential new members and states remaining outside. The Single European Market is predicated on the two elements of customs union theory, trade creation and trade diversion. The notion of 'Fortress Europe' and the present trading relationship with the lesser developed countries in the Third World feed the suspicion that trade diversion rather than creation may be a prime objective of the European Union.

The move towards European Monetary Union also poses difficulties for existing members of the EU. The imposition of monetary and fiscal convergence criteria puts up a further barrier to the wider integration of Europe. Wider integration also extends the periphery of the EU and subjects the core to difficult distributional questions.

Peripherality is not limited to the four poorer economies of the EU. By imposing nominal convergence criteria, particularly fiscal ones, greater economic divergence will occur between the regions of the EU. The prospect of a single European currency means that some kind of fiscal activism will be required. The restriction on discretion over economic policy is strengthened by enforcing fiscal rules, which limits managing the adjustment. Fiscal activism is an important component in the development policies of Europe's peripheral economies.[23]

Central and eastern European states may see the EU as a natural market for their exports and as an engine of economic growth. If these countries, however, are to be included in a wider European Union, then conforming to policy prescriptions may derail growth.[24] Furthermore, it is apparent that if they are to take advantage of fiscal activism to transform their regions, then a high degree of state intermediation is likely to be necessary.

23 There are, however, no plans for a centralised fiscal policy as in other monetary unions such as the US.

24 The European Council at its Luxembourg meeting in 1997 decided to open accession negotiations with a number of central and eastern European countries with the initial objective of aligning their national legislative framework with Community law.

## 3.4 CONCLUSIONS

The EU as an international institution has a long-established record of trying to develop an integrated regional policy across the Member States. Part of this has been in the form of explicit regional incentives, but of more importance have been a variety of other measures, such as the Common Agricultural Policy, that have exerted a *de facto* influence over the spatial allocation of resources in the EU.

In terms of assessing the impact of the various explicit and implicit measures it is difficult to say how successful they have been. One problem is that the objectives of many measures, especially those of a less explicit kind, have not always been transparent. Also, on the surface the amounts of resources devoted directly to EU regional policy have been relatively limited. Even when other less-direct policies are included the redirection of resources within the EU has still been relatively limited, especially between Member States. Having said that, however, the evidence does not point to the available resources always being used wisely.

Counter to this, the EU has been a fluctuating geographical area. Its membership has periodically changed and its own priorities have frequently shifted. National governments have been reluctant to surrender traditional powers and to give over resources. The problem of adjusting to new members is one that is only likely to increase as former communist states seek to join the Union.

# 4. Theories of Economic Development

## 4.1 INTRODUCTION

Economists over the years have expended considerable intellectual energies in attempting to explain economic growth. This concentration of minds is understandable given the importance of economic growth for furthering human well-being.[1] Equally, however, economists have been conspicuous by their failures in this field of endeavour. This does not mean that there is a shortage of sophisticated models or of intricate ideas attempting to explain the process of economic growth, but rather the problem is something of the opposite. That is, there is an abundance of theories that seek to account for economic growth and development, none of which, though, provide an entirely convincing explanation and, in some cases, give rise to contrary policy recommendations.

Many of the different theories have particular sectoral focuses, such as the importance of infrastructure (which is looked at in more detail in Chapter 8), or concentrate on particular driving forces, such as the export base of an area. One key element which is frequently missing from much of this literature, however, is the spatial and distance element. Even when such spatial factors are incorporated, they are often treated in a trivial fashion with the emphasis on the role of the price mechanism on factor mobility (Richardson, 1973).[2]

1 Durlauf and Quah (1998) argue that economists study growth across countries for three reasons: 'First, understanding the sources of varied patterns of growth is important: persistent disparities in aggregate growth across countries have, over time, led to large differences in welfare. Second, the intellectual payoffs are high: the theoretical hypotheses that bear on economic growth are broad and, perhaps justifiably, ambitious in scale and scope. Third, the first wave of new empirical growth analyses, by making strong and controversial claims, have provoked yet newer ways of analysing cross-country income dynamics. These newer techniques are, in turn, generating fresh stylised facts on growth with important implications for theory.' A parallel set of arguments could be made for studying growth across regions.

2 Martin and Sunley (1998) take this further and maintain that this is still a problem with more recent developments in growth theory, *viz*: 'As has often been the case when economists have turned their attention to regional

This latter approach was a notable feature, for instance, of work appearing in the 1960s and 1970s when a plethora of ideas appeared and numerous models were developed along these lines. More frequently spatial cost differentials have been ignored. Keynesian inspired economists, led by Kaldor (1961; 1975) and others, for instance, focused their attention in the 1950s and 1960s on the demand-side and on scale effects, and sought active regional public spending policies to assist slower growing regions where effective demand was thought to be deficient.[3]

As a result of these and other inadequacies, not only do we poorly understand the overall growth process, but we know even less about exactly why some regions prosper and why some sectors in their economies perform better than those in others. Indeed, explaining spatial differences in growth is inherently more complicated than explaining aggregate growth. This is because growth rates vary with location and over time as a consequence of the relative strength of agglomeration and dispersion factors altering over space and time. Agglomeration effects associated with scale, density and scope advantages, for example, tend to lead to the spatial concentration of growth while high friction costs, due for instance to poor transport, tend to foster dispersion and more equal growth.

The late 1980s saw an increasing interest in the importance of technological change and economic development. Influential articles by Romer (1986; 1990a; b) and Lucas (1988) led to the New Growth Theory. Variations on the theory emphasise the role of externalities in technological change, specialisation and trade, monopoly rents from innovation and 'creative destruction', human capital and government policy. Parallel to the development of these non-spatial economic growth theories, new ideas emerged attempting to explain the spatial distribution of economic activity, both in terms of urban systems and in terms of regional development. This 'New Economic Geography' has in common with the 'New Growth Theory' literature an emphasis on increasing returns, externalities and imperfect competition.

The general equilibrium models of the new growth theories allow a broader discussion of diverging growth than the demand-driven Kaldorian models of cumulative causation, which are still commonly used in the regional development debate. The models of endogenous technical change can generate results which are consistent with some of the predictions of the Kaldorian framework. Like the Kaldorian approach, they also point to a need for regional economic policies, although the new theories suggest that such policies would need to be supply-oriented and hence focus, *inter alia,* on

development, the recent interest by the new growth theorists in regional convergence has failed to take *geography* and *place* seriously' (italics in original).

3 The 1970s also saw economic geographers developing a number of Marxist models of regional development. These are not discussed here. Smith (1984) offers an overview.

infrastructure, innovation and ecological sustainability rather than the traditional tools of demand stimuli and subsidies.

The objective in this chapter is not to provide a comprehensive account of the rival theories of regional economic growth, which can be found in most of the main textbooks on regional economics such as Richardson (1973; 1974) and Armstrong and Taylor (1993). Rather, it is to set out some of the key elements of these theories which allow for their empirical testing and which are of specific relevance to many of the on-going debates in the European Union.

## 4.2 THE NEO-CLASSICAL FRAMEWORK

In the classical economic works of Smith, Ricardo, Marx and Malthus understanding the process that underlie economic growth was a core concern.[4] Of central importance was the study of the determinants of the growth rate of a country or region. It was important in years of the Great Depression when nations sought to understand why their economies were shrinking in the face of apparent surpluses of factor endowments. This topic also lay at the core of development economics during its heyday in the 1950s and 1960s when institutions such as the World Bank and the United Nations sought to reduce poverty and backwardness in many nations of the world. The subject then essentially lay dormant for two decades.

4 This was not to say that this meant there was a consensus on the underlying mechanisms determining economic growth. At the one extreme were the 'pessimists' who include such notable as West, Malthus, Ricardo and James Mill. Looking at what they saw as the pressure of population and nature's decreasing response to human efforts to increase the supply of food leading to falling net returns to industry, more or less constant real wages and ever-increasing absolute and relative returns to land the vision of the 'pessimists' was one of a static equilibrium at a subsistence income level. J.S. Mill was more optimistic in his earlier writings. He initially believed that mankind could learn and, in so-doing, would respond to Malthusian lessons. Further, he saw savings as the driving force behind the investment that was needed for further economic development. Later he took up the view that the private-enterprise economy had reached its limits and that a stationary state would emerge, albeit one purely in terms of population but with still gradually rising living standards due to technical change. The 'optimistic' school of thought (e.g. the work of Carey and List), although generally less technically sophisticated than that of the pessimists argued that the great strength of capitalism was its ability to create productive capacity. Marx was somewhat outside of the optimistic school although his ideas that the capitalist society had the 'privilege' to create a productive apparatus required for a higher form of human civilisation indicates ideas leading in the same direction. The motor behind his analysis, as it was with Mill, are savings that are promptly turned into investments.

In his Ohlin Lectures, Krugman (1995) offers an explanation of why spatial and development economics, together with economic geography, are 'almost completely absent from the standard corpus of economic theory'. He argues that the main reason that development and growth economics got pushed down a side road is that '...the founders of development economics failed to make their point with sufficient analytical clarity to communicate their essence to other economists, and perhaps to each other.' There was a communications problem in part brought about by the inability or reluctance of development economists in particular to enter into mainstream economic debates.

Romer (1994) offers a somewhat different explanation. He considers that following the considerable advances in growth theory some thirty years ago or so, there began a disinterest in part stemming from a disenchantment that arose from the difficulty in obtaining empirical data suitable for testing alternative theories. Whether this was a real problem or the inability of those concerned to make good use of the information they did have is open to some dispute – Romer largely seems to believe the latter, The availability of new data coupled with empirical analysis[5] that brought into question the neo-classical models of Solow (1956) and others stirred up new thoughts and ideas, not to say new thinkers.[6]

Durlauf and Quah (1998) take a somewhat different and broader perspective in arguing that economists now study growth across countries for three reasons, 'First, understanding the sources of varied patterns of growth is important: persistent disparities in aggregate growth across countries have, over time, led to large differences in welfare. Second, the intellectual payoffs are high: the theoretical hypothesis that bear on economic growth are broad and, perhaps justifiably, ambitious in scale and scope. Third, the first wave of new empirical growth analyses, by making strong and controversial claims, have provoked yet newer ways of analysing cross-country income dynamics. These newer techniques are, in turn, generating fresh stylised facts on growth with important implications for theory.' A parallel set of arguments could be made for studying growth across regions.

More recent economic theories attempting to explain the likely regional implications of European integration provide conflicting predictions of what

5 Indeed, Harberger (1998) seems to be of the mind that the stimulus for the new approach to economic growth lay in the improvements in growth accounting.

6 What the new data showed, or appeared to show is neatly summed up by Grossman and Helpman (1944), 'First, the growth rate of the world's technological leader has been rising over time, not falling, which can happen in the neoclassical model only if the pace of exogenous technological progress steadily accelerates. Second, countries appear not to be converging to a common level of per capita income, as they must be in the neoclassical model if the countries share similar savings behavior and technologies'.

may materialise in the long-term. If one adopts the traditional neo-classical view then freer economic markets, with accompanying reductions in institutional interventions, will allow regions to exploit their comparative advantage and ultimately there will be a long-run convergence in their economic performance.[7]

The neo-classical theory provides a parsimonious underlying basis for seeking out general causes of differential economic development[8]. It offers a benchmark against which one may attempt to define the crucial common characteristics of economic growth. Alternative approaches that, for example, rely on institutional considerations offer insights into special cases but generally have much less to say about the wider issues.

Neo-classical theory essentially argues that across regions with similar preferences and access to similar technologies, poorer regions will catch up wealthier regions and the marginal return from capital in the latter begins to diminish[9]. Poorer regions, since they have less capital, will attract mobile investment because of the relatively higher return that they offer. Equally, labour will migrate from regions where wages are low to those where wages are higher pushing, up wages in the former and reducing them in the latter. In effect, the increased factor mobility that would accompany economic integration would remove spatial variations in living standards.

The standard neo-classical model of economic growth was formulated in 1956 by Solow (1956) and independently by Swan (1956). The Solow–Swan model predicts that countries or regions with the same preferences and technology will converge to identical levels of *per capita* income. Trade and factor mobility would accelerate convergence. While there is empirical evidence of such convergence, at least within groups of countries or regions the process tends to be very slow while others argue that a reorganising of the data may in fact show up patterns of divergence.

It is generally accepted in explaining such patterns of growth that the accumulation of human capital and technological change have a more important role to play than growth in capital per worker. The neo-classical growth model for closed economies provides a simple explanation of labour productivity growth in terms of capital accumulation – which tends to grow

7 For example, see the models developed by Solow (1956), Borts (1960) and Koopmans (1965).

8 There are those who tend to think of neo-classical economics as a school and hence there is no single neo-classical theory. Lucas (1988) offers the counter argument:

> I prefer to use the term 'theory' in a narrow sense, to refer to an explicit dynamic system, something that can be put on a computer and *run*...the construction of a mechanical, artificial world, populated by the interacting robots economics typically studies, that is capable of exhibiting behaviour the gross features of which resemble those of the actual world.

9 For a detailed discussion of the neo-classical growth model as applied at the sub-national level, see McCombie (1988a).

faster than in aggregate hours supplied – and other factors, referred to collectively as the 'catch-all' term, technological change. If closed economies are similar with respect to preferences and technology, diminishing returns to reproducible capital will generate a long-run convergence in levels of per capita income.

Taking a closed economy with competitive markets and a constant return technology at date t, labour supply is L(t). The exogenously given rate of growth of L(t) is n. Real production Y(t) is assumed to result from combining inputs according to:

$$Y(t) = F\{K(t), L(t)e^{gt}\} \tag{4.1}$$

where K(t) is the stock of capital at time t and $e^{gt}$ is the effect of exogenous labour-augmenting technical progress. Neglecting labour-leisure choices and assuming full employment, population and labour force become equivalent concepts growing at rate n. Equation (4.1) can be rewritten as:

$$y = f(k) \tag{4.2}$$

where lower-case letters denote per capita variables and italics denote a quantity per effective unit of labour $L(t)e^{gt}$. If the rate of depreciation of capital is a fraction δ of the stock, net investment is given by:

$$\dot{K} = Y - C - \delta K \tag{4.3}$$

where a dot denotes a derivative with respect to time and C is the level of consumption. Hence, *k* evolves in accordance with

$$\dot{k} = f(k) - c - (n + g + \delta)k \tag{4.4}$$

Households are assumed to seek to maximise lifetime utility given by

$$W = \int u(c)e^{nt}e^{-\rho t}\,dt \tag{4.5}$$

where c = C/L and ρ is the constant rate of time preference. Household utility, rather, and not individual utility, is in the welfare criterion because per capita utility is multiplied by household membership which grows at rate n. Assuming that the utility function has the form

$$u(c) = (c^{1-\sigma} - 1)/(1 - \sigma) \tag{4.6}$$

marginal utility u'(c) has the constant elasticity minus σ with respect to c. Finding the consumption path c(t) which maximises (4.5) subject to (4.6) is an optimal control problem. The optimal time path for consumption is

$$\dot{c}/c = (f'(k) - \delta - \rho)/\sigma \tag{4.7}$$

With initial resources K(0) and L(0), the optimal path will converge to the steady state path asymptotically. In the steady state, the effective quantities $y$, $k$ and $c$ do not change. Thus, income, capital and consumption per capita each grow at the rate of technological progress, g. The absolute quantities Y, K and C grow at the rate g + n. The long-run rate of return to capital is $f(k^*)$ where $k^*$ is the steady state effective capital intensity found by setting the rate of growth in per capita consumption in (4.7) equal to g. Thus,

$$f(k^*) = \delta + \rho + \sigma g \tag{4.8}$$

A Cobb–Douglas production function, with $\alpha$ denoting the share of profits in income, yields

$$f(k) = \gamma k^{\alpha} \tag{4.9}$$

and, by substitution of (4.3) into (4.7):

$$k^* = \{(\delta+\rho+\sigma g)/\alpha\gamma\}^{(1/\alpha-1)} \tag{4.10}$$

The optimal propensity to save in the steady state is also constant:

$$s^* = (n + g + \sigma)k^* = (n + g + \sigma)\ \{(\delta + \rho + \sigma g\}/\alpha\gamma\}^{1/\alpha-1} \tag{4.11}$$

From equations 4.10 and 4.11 it can be seen that a low discount rate $\rho$ and a high intertemporal elasticity of substitution (a small $\alpha$) increase $k^*$ and $s^*$.

In terms of convergence, opening the economy within this framework leads to additional forces. If capital is mobile then it will move to the area offering the highest return. The Cobb–Douglas specification means a diminishing marginal productivity of capital and from this follows that countries that have a high capital-labour ratio, and hence a high level of per capita income, must have a low return on capital. Capital will flow from high-income to low-income regions. Similarly, labour will migrate from low income areas to high-income regions with a similar positive effect on convergence.

The model is open to criticism. It focuses on real capital accumulation in a closed economy and abstracts from monetary considerations. These limitations can be serious omissions in explaining growth differences between countries. Monetary considerations are less important at the regional level, since monetary conditions may be assumed largely constant across regions. However, the openness of the economy cannot be ignored at the regional level and the terms of trade, factor mobility and the generation and diffusion of technological change then become important issues.

The neo-classical framework also has the inherent limitation that it treats the macro or meso-economy in the same way as it treats a firm. In doing this it implicitly transfers assumptions regarding the nature of the production function, of the form of market competition and of the motivation, that of profit maximisation, of the actors involved. These types of assumption are frequently questioned at the microeconomic level and would seem even more limiting at a higher order of aggregation.

## 4.3 CUMULATIVE CAUSATION

In contrast to the neo-classical framework, and following the Keynesian oriented ideas of Myrdal (1957), Kaldor (1970)[10] and others, greater integration may permit the more prosperous regions to more completely exploit agglomeration economies (associated with traditional notions of economies of scale, scope and density) and as a result lead to further divergence in regional economic performances.[11]

Figure 4.1 provides a simple diagrammatic presentation of the theory. The rate of productivity growth is treated as a function of income because of agglomeration economies and increasing returns to scale. This is consistent with the Verdoorn model (Verdoorn, 1949) where the rate of productivity growth, $r$, is assumed as $r = a + by$ with $b$ being the Verdoorn coefficient. With efficiency wages growing inversely with technical progress ($w = c - dr$) and efficiency wage growth itself inversely related to the rate of growth

10 Kaldor (1970) rejected the neo-classical model on the grounds that: 'The prevailing distribution of real income in the world – the comparative riches or poverty of nations, or regions – is largely to be explained not by "natural" factors but by the unequal incidence of development in industrial activities. the 'advanced', high-income areas are inevitably those which possess a highly developed modern industry. In relation to differences in industrial development, explanations in terms of "resource endowment" do not get us very far. One can, and does, say that industrial production requires a great deal of capital – both in terms of plant and machinery, and of human skills, resulting from education – but in explaining such differences in 'capital endowment' it is difficult to separate cause from effect. It is as sensible – or perhaps more sensible – to say that capital accumulation results from economic development as that it is a cause of development. Anyhow, the two proceed side by side. Accumulation is largely financed out of business profits; the growth of demand in turn is largely responsible for providing the inducements to invest capital in industry and also the means of financing it.'

11 Young (1928) developed the first important growth model that embraced a production function displaying increasing returns to scale. The problem with increasing returns is that they are incompatible with perfect competition, since marginal costs (or prices in perfect competition) lie under average costs, which means that firms are earning negative profits. For a detailed discussion of neo-Keynesian regional growth theory, see McCombie (1988b).

of output ($y = e - fw$), so $y_{t+1}$ can be seen to equal $e + f(ad - c) + bdfy_t$. or $gy_t + h$. Setting an equlibrium growth path of $y_e = y_t = y_{t+1}$ and substituting gives a geveral solution of $y_t = (y_0 - y_t)g^t + y_e$, where $y_0$ is the initial growth rate. For cumulative growth $g > 1$ and $y_t > y_e$. The situation is seen in the diagram where the initial rate of growth exceeds the equilibrium level and $g > 1$. The rate of growth, therefore, accelerates along the path $y_0 => y_1 => y_2 =>$ etc.

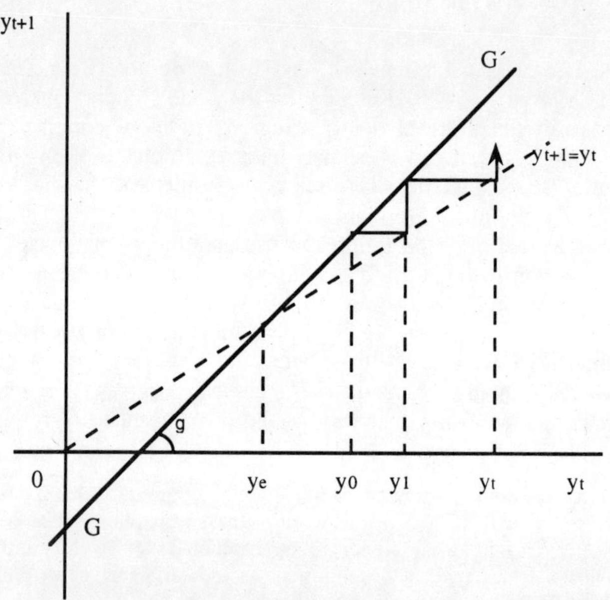


Figure 4.1 *Cumulative causation*

A number of changes in the nature of industry and trade since the development of the neo-classical approach are often cited as reasons for the greater applicability of this Keynesian style of looking at the issue.[12] The growth in intra-industry trade (the trading of similar products between countries and regions) is seen by some as favouring regions which already have a specialism in a particular form of production. This initial advantage

12 The growth of labour unions in the early part of the twentieth century also adds an institutional element to the argument for cumulative causation. The growth of national wage bargaining and downward rigidities in wage rates can be seen as an impediment to the mobility of labour from low to high income areas.

is often strengthened in a world of multinational producers who have established a dominant position in markets.[13]

The shift away from manufacturing (de-industrialisation) towards a more service oriented economy (Wabe, 1986) also introduces important complexities into the neo-classical framework, the latter having been essentially developed at the end of the nineteenth century to explain the behaviour of industrial undertakings.

There are a number of variations on the cumulative causation model. Krugman (1991), for example, focuses on the urbanisation process, arguing

[13] The basic issue has been the concern that the simple neo-classical mechanisms do not work to create pressures for economic convergence. In the very simple two region case seen as the left portion of the figure below the same good is being produced in each area involving the same constant returns to scale production function relating output to homogeneous inputs of capital and labour. Here A represents an initially 'rich' region with high marginal real wage rates (ω) but low marginal returns on capital (Π) and B is a 'poor' region with low wages but a high marginal return on investment. Market forces would result in capital flows from A to B with labour migrating in the opposite direction. This leads, under the normal assumptions of neo-classical economics of factor markets, perfect factor divisibility and so on, to factor returns converging across the regions.

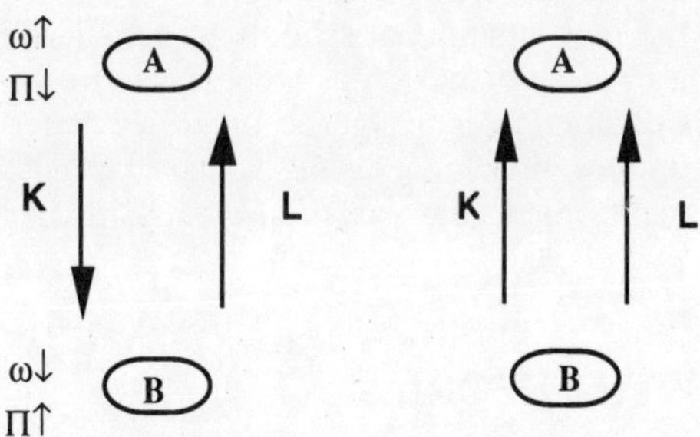


This is a useful conceptualisation for some purposes but avoids, at least for our uses, two important issues. It says nothing about how the regions in combination will grow other than that this is dependent on the availability of factors. This seems intellectually to run counter to what we have seen in history. Second, this idea of convergence defines much of the empirical evidence that is around us. Quite simply as many economists have noted in the past, and Lucas (1988; 1990) highlighted most articulately to put impetus into the current controversy, factor flows do not correspond to the simple model. Capital would seem to move to regions that already have a relative abundance and, as was Lucas's main point, individuals with human capital migrate from places where it is scarce to those where it is abundant. The right portion of the figure provides directional factor flows.

that cities are the core of any economic activity in a modern economy and links this to the costs of transportation to markets. The argument being:

> Given sufficiently strong economies of scale, each manufacturer wants to serve the national market from a single location. To minimize transportation costs, she chooses a location with large local demand. But local demand will be large precisely where the majority of manufacturing choose to locate. Thus there is a circularity that tends to keep a manufacturing belt in existence once it is established.

Krugman's arguments and variations proposed by others on this theme add refinements to the basic cumulative causation model but do little to tackle a core problem. They help explain why divergent growth rates may continue of widen but have very little to say why spatial growth diverged in the first place. they offer guidance as to why a pattern of development may continue but say little about where the pattern was initiated.

While some of these observations and ideas justify the need to look beyond the supply-driven focus of the neo-classical school, the more widespread concern with demand considerations that dominated macroeconomics growth theory in the 1960s and 1970s provided a positive incentive towards looking at Keynesian frameworks. It also tied into a period of active macroeconomic policy formulation where ideas of demand management dominated, but the details of exactly how and where to intervene in the economy had been less thoroughly thought through.

It is now useful to compare the more traditional schools of cumulative causation thought with the recent upsurge of work on endogenous growth that also points to the prospect of continual divergence in growth rates. While the two general models lead to similar conclusions, the endogenous growth approach would seem more relevant to the industrial composition of much of modern Europe.

## 4.4 ENDOGENOUS GROWTH THEORIES

The recent upsurge of policy based interest reflected in the new growth theories and related developments stems from a combination of factors. Economic restructuring, technological change and the shifts in regional growth patterns, for example, have exerted a major impact on resource allocation and welfare. At the global, national, regional and urban levels, economies have become more interdependent. Policy makers have also become more aware of the need to stimulate competitive behaviour: the move to economic deregulate being one such manifestation of this. Regional economic policies largely reflect responses to a permanent conflict between the relatively efficient use of scarce resources in core regions of the

EU and the resulting equity discrepancies with respect to peripheral regions.[14].

Production-oriented policies can exert both strong spatial and sectoral pressuress. A regional innovation policy, for eaxample, promoting the microelectronics industry or the telecommunications sector can target areas with a favourable 'seedbed' potential for these sectors. Technological innovation is, therefore, not manna from heaven as in the Solow–Swan neo-classical model, but can be promoted by public policy.[15] Regions in this framework are competitive geographical units that try to obtain an economic advantage through developing or adopting technologically advanced products or processes. Questions emerge as to what type of spatial selection environment induces such 'technogenesis'.

The reason why technological change can create spillovers and can lead to increasing returns is that technological inputs are non-rival goods. New inventions are produced at a high cost for the first unit but subsequent units can be produced at virtually zero cost. This generates non-convexities in production (Romer, 1990a) even if such goods are partially excludable. The technological spillover phenomenon is better captured by human capital accumulation or the introduction of new goods rather than by conventional notions of physical capital accumulation.[16] The characteristics of dynamic competitive equilibrium can be traced by setting up an optimal control problem. Where a steady state exists, the presence of an externality, for example through R&D, creates a divergence between the private and social rates of return and the competitive equilibrium may not in this case be Pareto-optimal.

To highlight a common feature of most of the endogenous growth models a simple model of endogenous technological change can be formulated in which the existence and properties of the steady state are

14 While the new growth theories attempt to handle some of these issues they have been critiqued on at least three fundamental grounds. First, they are preoccupied with supply considerations. Second, there are other explanations of differential growth rates that do not require assumptions of increasing returns. Third, they rely on static formal equilibrium frameworks that take no account of institutional context.

15 Kaldor and others did introduced more sophisticated notions of technical progress into growth theory. Kaldor (1957), in a framework later refined by Arrow (1962), attempted to bring it in as an endogenous process. Essentially he has a vintage model with fixed coefficients where the productivity of factors working on new machines is related to total past investment – the technical progress function $\dot{Y}/Y = g(\dot{K}/K)$.

16 Economies of scale internal to the firm may generate some increasing returns to capital, but their extent is likely to be limited. Thus, the new models of growth emphasise the external benefits of formal education, public knowledge, entrepreneurial imitation and the introduction of new goods (Romer, 1986).

readily established without having to explicitly solve the underlying dynamic optimisation problem.[17]

Technological change is considered a labour augmenting process.[18] N measures the effective labour input, N = L T, where L is the quantity of workers and T is an index of the average quality of labour input, that depends on the stock of knowledge and practices. The neo-classical model set out above is a special case in which T grows at the exogenous rate g. Here this assumption is relaxed. Important to the current view of the process of technological innovation is that a change in T requires a production process with real resource inputs, a multi-product output, its own technology, market structure, spatial differentiation and its own changing technology. A change in T is, thus, generated by the following process of knowledge creation:

$$\dot{T} = H(R/L, T) \tag{4.12}$$

17 The endogenous approach to economic growth represents only one of several strands of the growing literature on economic development. It has also brought with it a new set of empirics, see Durlauf and Quah (1998) on methodologies, while Temple (1999) summarises the empirical findings. While much of this literature relates to macroeconomic growth it is also of considerable relevance for analysing regional dynamics. Martin and Sunley (1998) offer the following brief outline of the various frameworks that now exist.

| Type of growth theory | Features |
|---|---|
| Augmented neoclassical | Physical and human capital, exogenous technical progress universally available. Slow and conditional convergence within clubs of countries with similar socioeconomic structures |
| Endogenous broad capital | Capital investment, constant returns through knowledge spillovers. Cummulative divergence, but shaped by government spending and taxation. |
| Intentional human capital | Spillovers from education and training investments by individual agents. Convergence dependent on returns to investment, public policy, and patterns of industrial and trade specialization. |
| Schumpetarian endogenous innovation | Technological innovation by oligopolistic producers, with technological diffusion, Transfer, and imitation. Multiple steady states and persistent divergence likely. Possible club convergence and catch-up. |

18 Technology here has a very broad meaning: 'The word technology invokes images of manufacturing, but most economic activity takes place outside of factories. ideas include the innumerable insights about packaging, marketing, distribution, inventory control, payment systems, information systems, transaction processing, quality control and worker motivation that are all used in the creation of value in a modern economy' (Romer, 1993),

where R/L is expenditure per worker on activities such as education, training and R&D. The change in T is, thus, positively related to the intensity of the effort devoted to the enhancement of labour quality as well as the current level of labour quality.[19]

The public sector and private sector in the economy both carry out knowledge creating activities, financed by taxes and retained profits respectively. For simplicity, these activities are combined and it is assumed that a fraction m of national income is allocated to this process of technical change:

$$R = mY \tag{4.13}$$

As with the accumulation of physical capital, a trade-off arises because a large value of m reduces current consumption, but yields a higher level of output in the future. If the production function relating effective per capita output to effective per capita capital is as in equation (4.2), $y = f(k)$, then using equation (4.13):

$$\dot{T}/T = H(R/LT, 1) = H(my,1) \equiv h(mf(k)) \tag{4.14}$$

Households maximise lifetime utility according to equation (4.5), but consumption per capita at any time cannot exceed $f(k) - \delta k - \dot{k} - mf(k)$. There now two decision variables: the propensity to save and the propensity to allocate resources to technical change. Both propensities will be constant and on a steady state growth path. As in the standard neo-classical model, income per head will grow in the steady state at a constant rate, but equation (4.14) shows that this rate is now a function of both m (the proportion of resources devoted to education, innovation, etc.), and $k$ (the effective capital intensity). It is straightforward to show how savings behaviour affects $k$ and, therefore, the rate of growth of income per capita. The propensity to save for physical capital accumulation, s, equal to

$$s \equiv (\dot{K} + \delta K)/Y \tag{4.15}$$

Turning to the steady state growth path on which s and m are constant we assume that the labour input L again grows at an exogenous rate n. The 'fundamental growth equation', similar to the Solow–Swan model, is, for given s and m, the path of the effective capital intensity k:

$$\dot{k} = sf(k) - \delta k - [n + h(mf(k))]k \tag{4.16}$$

[19] The function is assumed to be homogeneous of degree one, twice differentiable and concave.

The long-run equilibrium level of the relative capital intensity is given by $k^*$ for which $\dot{k} = 0$. Under the specified conditions, such an equilibrium exists and is stable.

In this model the positive feedback loop from output growth to technological change is still consistent with a steady state due to diminishing marginal returns to physical capital, combined with constant returns to scale. At very high levels of effective capital intensity, capital accumulation does not proceed fast enough to accommodate growing effective labour input. This reduces the capital intensity.

If, however, there are increasing returns to scale in production, ever-increasing growth rates emerge. Romer (1986) justifies such a model by the observation that over several centuries world-wide labour productivity growth has been accelerating (see also Kremer 1993), although it is equally true that during the last forty years productivity growth exhibited a downward trend. Nijkamp and Poot (1993) formulate a model of increasing returns in which such ever increasing growth is eventually checked by technological, social and economic capacity constraints.

The merit of the simple model is that it shows how endogenous technical change generates a link between thriftiness and per capita growth: for example, if the removal of a tax distortion raises the optimal steady state savings ratio, the per capita growth rate becomes permanently higher. By means of Figure 4.2 it can be established that;

- if the savings propensity s increases, $k^*$ and the rate of growth of output per worker h( m f($k^*$) ) increase;
- if the rate of depreciation $\delta$ increases, $k^*$ and the rate of growth of output per worker h( M f($k^*$) ) decreases;
- if the rate of growth of labour supply n increases, aggregate output will grow faster, but $k^*$ and the rate of growth of output per worker decline;
- if the optimal proportion of income devoted to the production of technical change m increases, the growth rate of aggregate output increases, $k^*$ decreases, but here the rate of growth of output per capita increases.

This assumes that the rate of population growth, n, is exogenous. Theories have been formulated that explain fertility decisions in an intertemporal optimisation framework similar to that for the neo-classical growth model (Barro and Becker, 1989). What is required is the notion of dynastic utility: parents care about the utility attained by their children when reaching adulthood and by subsequent generations (Becker and Barro, 1988). Becker *et al.* (1990) show that if endogenous fertility is combined with human capital accumulation and the latter process exhibits increasing returns, multiple steady states emerge: an undeveloped steady state with little human capital and high fertility and a developed state with growing human capital and low fertility. A common feature of these increasing returns to scale models is a sensitivity to initial conditions.[20] In increasing returns models such as in Becker *et al.* (1990), historical endowments and 'luck' are critical determinants of differentials in growth which we may observe between countries or regions.

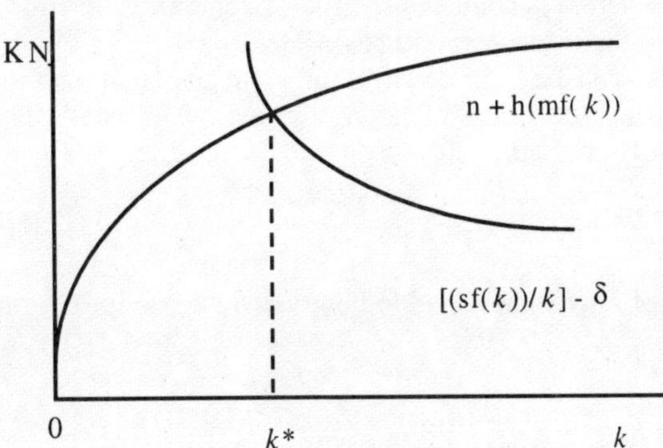


Figure 4.2 *Thriftiness and per capita income growth*

## 4.5 OPEN ECONOMY GROWTH MODELS

The model developed above has artificially been confined to the case of a closed economy. The growing importance of trade, capital flows, a diffusion of product and process innovations, and net migration at the inter-regional and international levels suggest that spatial interactions need to be explicitly considered, both in terms of their direct effects on growth and their effects on technological change. In this section we address these issues by considering, in this order: factor mobility, diffusion and trade. We also briefly note the implications for policy.

If inter-regional differences in technological change generate inter-regional differences in growth rates, a reallocation of production factors may be expected. In the neo-classical model such a reallocation would generate a convergence in the rate of technological change. This can be demonstrated by means of the model of the previous section.

If production factors are paid their marginal product and the effective amount of capital per worker is k, the real rate of return on capital is $f(k)$ and the real wage at time t is $[e^{h(Mf(k))t} f(k) - k f'(k)]$. Net capital movements would thus be in the direction of low-income regions (with low values of k) while net labour migration would be in the direction of high income regions. It is well known, however, that capital often does not flow from

20 Initial conditions do not matter in the Solow model.

rich to poor countries as the neo-classical model predicts. It can be argued that, given differences between countries in human capital accumulation, the external benefits of human capital, capital market imperfections and political uncertainties, real risk-adjusted rate of return differentials are in fact small (Mankiw, 1995). Similarly, human capital may migrate from places where it is scarce to places where it is abundant (a process sometimes referred to as the brain-drain), rather than vice versa (Lucas, 1988).

Labour migration can be considered to offer an explanation for such observations. Separating the effect of natural growth and migration, the change in labour supply is given:

$$\dot{L} = nL + M \tag{4.17}$$

where net migration M may be assumed to be given by a gravity-type model of the form:

$$M = (LL^f/q)(w - w^f) \tag{4.18}$$

where (1/q) is the speed of response of the imperfectly mobile production factor q labour to a real wage differential. The parameter q may be, for example, positively related to the distance between the regions. Job search models of migration readily lead to such a specification (Borjas, 1989; Poot, 1993). Combining equations (4.17) and (4.18) with the earlier model, the fundamental growth equation now becomes (in growth rate form):

$$\dot{k} = (sf(k)/k) - \delta - n - 1/q\{e^{h(mf(k))t}[f(k) - kf'(k)] - w^f\}L^f - h(mf(k)) \tag{4.19}$$

Equation (4.19) shows how migration would act as an equilibrating mechanism: in low-income regions the real wage would be low and grow slowly (due to a lower rate of technological change). Outward migration raises the effective amount of capital per worker k and therefore raises the level of the real wage as well as its rate of change. The reverse is true for high-income regions. The parameter q would measure how fast this process occurs.

A problem with this model is that it ignores the effect of migrants on technological change. If migrants provide new ideas and encourage investment embodying new technologies, there are dynamic gains from inward migration not captured in the equation. These effects may lead to the 'brain drain' effects. Empirical findings indicate that there are dynamic gains from migration which implies that migration may have a diverging rather than converging effect on real income disparities.[21] The regional literature suggests that migrants on balance move in the right direction, but that this

21 The evidence is, for example, that net immigration in developed countries has raised per capita incomes.

reallocation does not reduce inter-regional disparities. This conforms to a cumulative causation process rather than neo-classical convergence. However, recent work by Persson (1994) and Cashin and Loayza (1995) finds empirical evidence for migration aiding convergence within Sweden and between South Pacific countries.

Introducing diffusion in the simple model of endogenous technological change provides additional insights on the growth paths. Diffusion analysis has recently become an important field of research in industrial economics. At the microlevel, this work not only focuses on the distribution and adoption of new technologies, but also on business services and networks related to technological transformations (Cappellin, 1989). In most diffusion studies the conventional S-shaped curve forms a central component (Davies, 1979; Metcalfe, 1981; Morrill *et al.,* 1988). The adoption time and the adoption rate can be captured by this curve. The precise shape of the S-curve can then be explained by such factors as firm size, market structure and the profitability of innovations (Kamien and Schwartz, 1982). An important negative influence can be exerted by barriers to information transfer in a multi-region system.

At the macro-level, the model so far has simply interpreted technology as know-how augmenting the labour input. Equation (4.14) can be modified to explicitly consider the transmission of the accumulation of know-how from one region to another. It is then straightforward to show that diffusion is compatible with a steady state in which both regions could grow at different rates. The equilibrium effective capital $k^*$ and $k^{f*}$ can then be found as the steady state solution to the simultaneous differential equations.[22]

$$\dot{k} = \mathrm{sf}(k) - [\delta + \mathrm{n} + \mathrm{h}(\mathrm{mf}(k) + \mathrm{dh}(\mathrm{m^f f}(k^{\mathrm{f}}))]k \qquad (6.20a)$$

$$\dot{k}^{\mathrm{f}} = \mathrm{sf}(k^{\mathrm{f}}) - [\delta^{\mathrm{f}} + \mathrm{n^f} + \mathrm{h}(\mathrm{m^f f}(k^{\mathrm{f}})) + \mathrm{dh}(\mathrm{mf}(k))]k^{\mathrm{f}} \qquad (6.20b)$$

The existence and stability of a solution ($k^*$, $k^{f*}$) depends on the properties of the functions f and h and the values of the parameters. If the diffusion parameter is very large, for example, overshooting may take place and the trajectories of the effective capital per worker could become unstable.

In most cases, trade, factor mobility and diffusion of technical change occur simultaneously. Freeman (1988) finds that trade theory offers two quite different views of the interrelationship between these flows. The Heckscher–Ohlin theory suggests that trade and factor mobility are substitutes in achieving factor price equalisation and a final equilibrium with a static allocation of factors. If trade results, though, from differences in technology between regions, the flows are likely to be complementary. Increases in net migration can then increase trade and generate capital inflows.

22 Where d is a diffusion parameter.

A key issue involving the relation between trade and growth is whether regional openness leads to inter-regional convergence. The traditional neo-classical trade-and-growth model (Oniki and Uzawa, 1965), suggests that two trading regions with an identical rate of growth of labour supply would, under standard conditions, move towards a long-run balanced growth path. The two regions grow on this path at identical rates and the pattern of specialisation is determined by the equilibrium factor intensities, i.e. the regions would produce relatively more of the good which uses the abundant production factor more intensively.

The extension of this two-good, two-factor model to incorporate endogenous technical change is straightforward. In the trade model, there are two goods: a consumption good and an investment good. The consumption good is chosen as *numéraire* whilst the relative price of the investment good (i.e. the terms of trade) is p. In the steady-state, capital intensities $k^*$ and $k^{f*}$ will exist if and only if both regions grow at the same rate, otherwise p continues to change.

This is the generalisation of the usual assumption that the natural growth rate in both regions must be identical for the existence of a steady-state. While differences in the growth rates of labour supply n and $n^f$ may be small between regions, the introduction of endogenous technical change is a disequilibrating factor in a trade model. From any given starting position the growth rates of effective labour supply in the two regions may not converge.

With a positive diffusion parameter d, the process of innovation diffusion increases the rate of growth in income per head. There are similarly dynamic gains from trade. These are not captured in the trade model.[23]

The neo-classical trade model assumes that the labour-augmenting technical change affects the consumption and the investment goods sectors equally. It is more realistic to assume that labour productivity improvements could vary between sectors, or that a trade advantage is generated by product innovations. Alternatively, the level of activity in specific sectors may provide a learning-by-doing benefit for the whole economy. In this case an increase in the supply of the resource used intensively in the knowledge generating sector speeds up growth. Similarly, the market allocation of resources to this sector is sub-optimal because firms do not take spillover benefits into account.

In an open economy, the capture of spillover benefits from other regions increases growth, but what matters from a policy perspective is which of the regions has a comparative advantage in R&D. If subsidies are

23 The dynamic gains from economic integration have been formally modelled by Rivera-Batiz and Romer (1991), who show that integration of regional economies raises the average growth rate. It is, though, possible that a specialisation based on comparative advantage leads to a sub-optimal investment in R&D activities by resource-rich economies (Grossman and Helpman, 1994).

given to regions that are better at manufacturing than innovating, the overall growth rate may decline.[24]

With technical change positively related to output, a feedback mechanism is generated in which production exhibits increasing returns to scale. Uneven development is a necessary outcome of such a situation: an initial discrepancy in capital–labour ratios between regions will be reinforced over time.

Trade specialisation may also generate such uneven development. An example of such a situation is a model formulated by Krugman (1981). Krugman assumes that an agricultural good and a manufactured good can be produced by means of Ricardian production techniques, with increasing external economies of scale.[25] In either case, the technical coefficients representing the input requirements per unit of output decline as the capital stock increases. The region with the larger initial capital stock has the higher profit rate and, if all profits are saved, generates the fastest capital accumulation. The result is an ever-increasing divergence between the regions, which only ends when a boundary of some kind has been reached. Krugman assumed this to be a limit to labour supply.

Moreover, factor mobility and commodity trade may reinforce each other through technical change. Lucas (1988) suggests that a difference in human capital accumulation is one of the main causes of difference in growth rates between regions. Different goods have different potentials for human capital growth through on-the-job training or through learning-by-doing. Consequently, the comparative advantage that determines which goods get produced also determines the rate of growth in human capital (and therefore technical change).

Lucas's model of trade and growth has features similar to Krugman's (1981) model, although the increase in the efficiency of the Ricardian production technology in the former is due to human capital accumulation through learning-by-doing, rather than economies of scale through physical capital accumulation. Nonetheless, if two goods are produced which are close substitutes (i.e. they have a substitution elasticity greater than one), there will be a tendency for complete specialisation with the outcome determined by the initial conditions.

24 A more in-depth analysis of comparative advantage and long-run growth is provided by Grossman and Helpman (1990). In their model, there are three sectors: an R&D sector, which produces blueprints for new products and also generates increases in the stock of knowledge, an intermediate aoods sector and a final consumption goods sector. Resources devoted to R&D increase the varieties of differentiated inputs in final production and this in turn raises total factor productivity. Applying this to two regions, each with fixed primary resources, a steady-state growth rate can be computed.

25 Such external economies are often empirically indistinguishable from technical change.

The implication of many of the 'New Growth Theory', 'New Economic Geography' and 'New International Economics' is that policy has a role in ensuring that initial conditions on the growth path are created that take into account the possibility of a technological comparative advantage. To ensure, for example, that more resources are devoted to goods with a high learning-by-doing propensity, an industrial policy of picking winners would appear helpful in the Lucas model. The introduction of trade also generates complete specialisation. Over time, the terms of trade change continuously to reinforce the pattern of comparative advantage. Provided the goods are good substitutes, regions that produce goods enjoying a faster technical change will continue to have a higher growth rate, resulting in a persisting change in the terms of trade. This dynamic trade model again suggests a persistent pattern of uneven development.[26]

There is a fairly long tradition of emphasising uneven development in the regional growth literature, such as expounded in Myrdal's (1957) cumulative causation theory discussed above. The current challenge in this type of modelling is to be able to endogenise changes in the position of individual regions in this growth continuum. Possibilities for such growth switches would include the introduction of different income elasticities for different classes of goods on the demand side and, on the supply side, the continuing introduction of new goods, with learning potentials declining as production increases. Such factors could continuously shake up the existing pattern of specialisation. Kaldor's (1961) stylised facts of growth, which include the observation of a large inter-country variance in productivity growth rates, led at the regional level to a search for explanations in terms of export demand and patterns of specialisation.

Since this literature was influential in traditional thinking about regional policies, it is important to compare it with the modern approaches that are supply and technology-oriented.

Traditionally, the regional growth literature has tended to proceed along Keynesian lines with a heavy emphasis on demand considerations. Output growth in a region is driven in the well known Kaldor–Dixon–Thirlwall model by relative competitiveness and income growth outside the region (Dixon and Thirlwall, 1975). In such an export-led growth model, supply-side factors play only a role in terms of the effects of cost inflation and productivity on relative competitiveness.[27] This model explains differences in equilibrium growth rates between regions in terms of differences in price and income elasticities in the demand for exports and differences in rates of autonomous productivity growth.

26 Markusen (1996) emphasises that industrial policy consequently favours the highly urbanised high-income regions and that a top-down regional policy continues to be desirable to avoid increasing inequities between regions.

27 The latter effect being by means of Verdoorn's law (Verdoorn, 1949).

Output growth is assumed to be export-led with the export demand function having constant price and income elasticities. Price inflation results from fixed mark-up pricing on production costs, which in turn depend on unit wage costs and labour productivity. Central to this growth model is that labour productivity is partly dependent on growth of output itself, i.e. Verdoorn's Law.

The empirical literature regarding this later relationship suggests that the observed relationship may be the result of simultaneous responses in output and labour markets to changes in demand, combined with the effects of economies of scale and technical progress. Dynamic increasing returns appear to exist, but what is missing is an explicit specification of economies of scale and the link between output growth and technological change.[28]

This model has unrealistic implications if it is considered in an explicit two region situation in which income growth in either region affects growth in the other region through trade.[29] Krugman (1981) observes that long-run balance of payments equilibrium in such a regional growth-and-trade framework necessitates a strict relationship between differences in growth rates between regions on the one hand and income elasticities of the demand for exports and imports on the other. The Kaldor–Dixon–Thirlwall model is not informative about the processes that would ensure that the growth rates generated by this model would be consistent with long-run balance of payments equilibrium.

If, for instance, technical change proceeds at a different pace in two regions, growth in the more innovative region could be hampered by lower demand for its output from the less innovative, and competitive, region. Indeed, if the Verdoorn effect is strong enough, a situation may be created in which a detrimental shock in the trading partner's economy (e.g. a rapid growth in nominal wages) is more than compensated by a negative effect on the local economy.

The model does not explicitly take into account the possibility of migration between regions, nor the diffusion and adoption of technological advances. These phenomena cannot be readily introduced. For example, net migration would respond to the difference in growth rates in per capita incomes, but the latter are likely themselves to be affected by net migration. Moreover, production capacity limits are assumed unimportant. In essence, the model describes the properties of a demand-driven steady state growth

28 Moreover, Scott (1989) finds that the link between productivity and competitiveness implied by the Verdoorn relationship and the export demand function is too strong: nominal wages can react to an increase in productivity, which could partly offset the effect of productivity growth on export growth.

29 It is straightforward to compute the reduced form for the per capita income growth rates in both regions, but dependent on the choice of parameters, these growth rates could differ and would suggest a persisting trade imbalance (Nijkamp and Poot, 1993).

path rather than full dynamics. Yet it does make explicit that an exogenous shock to trade can have a long-term impact on the equilibrium growth rate, although the introduction of simple explicit feedback effects can strongly modify the behaviour which may be expected in the absence of such effects.

## 4.6 GROWTH THEORIES AND THE EU

The EU has developed over a period when there has been considerable debate about the driving forces behind economic growth. It was formed at a time when the Keynesian school of economics was coming to the fore; it then went through a period of demand-focused macroeconomic thinking followed by reactive supply-side concerns, and now finds itself in the steam of new growth theory thinking. The mainstream theories certainly have provided no continuity or consensus as to the causes of economic growth nor to the policies that would be useful in stimulating it.

More recent economic work, while elaborating on these ideas, provides little more by way of consensus. Balassa (1961) focuses on the opportunities and low factor costs often found in more backward regions and argues that frontier regions could well be the main beneficiaries of the spread effects induced by greater economic integration.

Krugman and Venables (1990) use similar arguments to reach different conclusions. They argue that, while economies of scale may well exist, the removal of impediments to trade could mean that these can be reaped at peripheral locations where factor costs are low as well as at the existing core regions where agglomeration advantages have previously dominated. This may, therefore, lead to convergence in economic performance of periphery and core regions, but leave regions located between them at a disadvantage – effectively a sort of doughnut of economic depression results.

The importance of monetary union, of the type currently being undertaken in the EU, for regional economic performance has attracted a particularly extensive literature.[30] In broad terms the argument is that the development of a common trade policy linked with a monetary union deprives Members of trade-policy instruments which are often used in support of spatially concentrated industries (Williamson, 1976). Put another way (Pearce, 1972), a common currency destroys 'monetary illusions' which allow different real wages to exist. Such differences in real wages are seen to off-set variations in productivity levels and hence allow regions with relatively low productivity to compete successfully with those with higher productivity. A common currency, if it were to lead to labour in the less-productive regions demanding equal money wages because of equalisation of price levels, makes the maintenance of tolerable prosperity in such regions

30 A clear analysis of the implications of monetary integration on real economies is contained in De Grauwe (1997).

impossible. Effectively it means real wages would be pushed up, making these regions uncompetitive.

Another argument found by Balwin (1994) is that monetary union will eliminate exchange rate uncertainty, which will in turn reduce the real rate of interest. This will give rise to a temporary increase in growth as capital is accumulated. In the context of a neo-classical model, however, once the new equilibrium is reached the growth rate of output returns to its former level. Furthermore, it may be argued that a fall in the real rate of return on investment will reduce the level of investment. Hence, the removal of exchange rate uncertainty may lead to a lower rate of economic growth. Thus monetary union is likely, at best, to have an ambiguous effect on the rate of economic growth.

From a policy perspective, however, whichever theory is favoured there are still grounds for market intervention. If, indeed, economic integration in Europe does follow the neo-classical scenario and economic efficiency and social equity coincide with converging regional economic performance, then the mechanism which produces that (factor mobility) is a slow and gradual one.[31] Policies to lubricate the mechanism could be justified as yielding a positive economic return. Alternatively, if forces of circular-and-cumulative causation are in fact at the fore then active regional policies are needed to limit economic divergence and the adverse social and political (and possibly economic) consequences likely to accompany it. The nature, timing and strength of intervention, though, may well depend upon the basic, underlying economic mechanisms at work. To gain insights into these it is important to have a good appreciation of the on-going trends in EC regional economies.

## 4.7 CONCLUSIONS

Economists are good at many things but they have yet to really offer an acceptable account of why nations or regions grow at different rates. Understanding regional growth processes is a key element in devising appropriate regional economic policies irrespective of the underlying objectives of those policies. In practice, however, and also very much in line with the problems of macroeconomists, regional economists have only a very partial understanding of these processes. The problem is also more difficult than that confronting many macroeconomists because of the openness of most regional economies and the importance that such factors as trade, transfer payments and migration might play.

[31] The factors motivating labour migration behaviour are complex and in addition to it tending to be long term in nature there are circumstances, especially when the role of expectations are brought into the analysis, when it can be apparently perverse in its nature (Molho, 1986).

To put it bluntly, while there are no shortages of economic and social theories that seek to explain economic growth and to account for spatial variations in the growth process, there is no one dominant explanation as to why one region or country should grow faster than another. It is, therefore, from a policy perspective important to be wary of rushing into actions based upon an inflexible adherence to any particular school of thought.

Empirical testing of regional growth theories is relatively limited in the sense that until recently the techniques and the data available were restricted. It has also been limited because the nature of the theories themselves have changed over time in response to new thinking and to changes in background conditions such as prevailing technologies. In the EU context there have also been accompanying institutional developments, not only in terms of regional policies but also with regard to matters such as the environment and social policies. At a more practical level it is only recently that the long-run, comparable data series required to undertake econometric analysis at the sub-national level have begun to emerge.

# 5. Regional Economic Performance in the European Union

## 5.1 INTRODUCTION

The evidence presented in the previous chapters provides clear indications of the diversity in performance across the individual regions of the European Union. These variations in the economic performance of the Union's regions have long been recognised to exist but there is now a more concerted effort to reduce them. This, for example, was made explicit in the White Paper on employment produced by the Commission (Commission of the European Communities, 1993).

The statistical accounts of regional diversities, though, have tended to be descriptive and have provided very little by way of analytical assessment of how regional economies have performed relative to each other or to the European economy as a whole. The rigorous analysis of economic convergence has, therefore, in the past been, rather surprisingly, a neglected and under-researched topic in economics, although there has been something of an up-swell of interest at the aggregate level following Baumol's work on the convergence of OECD economies (Baumol, 1986).

The more rigorous analysis that has been conducted on EU convergence, however, has tended, until quite recently, to be on monetary phenomena and at the national rather than regional level (such as the work of Haldane and Hall, 1991, and Hall *et al.*, 1992 on nominal exchange rate and inflation convergence in the EU). More recently, though, rigorous empirical studies of real convergence at the regional level have emerged. These include work on the EU (Simms, 1995), on Italian regions by Mauro and Podrecco (1994) and Paci and Pigliaru (1995); on Spanish regions by Garcia-Milà and Marimon (1995) and Jimeno and Bentolila (1995); and on Portuguese regions by Barros and Garoupa (1995).[1]

The studies of Japanese, US and European regions by Barro and Sala-i-Martin (1991; 1995) are, however, the most cited studies in the field. They conclude that there is conditional convergence whereby regions are

1 Similar work has also looked at Mexican states (Mallick and Carayannis, 1994); Canadian regions (Milne, 1993); Australian colonies (Cashin, 1995; Oxley and Greasley, 1995) and US states (Carlino and Mills, 1992).

converging towards their steady state at an annual rate of about 2 per cent. Conditional convergence is relevant when economies are not structurally similar and GDP per capita does not converge to the same levels but differences between countries become stationary so that growth rates are the same in the long-run.[2] Aggregate convergence, in contrast, is consistent with a neo-classical framework whereby each region, while having differing initial positions, converge to a common per capita rate, determined by exogenous technical progress.

While Barro and Sala-i-Martin's econometric analysis of European regions offers interesting insights into convergence, it is forced to rely for its empirical analysis on several disparate data sets and to use a number of alternative proxies for variables such as industrial composition in different time frames as explanatory variables. In contrast, a consistent data base is employed in this chapter to both re-examine and up-date the findings of their study and to extend the analysis to embrace a wider set of variables that are often thought to have an influence on the convergence process. In particular, the calculations offered by Barro and Sala-i-Martin relate to a period before the creation of stronger monetary ties between some Union Members that have changed the long-standing nature of national regional policy instruments.

## 5.2 PROBLEMS IN TESTING FOR REGIONAL ECONOMIC CONVERGENCE

As we have seen, in recent years there have been a number of moves towards greater economic integration amongst groups of nations. While the creation of the Single European Market is one clear manifestation of this, and the North American Free Trade Agreement is another, the efforts at attaining a more liberal General Agreement on Tariffs and Trade (GATT), the creation of the General Agreement for Trade in Services (GATS), and the establishment of the World Trade Organisation (WTO) also fit into the general trend. Given this concern with integration and the inevitable implications of such changes on the distribution of economic welfare, it is not surprising that the analysis of economic convergence has become very topical in the 1990s.

Initially, it is important to point out that measuring degrees of regional convergence or divergence is not a straightforward task.

First, in economic terms there are strictly two aspects of convergence, nominal convergence (such as Hall *et al.*, 1992) and real convergence (such

2 Sala-i-Martin (1994) and Martin and Sunley (1998) offer discussions of the various notions of convergence. To test for conditional convergence it is necessary to hold the steady state of each economy and one method of doing this is to introduce additional structural-type variables that proxy for the steady state.

as Durlauf and Johnson, 1992). The former, in the European Union context, is generally seen to concern such things as national convergence in Members' exchange rates, interest rates and inflation rates. It is convergence in the real economy which is of interest here and this ties in with issues such as that of wealth creation, unemployment and productivity growth.

Second, general methods of examining convergence include using such indicators as changes in the coefficient of variation of the dispersion of regional performance over time (sometimes called 'sigma' convergence) or changes in Theil's U-statistic. Such techniques, for example, were employed by Emerson *et al.* (1992) when assessing the spatial implications of a single European currency and by Cingolani (1993) with respect to EU convergence more generally. While useful in some contexts, they generally provide a rather incomplete picture of whether convergence is occurring.

Some of the problems with these more basic measures can be seen by taking a very simple hypothetical example. If there are two countries, J and K, each comprising four regions with their income growth profiles depicted as in Figure 5.1, then, while they may show identical changes in parameters such as their standard deviations[3] or inter-quartile ranges, it is still not altogether clear whether one cannot say that the regional economic performances in J is converging more than in K. For a complete analysis more detailed considerations need to be taken into account.

Accepting these caveats, descriptive measures of convergence show that there has been a degree of convergence in EU regional incomes since the mid-1970s. In Tables 2.6 and 2.7, for example, we have already seen the estimated coefficients of variation for regional household gross domestic product (at levels 1 and 2 of regional aggregation) within the Union for the period 1977 to 1990. The limitations of the level 2 data suggest that the higher level of aggregation is, from a statistical perspective, superior but even so there is a reassuring consistency about the results obtained. The size of the coefficients generally decline over time, albeit very gradually, suggesting that there has been a general trend towards income convergence.

3 Because the type of data set generally used is not generally index number based, however, there is not the problem, using standard deviations in the data over time across regions, of convergence to the base year. In terms of variable $X$ in region i at time t, the formulae employed is to compute:

$$\sigma_t = S_i(X_{it} - m_t)/n - 1 \quad \text{with } i = 1,\ 2,\ ....,n$$

$$q_t = s_t/m_t$$

where : $\sigma_t$ is the standard deviation; $m_t$ is the sample mean across the n regions in each time period; and $q_t$ is the coefficient of variation.

The major problem with this type of measure is that it can be subject to outliers. Hence convergence or non-convergence may be excessively influenced by an outlying region.

The tables also show the implications for regional income disparities as successive enlargements have brought more peripheral regions into the Union (see Keeble *et al.*, 1988). Similar pictures emerge using other standard measures of dispersion such as ratios of deciles.

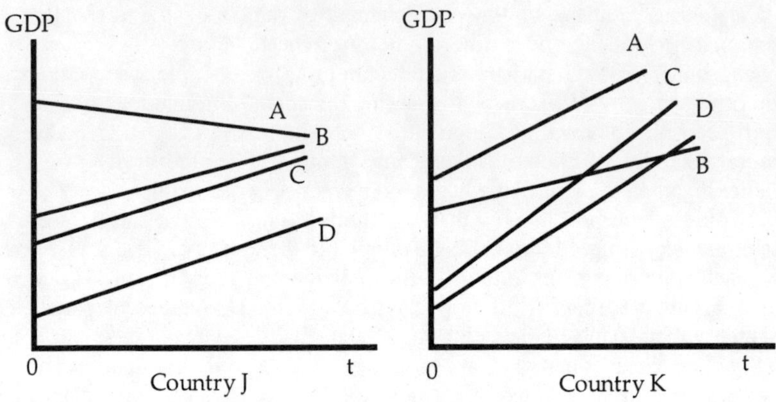


Figure 5.1 *Alternative paths of regional income growth*

There are, however, significant differences in the degrees of convergence exhibited within Member States. Table 2.6, for instance, showed the coefficients of variation for GDP per capita across the larger Member countries and Table 2.10 added to this by taking variations within countries. This type of measure is an indication of the variations in the dispersions of income per capita across EU members and the extent to which it has changed over that sample period. For example, although in 1975 the Netherlands had the lowest dispersion of income per capita in the Union, by 1990 not only had income become more dispersed across Dutch regions than in 1975, but also France, the United Kingdom and Italy now exhibited a lower degree of dispersion. Spain demonstrates the greatest level of convergence in per capita incomes, although it still had the greatest degree of dispersion of income per capita within the Union in 1990.

This type of cross-sectional convergence is often called sigma-convergence and denoted as 'σ-convergence'[4] and, for example, it shows simply that the dispersion in the level of incomes per head has broadly decreased over time between the EU level 1 regions. This is a finding which

4 Although not reported here, changes in the standard deviation of the preferred indicator is often used as an indicator of σ-convergence with convergence occurring if $\sigma_{yt+T} < \sigma_{yt}$ where $\sigma_{yt}$ is the standard deviation of $\log(\psi_{it})$ at time t.

conforms to the more macro analysis, for instance, of Dowrick and Nguyen (1989) across OECD states.

The changing coefficients in these types of analysis can, therefore offer general guidelines, for example, relating to the implications for regional income disparities as successive enlargements have brought more peripheral regions into the Union (Commission of the European Communities, 1988), but offer little beyond this. The major difficulty with these types of measures is that they can be subject to outliers. Hence, convergence or non-convergence may be excessively influenced by an outlying region. Further, it is not possible, or at least very difficult, to consider any causes of change through time.

## 5.3 $\beta$-CONVERGENCE

It is important to be clear on the nature and form of economic convergence that is under study. For the reasons cited above, we are less concerned here with further developing $\sigma$-convergence indicators in this chapter, but rather focus on the concept of $\beta$-convergence. This latter form of convergence occurs when poor economies' per capita incomes tend to initially grow faster than rich economies, such that they catch up with the richer ones. $\beta$–convergence tends towards $\sigma$–convergence, but may be offset by new disturbances that temporarily increase cross-sectional dispersion (Quah, 1996; Sala-i-Martin, 1996). In the long term the regions can have different income levels but are growing at the same rate.

More strictly, Barro and Sala-i-Martin (1991) define the two principal concepts of economic convergence. $\sigma$-convergence refers to a decline in the regional dispersion of real income per head across groups of economies or regions over time, that is $\sigma_{t+T} < \sigma_t$, where $\sigma_t$ is the standard deviation of real income per head over time across the regions. $\beta$-convergence, on the other hand, implies a negative relationship between the growth in income per head and the initial level of income per head in a cross-section of countries or regions. Where this is the case the poor economies are growing faster than the rich economies and hence there is convergence in income per head over time.

In most instances there is no automatic reason why $\beta$- and $\sigma$-convergence should coincide with all economies converging smoothly towards the common steady-state growth path and with the dispersion of the cross-section declining to zero (as seen in Figure 5.2). Indeed, Durlauf and Qhah (1998) provide a number of possibilities for the same $\beta$-convergence statistic.

The two concepts of convergence are not, however, unrelated. Suppose there are N regions, then the real per capita income for regional economy i can be approximated by:

$$\ln(y_{it}) = \alpha + (1 - \beta)\ln(y_{it-1}) + e_{it} \tag{5.1}$$

where the dependent variable in the equation is the natural logarithm of per capita income, $\alpha$ and $\beta$ are constants, with $0 < \beta < 1$ and $e_{it}$ is the random disturbance term. The condition $\beta > 0$ implies $\beta$-convergence because the annual rate of growth is inversely related to $\ln(y_{it-1})$. A higher value of $\beta$ implies a greater degree of convergence. The disturbance term captures temporary shocks to the production function, saving rate and so on, and it is assumed to be independent over time and across regions with a mean of zero and a variance of $\sigma_\varepsilon^2$ for all regions.

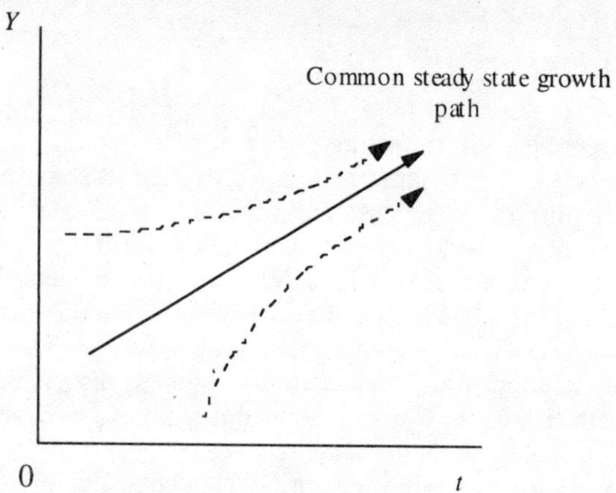


Figure 5. 2 *Coincidental $\beta$ and $\sigma$ convergence*

In order to measure the cross-section dispersion of real income per capita, the sample variance of the log of income is

$$\sigma^2 = (1/N)\Sigma[\ln y_{it} - \mu\_]^2 \tag{5.2}$$

where $\mu$ is the sample mean of $(\ln y_{it})$. If N is large, then the sample variance is close to the population variance and from equation (5.1) the equation for $\sigma_t^2$ can be defined as:

$$\sigma_t^2 = (1 - \beta)^2 \sigma_{t-1}^2 + \sigma_\varepsilon^2 \tag{5.3}$$

This is the first-order difference equation that is stable if $0 < \beta < 1$. Thus if there is no $\beta$-convergence there can be no $\sigma$-convergence. This is, $\beta$-convergence is a necessary condition for $\sigma$-convergence. It is, however, not a sufficient condition, since $\sigma_t^2$ may rise or fall towards the steady state depending on whether the initial value of $\sigma_t^2$ is above or below the steady state.[5]

5 The figures below (based on Sala-i-Martin. 1996), and essentially an extension of Figure 5.1) provide an illustration of this by looking at the behavior of income per head in two economies A and B over time. In the upper left panel at time t the level of per capita income in A exceeds that in B but by time t + T the levels have come closer together because region B has grown faster than A. That is, there has been $\beta$-convergence, the poorer economy has grown faster than the richer one. Moreover, because the dispersion of per capita income at t + T is smaller than at time t, there has also been $\sigma$-convergence. The top right element of the figure shows a different situation with both economies growing but with A growing faster than B. As a result the difference in per capita income is larger at t + T than at the initial time period. Here there is both $\beta$-and $\sigma$-divergence. There is the third case, seen in the bottom elemen,t where the poor economy at time t grows while the richer one declines. The income dispersion between the regions may not have declined if the distance between the curves is the same at t + T as it was at t but there is no $\sigma$-convergence.

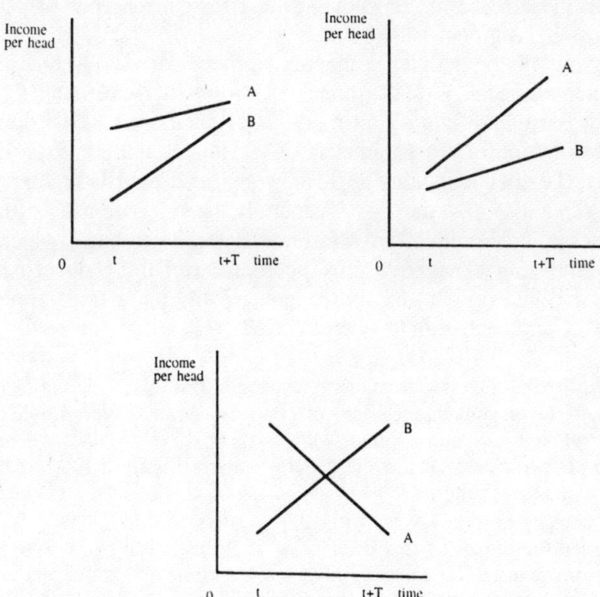


The reason that there is a difference between $\beta$-and $\sigma$-convergence is that they measure different aspects of the world. $\sigma$-convergence is related to the cross-regional distribution of income and how this changes over time. $\beta$-convergence relates to the mobility of different economies within the given distribution of country incomes. The upper elements of the figure are examples of this when the movements in the various economies change the final distribution over time. The lower element is an example in which there is mobility within the

It is important to note that any permanent shocks to the regional economies may preclude $\beta$-convergence from ever being attained. While acknowledging that $\beta$-convergence is not meaningful if shocks to relative regional per capita incomes are persistent, data limitations prevent the use of more powerful stochastic measures of convergence (see, for example, Bernard and Durlauf, 1991; Haldane and Hall, 1991; Hall *et al.*, 1992) across EU regions although analysis using this approach at a national level is provided in later chapters. Although stochastic approaches using, for example, time-varying parameter techniques are not used in this study, because of their veracious need for time series data, it is possible to approximate such an approach by running a series of 'rolling' cross-section regressions and to test whether the $\beta$s estimated are stable over time.

This type of methodology has attracted increasing interest. In the recent past a series of econometric studies, using cross-sectional regression analysis, have been conducted to test for either global economic growth convergence across countries (Baumol, 1986; Barro, 1991; Barro and Sala-i-Martin 1992a; 1995; Dowrick and Nguyen, 1989) or regional convergence (Barro and Sala-i-Martin, 1991; Milne, 1993).[6] Following Baumol (1986), we make use of this mean reversion procedure to test for convergence of per capita income across EU regions.

We proceed by initially developing a theoretical model of $\beta$-convergence founded in the neo-classical growth model of Solow (1956) and the subsequent work of Barro and Sala-i-Martin (1992a). It then outlines the data base used for the estimation of the parameters of the model and proceeds to examine the empirical evidence relating to $\beta$-convergence across EU regions.

Work in this area has, in the past, generally been concerned with determining whether poor economies grow faster than wealthier ones, which is equivalent to identifying a negative cross-section correlation between a country's initial per capita output and subsequent growth for a fixed time period.[7] This type of approach should, therefore, be well-suited for testing

distribution, but the distribution itself remains unchanged. With a larger number of economies the patterns of convergence can, of course, become more complex with some groups of regions converging while others diverge and where outlying or peripheral regions can distort the general pattern. Figure 5.1 offered, for example, a more complex pattern.

6 The empirical work is not, however, without its critics. Solow (1994), for instance, has expressed the view that this body of work '...seems altogether too vulnerable to bias from omitted variables, to reverse causation, and above all to the recurrent suspicion that the experiences of very different national economies are not explained as if they represent different "points" on some well-defined surface'.

7 Barro (1991) offers a fairly typical example of the type of cross-sectional models examined at the national level:

$$\gamma_{it,\, t-T} = \alpha + \beta . y_{it-T} + \delta . X_{it-T} + \varepsilon_{it}$$

for convergence of income across European regions. Indeed, one of the main concerns of this chapter is with extending the regional economic literature in this area and may, in part, be seen as an update of the EU aspects of Barro and Sala-i-Martin's 1991 study, although it differs from this earlier study in three important ways:

- First, the data set is extended both temporally forward and spatially to embrace all current EU member states and, therefore, includes Greece, Spain and Portugal. This enables the undertaking of some tentative analysis of the effects of enlargement on Union economic convergence in the 1980s.
- Second, a consistent data set is used for the period from 1975 which, although this constrains the time span of the study, has the advantage over the series used by Barro and Sala-i-Martin in that it does not require different sources of data being spliced together. It is based on official EU level 1 administrative regions rather than the mixed system of regions employed by Barro and Sala-i-Martin.
- Third, the GDP per capita data is measured relative to the EU average so that convergence is measured across the EU as a whole and not just within the country, as in Barro and Sala-i-Martin (1991). This enables us to interpret our results in terms of the EU as an entity and not in relation to a specific country. This is arguably a more relevant measure of convergence in terms of EU regional policy.
- Finally, rather than following Barro and Sala-i-Martin in the use of ten-year averages of per capita income, three, or four-year periods are used to pick up the differences in speeds of convergence over shorter time periods. Indeed, although the data may exhibit convergence over the long run, in the short run convergence may be faster or slower than on average or may even display divergence over specific time periods. In general it seems that these differences in convergence may be associated with the business cycle, with divergence commonly occurring in recessionary periods and faster convergence in periods of relatively high economic growth in the Union.[8]

where: $\gamma_{it,t-T}$ is country $i$'s growth rate of per capita GDP between $t-T$ and $t$; $y_{it-T}$ is its level of per capita GDP at time $t-T$; and $X_{it-T}$ is a vector of explanatory variables such as investment rates, number of political assassinations, and secondary school enrolments. Jin (1995) offers a different approach focusing on cointegration issues.

8 Indeed, the EU explicitly recognises this longer-run effect in its policy discussions when it talks of the 'stylised facts' of convergence (Commission of the European Union, 1998). It argues 'that convergence occurs and is more rapid during periods of increasing integration and when the economic climate is good'. The reasons for this are seen to stem from the basic forces that lead to convergence, namely: (a) the attraction of investment to regions when costs are lower; (b) the transfer of technology and best practice from leading to lagging

## 5.4 A THEORETICAL MODEL

In theoretical terms a model of spatial convergence in per capita output can be developed from the neo-classical growth model of Solow (1956), Cass (1965) and Koopmans (1965). Follow the notation of Barro and Sala-i-Martin (1992a). The production function, in intensive form, is given by:

$$\hat{y} = f(\hat{k}) \qquad f'(\hat{k}) > 0, \quad f''(\hat{k}) < 0 \tag{5.4}$$

where $\hat{y} = Y/E$, $\hat{k} = K/E$ and where $Y$ is output, $K$ is capital and $E$ represents units of effective labour. There are two exogenous sources of growth in effective labour units. The first is the rate of technical progress, $x$, and the second is the growth rate of the working population, $n$. Therefore,

$$E = Le^{xt} = L_0 e^{(n+x)t} \tag{5.5}$$

In a closed economy, without government, the rate of new investment must equal the rate of saving, defined as income, $Y$, less consumption, $C$. Hence:

$$\dot{K} - \delta K = Y - C \tag{5.6}$$

where $\dot{K}$ is the change in the capital stock, $\delta$ is the rate of depreciation so that $\dot{K} - \delta K$ represents new investment. In terms of effective labour units this equation can be written as:

$$\dot{\hat{k}} = f(\hat{k}) - \hat{c} - (\delta + n + x)\hat{k} \tag{5.7}$$

where $\hat{c}$ is consumption per effective unit of labour ($C/E$).

The representative household is assumed to maximise utility given by:

$$U = u(c) \quad u'(c) > 0, \quad u''(c) < 0 \tag{5.8}$$

where $c$ is consumption per head, $C/L$. Total social utility in each period is weighted by the size of the population and the rate of time preference, $\rho$, in each period. Therefore social utility is maximised by adding social utility over all future time periods, that is:

regions; and (c) migration of workers from regions with low pay and low job opportunities to those with high pay and opportunities - this promotes convergence in wages (and hence costs) rather than in employment and output.

$$u = \int_0^\infty u(c)e^{-(\rho-n)t}dt \tag{5.9}$$

where $L_0$, the base period labour supply, has been normalised to unity. The optimal growth path which maximises social welfare is now obtained by maximising 5.9 subject to the constraint given by equation (5.7). The current value Hamiltonian for this problem is:

$$H = u(c) + m[f(\hat{k}) - \hat{c} - (\delta + n + x)\hat{k}] \tag{5.10}$$

In this case, the maximum principle requires that:

$$\frac{\partial H}{\partial c} = u'(c) - m = 0 \tag{5.11}$$

This condition does in fact maximise $H$ because $u''(c) < 0$ by equation 5.8. The two equations of motion are given by:

$$\begin{aligned} \frac{\partial H}{\partial m} &= f(\hat{k}) - \hat{c} - (\delta + n + x)\hat{k} = \dot{\hat{k}} \\ \frac{\partial H}{\partial k} &= m\left[f'(\hat{k}) - (\delta + n + x)\right] - (\rho - n)m = -\dot{m} \end{aligned} \tag{5.12}$$

Differentiating equation (5.11) with respect to time gives:

$$u''(c)\dot{c} = \dot{m} \tag{5.13}$$

Using equations (5.8) and (5.10) to eliminate $m$ and $\dot{m}$ in equation (5.12) gives a pair of dynamic equations in $c$ and $\hat{k}$ as follows:

$$\dot{\chi} = -\frac{\upsilon'(\chi)}{\upsilon''(\chi)}\left[\phi'(\hat{\kappa}) - (\delta + \xi + \rho)\right] \tag{5.14}$$

$$\dot{\hat{k}} = f(\hat{k}) - \hat{c} - (\delta + n + x)\hat{k} \tag{5.15}$$

Although this non-linear dynamic system can be linearised using Taylor's expansion and the signs of the characteristic roots used to determine the stability of the system, the characteristic roots can not be computed unless specific functional forms are assumed for $u(c)$ and $f(k)$. Therefore, following Barro and Sala-i-Martin (1992a), the utility function is assumed to have the form:

$$u(c)=\frac{c^{1-\theta}-1}{1-\theta} \tag{5.16}$$

Since $u'(c)=c^{-\theta}$ and $u''(c)=-\theta c^{-(1+\theta)}$ equation (5.14) now becomes:

$$c=\frac{c}{q}[f'(k)-(d+x+r)] \tag{5.17}$$

Equations (5.15) and (5.17) give the steady state growth paths for *k* and *c*. In the steady state the effective quantities, $\hat{y}$, $\hat{k}$ and $\hat{c}$, do not change and the per capita quantities, *y*, *k*, and *c* grow at the rate *x*.

To check the stability of the model, one can linearise in the neighbourhood of the steady-state equilibrium $(\bar{c},\bar{k})$. This generates the system:

$$\begin{pmatrix}\dot{k}\\ \dot{c}\end{pmatrix}=\begin{pmatrix}\psi & -1\\ \frac{c}{\theta}f''(k) & 0\end{pmatrix}\begin{pmatrix}k-\bar{k}\\ c-\bar{c}\end{pmatrix} \tag{5.18}$$

where $\psi=\rho-n-(1-\theta)x$, which is assumed to be positive (see Barro and Sala-i-Martin, 1992a) and in the steady state $f'(k)=\delta+\rho+(1+\theta)x$ so that the last term in the 2x2 A-matrix is zero. This system exhibits saddle path stability since the trace and determinant of A are positive and negative, respectively. That is,

$$\begin{aligned}&\mathrm{Tr}(A)=\psi>0\\ &\mathrm{Det}(A)=-\frac{c}{\theta}f'(k)<0\end{aligned} \tag{5.19}$$

The stable root, $\beta$, is given by the formula:

$$\beta=\frac{-\mathrm{Tr}(A)+\{\mathrm{Tr}(A)^2-4\mathrm{Det}(A)\}^{1/2}}{2}$$

which, assuming a Cobb–Douglas technology, such that $\hat{y}=f(\hat{k})=A\hat{k}^{\alpha}$, can be shown to be equivalent to:

$$\beta=\frac{1}{2}\left\{\psi^2+4\left(\frac{1-\alpha}{\theta}\right)(\rho+\delta+\theta x)\left[\frac{\rho+\delta+\theta x}{\alpha}-(n+\delta+x)\right]\right\}^{1/2}-\frac{\psi}{2} \tag{5.20}$$

Because of the Cobb–Douglas technology, the dynamic path of *y* will be the same as that for *k*. Therefore, in discrete time, the solution for log[ $\hat{y}(t)$] is of the form:

$$\log[y(t)] = \log[y(0)]e^{-\beta t} + \log(\bar{y})(1 - e^{-\beta t}) \tag{5.21}$$

The average rate of growth of *y* over the period between 0 and T is:

$$\frac{1}{T}.\log\left[\frac{y(T)}{y(0)}\right] = x + \frac{1 - e^{-bbT}}{T}.\log\left[\frac{\bar{y}}{y(0)}\right] \tag{5.22}$$

The higher the value of $\beta$ the greater the responsiveness of the average growth rate to the gap between the long-run equilibrium level log( $\bar{y}$) and the initial level of income, log(y(0)). The model implies conditional convergence in that for given values of *x* and $\bar{y}$, the growth rate is higher the lower is log(*y*(0)). For the empirical work we estimate:

$$\frac{1}{T}\log\left(\frac{y_{it_0+T}}{y_{it_0}}\right) = \phi - \left(\frac{1 - e^{-\beta t}}{T}\right)\log\left(y_{it_0}\right) + u_{it_0,t_0+T} \tag{5.23}$$

where $\phi = x + \left[\left(1 - e^{-\beta t}\right)/T\right]\left[\log(\bar{y}) + xt_0\right]$, $u_{i,t_0,t_0+T}$ is the error term and i denotes regions. The coefficient on log ($y_{it0}$) in equation (5.23) declines as T increases, for a given $\beta$. As T gets larger the effect of the initial position on average growth rates becomes smaller. $\beta$ is estimated non-linearly to allow for this effect, such that the value of $\beta$ should be independent of the size of T.

At the empirical level, Levine and Renelt (1992) cast some doubts over the mean reversion approach, pointing to their finding of a lack of any robustness in the results that they had derived. They were particularly concerned, using an extreme-bounds test on macroeconomic data, about whether one could actually say much about the variables that influence economic growth. In an analysis of the robustness of variables in explaining spatial economic convergence, and looking at some 62 variables (using three in each regression and the remainder in various combinations of threes to keep the number of permutations within manageable bounds) deployed in 30,856 regressions per variable, Sala-i-Martin (1997) found 'a substantial number of variables can be found to be strongly related to growth'.[9]

9 Although only one of the tested variables passed the extreme bounds test, Sala-i-Martin points to the fact that on t-test criteria some variables were significant almost all of the time while others were consistently insignificant.

## 5.5 β-CONVERGENCE ACROSS EU REGIONS

For estimation purposes, the test equation has the general form:

$$\Delta x_{it} = \alpha + \beta x_{it-j} + \Delta_i G + e_i \qquad (5.24)$$

where: $x_i$ is the variable being tested for convergence; $D_i$ is an (n x k) matrix of k dummy variables capturing regional economic heterogeneity; G is a (k x 1) vector of parameters; $e_i$ is a white noise error term; and i denotes the region. In this modelling framework, $b < 0$ is a necessary, although as Bernard and Durlauf (1991) have shown, not a sufficient condition for convergence.

The basic model specification of equation 5.24 that is examined is:

$$[Y_{iT} - Y_{iT-j}](1/j) = \alpha + \beta Y_{iT-j} + \beta_E[ERM_i . Y_{iT-j}] + \beta_a A_i + \gamma_q N_q + e_i \qquad (5.25)$$

where $Y_{iT}$ is the natural logarithm of gross domestic product per head (relative to the EU average) in region i at time T, and $(Y_{iT} - Y_{iT-j})/j$ is, therefore, the average per annum growth rate in GDP per capita between T and T–j. This specification differs, for example, from the Barro and Sala-i-Martin specification which looks at deviations from national means and thus looks at convergence within countries rather than strictly convergence between countries.

$A_I$ is an agricultural employment variable, which is defined as the proportion of each region's employed population that works in agriculture; $ERM_i$ is a slope dummy with a unitary value reflecting national membership of the Exchange Rate Mechanism, and $N_q$ is a vector of q–country dummies with Denmark the omitted country. The agricultural employment variable is included to allow for the differing composition of economic activities within EU regions. It attempts to capture the structure of regional economic activity. In addition to pure structural considerations, the potential importance of this may also be seen to stem from the substantial transfer payments that are made through the Common Agricultural Policy.

The $ERM_i$ variable reflecting membership of the Exchange Rate Mechanism (ERM), specified as multiplicative with the initial level of regional income, is included to reflect the possible importance in changes in the nature of the institutional restrictions operating in the Union. If one adopts the traditional neo-classical view, then freer economic markets, with reductions in institutional interventions, will allow regions to exploit their comparative advantage and ultimately there will be a convergence in their economic performances. Alternatively, it is often argued that a common trade policy linked with monetary union deprives Members of trade-policy instruments that are often used in support of spatially concentrated industries (Williamson, 1976).

Put another way, a common currency destroys money illusion that allow different real wages to exist. Such differences in real wages are seen to off-set variations in productivity levels and, hence, allow regions with relatively low productivity to compete successfully with those with higher productivity. A common currency, if it led to labour in the less-productive regions demanding equal money wages because of equalisation of price levels, makes the maintenance of tolerable prosperity in such regions impossible. Effectively it means real wages would be pushed up, making these regions uncompetitive. The inclusion of the $ERM_i$ variable allows such ideas to be explored.

In particular, since the $ERM_i$ is not a Union-wide system, in that during the period under review some Members of the EU remained outside it (UK and Greece) while others operated only within a wide exchange rate band (Italy), this may have allowed these countries greater flexibility in domestic policy and, thus, in their approach to national regional policy. The $ERM_i$ dummy is set at zero for all regions of the UK, Greece and Italy for this reason.

The set of country dummies, N, was included to reflect both potential differences in domestic regional policy and variations in national technologies and preferences.

For analytical purposes the definition of a region has been the subject of considerable theoretical debate, but even at the more pragmatic level of our analysis the need to employ standard administrative definitions is not without its difficulties. The Commission of the European Union collects data at several levels of spatial aggregation but at the lower levels the times series are incomplete in the cases of several member countries.

Furthermore, while data are generally collected by national governments at the level 1 aggregation, for domestic administration reasons many time series relating to such variables as income have not traditionally been gathered at lower levels of aggregation. They are, therefore, often synthesised and their reliability is consequently much less robust. Thus, while ideally spatial disaggregation is desired in the data set, often rather larger regions must form the basis of analysis.

The data set initially used for the analysis is, therefore, based on the EU level 1 aggregation. This provides useful annual data on 50 regions in nine countries: the UK (11 regions), West Germany (10 regions), France (8 regions), the Netherlands (4 regions), Belgium (3 regions), Italy (11 regions), Denmark (1 region), Luxembourg (1 region), and Ireland (1 region), for the period 1975–90. In addition, from 1980 data are also available on Greece (3 regions, and from 1983 on Spain (6 regions) and Portugal (1 region) – this gives a cross section of 61 (observations) regions between 1983 and 1990.

It is important to note that (a) West Berlin is excluded from the sample because data are not available for 1990 and, although Greece consists of four regions, the 1980 and 1983 samples only provide data on three regions and these are used throughout. For convenience, these sub-samples are subsequently referred to as EU(9), EU(10) and EU(12) respectively.[10]

Initially, parameters were estimated for each model using cross-sections of European regional data for the years 1975, 1981 and 1988. Regression analysis permits the estimation of the relevant coefficients across 51 EU regions.[11]

Besides enabling a long-term look at convergence over the entire time period, the data enables comparison of the levels of convergence in the real regional economies that took place in the pre-effective Exchange Rate Mechanism period – that is, 1975 to 1981 – with that during the period when the ERM was fully operational – that is, 1981 to 1988. Strictly the ERM came into existence in 1979. The division adopted here reflects both the potential lagged effects of its impact on real regional economies and the fact that there were frequent realignments prior to 1981. Table 5.1 sets out some basic results for the sub-periods,[12] where the structural and country dummies are excluded so that $b_E = b_A = \gamma_q = 0$

In terms of output per capita, the overall explanatory power of the model is not especially high. Given the particular specification of our model, the negative (and significant) $\beta$ coefficients show convergence in per capita gross domestic product across the 51 European Union's regional economies over the time periods estimated. Estimation of the equations at the more disaggregate NUTS 2 level proved possible for a part of the data set and similar indications of convergence in per capita gross domestic product were found.

Convergence would appear, from the size of the $\beta$ coefficients, stronger in the late 1970s (3.7 per cent) than in the 1980s (2.8 per cent) when the introduction of the ERM began to exert an influence. These are also figures that are much higher than, for example, the 1.8 per cent implied by the basic models of Barro and Sala-i-Martin (1991) for the 1950–85 period, although less than the 9.5 per cent found for their last five-year sub-period from 1980–5.

10 The main series employed in this work is gross domestic product per head at market prices in purchasing power parities standard. The original source of these data is the Statistical Office of the European Communities, although it is reproduced in various issues of *Regional Trends*. It is not, however, available for all years in the sample.

11 Estimation was done using SHAZAM: see White (1978).

12 The findings here are presented in more detail in Button and Pentecost (1995b).

Table 5.1. *Initial estimates of regional output (GDP) convergence*

| Coefficient | 1975–81 | 1981–88 | 1975–88 |
|---|---|---|---|
| $\alpha$ | 0.1779 | 0.1332 | 0.1458 |
| | (5.717) | (5.683) | (8.309) |
| $\beta$ | −0.0375 | −0.0276 | −0.0306 |
| | (−5.460) | (−5.461) | (−8.085) |
| $R^2$ | 0.03532 | 0.2341 | 0.4776 |
| $\sigma$ | 0.0153 | 0.0126 | 0.0096 |
| ESS | 0.0116 | 0.0078 | 0.0046 |
| LLF | 141.545 | 151.699 | 165.115 |
| BJ(2) | 3.2494 | 1.1080 | 3.8970 |
| | (5.99) | (5.99) | (5.99) |

*Notes*:
White's heteroscedasticity-consistent t-values in parenthesis
$\sigma$ is the standard error
ESS is the residual sum of squares
LLF is the log likelihood function
BJ(2) is the Bera-Jacque test for normality of the residuals (distributed as Chi-squared with two degrees of freedom)

Table 5.2 shows the effect of dropping the restrictions ansd hence permits analysis of structural differences in the economies and the partial nature of the ERM system. The first three columns of results look at convergence for the entire 1975–88 period for the nine Union member countries. The inclusion of the ERM variable and country dummies, together with the structural dummy, clearly improves the explanatory power of the model and the other diagnostic statistics are reassuring. The agricultural employment variable, while significant, is small. Equally, many of the country dummies are significant.

The evidence on the $\beta$-coefficient is that it is significant but also is sensitive to the set of other variables included. The inclusion of the country specific dummy variables, for instance, removes the statistically significant convergence effects found in Table 5.2. Membership of the ERM, however, seems to foster convergence of the relevant regional economies, rather than acting to limit convergence. This may be due to the fact that the ERM only functioned for a part of the period reviewed and that the economic convergence actually took place in the late 1970s before the ERM really operated effectively.

Focusing on the more recent period of data (1981–88), when the ERM was operational for the whole time, also enables the inclusion of Greece in the model. The results (columns 4 to 6 in Table 5.2) present a slightly different picture to that found for the whole period.

Table 5.2. *Model specifications including country explicit dummies and interactive ERM variable*[13]

| | **A** | | | **B** | | |
|---|---|---|---|---|---|---|
| | 1975–88 (ex. Greece) | | | 1981–88 (inc. Greece) | | |
| Coefficients | (1) | (2) | (3) | (4) | (5) | (6) |
| $\alpha$ | –0.042 | 0.079 | –0.019 | –0.002 | –0.002 | 0.0115 |
| | (–1.641) | (4.714) | (–0.811) | (–0.506) | (–0.080) | (0.236) |
| $\beta$ | 0.006 | –0.014 | 0.019 | –0.001 | 0.005 | 0.005 |
| | (1.193) | (–3.551) | (2.295) | (–0.063) | (0.829) | (0.485) |
| $\beta_{ERM}$ | | –0.003 | –0.018 | | –0.005 | –0.008 |
| | | (–5.184) | (–2.284) | | (–9.314) | (–0.634) |
| $\gamma_{AEM}$ | 0.001 | | 0.001 | 0.000 | | 0.001 |
| | (2.720) | | (3.531) | (0.953) | | (1.074) |
| $\gamma_{IR}$ | 0.007 | | 0.002 | –0.001 | | –0.003 |
| | (2.414) | | (0.923) | (–0.215) | | (–0.515) |
| $\gamma_{UK}$ | 0.0214 | | –0.058 | 0.021 | | –0.015 |
| | (6.847) | | (–1.676) | (5.029) | | (–0.267) |
| $\gamma_{BE}$ | 0.005 | | 0.004 | –0.006 | | –0.006 |
| | (2.277) | | (2.804) | (1.971) | | (–1.793) |
| $\gamma_{FR}$ | 0.005 | | 0.006 | –0.004 | | –0.004 |
| | (3.064) | | (3.358) | (–1.659) | | (–1.615) |
| $\gamma_{NE}$ | 0.00 | | 0.006 | –0.003 | | –0.003 |
| | (2.825) | | (2.597) | (–0.485) | | (–0.513) |
| $\gamma_{LU}$ | 0.012 | | 0.013 | 0.010 | | 0.010 |
| | (14.18) | | (15.830) | (10.930) | | (9.728) |
| $\gamma_{GE}$ | 0.008 | | 0.009 | 0.001 | | 0.001 |
| | (5.868) | | (6.022) | (0.021) | | (–0.501) |
| $\gamma_{IT}$ | 0.033 | | –0.044 | 0.021 | | –0.016 |
| | (11.390) | | (–1.355) | (6.243) | | (–0.267) |
| $\gamma_{Gr}$ | | | | –0.005 | | –0.041 |
| | | | | (–0.375) | | (–0.679) |
| $R^2$ | 0.868 | 0.671 | 0.884 | 0.712 0.619 | 0.714 | |
| adj $R^2$ | 0.835 | 0.657 | 0.851 | 0.636 0.604 | 0.631 | |
| $\sigma$ | 0.0054 | 0.0078 | 0.0051 | 0.0087 | 0.0091 | 0.0088 |
| ESS | 0.0012 | 0.0028 | 0.0010 | 0.0032 | 0.0042 | 0.0032 |
| LLF | 200.161 | 176.910 | 203.419 | 186.321 | 178.814 | 186.564 |
| BJ(2) | 1.840 | 1.437 | 1.689 | 0.552 | 14.826 | 1.194 |
| | (5.99) | (5.99) | (5.99) | (5.99) | (5.99) | (5.99) |

*Notes:*

(1) Excludes ERM slope dummy variable, but includes structural and country dummies.

(2) Includes ERM slope dummy variable, but excludes all country and structural dummies.

(3) Includes all dummy variables.

13 See also the notes to Table 5.1.

The number of significant variables, for example, diminishes and not all the diagnostic statistics are below their critical levels. Overall, the case for convergence in regional incomes, as indicated by the sign and significance of the $\beta$ coefficient, is removed. Equally, the role of the ERM in influencing regional economic performance is removed when allowance is made for specific national effects. These results suggest that there has been little convergence in EU regional performance in the 1980s. This may be a general reflection of the more difficult macroeconomic environment.

The move, albeit an uneven one, towards closer economic ties within Western Europe raises a number of important questions concerning the nature of the Union's regional policy. In particular, matters of distributional equity have come to the forefront of debates that formerly focused almost entirely on the more general development of the European economy.

The EU has put in place regional policies but the amount of detailed analysis looking at patterns of economic convergence (or divergence) which has taken place over recent times is relatively sparse. It has been suggested that, by removing the devaluation instrument, GDP convergence has not been assisted by the ERM, although membership of the exchange rate mechanism may have enhanced overall economic growth. The findings here, though, do not support this view.

Equally, when the results of our analysis are compared to other studies, and particularly the work of Barro and Sala-i-Martin (1991), the evidence of convergence found here is much less convincing. This may be explained by the somewhat different data base employed, the detailed model specification adopted and the time periods considered. Given the aggregate nature of the data base it is not possible to isolate the specific factors involved.

The parameters of the equation (5.24) are also estimated for three different samples and over several other sub-periods to test for different speeds of convergence or, indeed, periods of short-run non-convergence. The model is again also run with country-specific dummies and with structural variables designed to capture the changing pattern of industrial structure in regions over the sample period.

Tables 5.3, 5.4 and 5.5 show the results for each of three sub-periods corresponding to the changes in Union membership. In each case the results in column A are for the model without dummy variables; those in column B are with the incorporation of two industrial structure variables, measured as the proportion of the employed labour force in agriculture and the proportion of the employed labour force in the industrial sector; those in column C are with eight, nine and eleven country dummies; and those in column D are for the model when all country dummies and employment variables are included. For ease of exposition the coefficients associated with the dummies and structural variables are omitted from the tables.

Table 5.3 relates to the nine countries which have been members of the Union for the entire period of the data set, 1975–90. The likelihood-ratio test (LR) indicates that model specification C dominates the other three.

This equation, together with both specifications A and B, show evidence of convergence, with negative values of $\beta$, although this is only just significant at the 5 per cent level in equation C.

Table 5.3. *$\beta$-convergence in GDP per capita in the EU (9) countries, 1975–90*

| | [A] | [B] | [C] | [D] |
|---|---|---|---|---|
| $\alpha$ | 0.113 | 0.069 | 0.023 | -0.016 |
| | (6.398) | (2.397) | (1.239) | (-0.045) |
| $\beta$ | -0.024 | -0.017 | -0.007 | 0.0002 |
| | (-6.693) | (-2.938) | (-1.972) | (0.028) |
| $R^2$ | 0.447 | 0.486 | 0.814 | 0.828 |
| se | 0.008 | 0.008 | 0.005 | 0.004 |
| LR | – | 3.655 | 54.368 | 58.370 |
| | | (5.99) | (15.5) | (18.31) |

*Notes:*

1. Critical values in parentheses below the $\alpha$ and $\beta$-coefficients are t-statistics.
2. se is the standard error of the regression
3. LR is the likelihood ratio test for significance of dummy variables (critical values in parentheses)

The inclusion of country-specific dummies seems to reduce the extent of EU growth convergence, although only the dummy for Italy was individually significant at the 5 per cent level. Ignoring country-specific effects, this equation shows a growth rate of about 2 per cent per annum over the sample period. Table 5.4 shows the pattern of the convergence across the ten EU countries' NUT 1 regions (the nine plus Greece, which became a member in 1981) from 1980 to 1990. It reveals a similar pattern to Table 5.3 with all $\beta$-coefficients emerging as negative, but with only one appearing as statistically significant at the 5 per cent level. The agricultural employment variable has a negative and consistently significant coefficient in the B specification when industrial structure dummies are included, that is not present over the sample of nine countries. This suggests that Greece's accession had a significant and negative impact on growth in the EU.

It is also noticeable that in these regressions the average growth rate is lower than when only the EU of nine Members was considered, being less than 1 per cent per annum. This may be a reflection of the slower economic growth in the 1980s and suggests that, for the 1975–90 sample, most of the growth came in the late 1970s between the two oil-price shocks. Table 5.4

also shows slower convergence in EU GDP per head after the enlargement when all dummies are excluded, but faster convergence when different sectoral and country effects are permitted.

Table 5.4. *β-convergence in GDP per capita in the EU (10) countries, 1980–90*

| | [A] | [B] | [C] | [D] |
|---|---|---|---|---|
| $\alpha$ | 0.033<br>(1.499) | 0.095<br>(2.918) | 0.019<br>(0.944) | 0.002<br>(0.054) |
| $\beta$ | -0.007<br>(-1.492) | -0.020<br>(-2.973) | -0.006<br>(-1.846) | -0.005<br>(-0.839) |
| $R^2$ | 0.040 | 0.156 | 0.638 | 0.648 |
| se | 0.010 | 0.009 | 0.006 | 0.006 |
| LR | – | 6.813 | 51.617 | 52.213 |

*Notes*: As for Table 5.3.

Table 5.5 provides results for the twelve EU countries which have been members of the European Union from 1986 to 1990. There is evidence of significant, rapid convergence in versions A and B of the model, with an annual average growth rate of between 5 and 8 per cent. These results also indicate strong country effects (indicated in column C) with seven of the eleven country dummies being significant at the 5 per cent level. In particular Spain, Portugal and, to a lesser extent, Italy all helped to raise the rate of GDP growth over the period, whereas all other country dummy coefficients exhibited negative signs. This is evidenced by diverging growth rates across the Union as a whole with strong growth in the Mediterranean regions and slower growth in the northern regions. These results are robust across the sub-periods 1983–86 and 1986–90.

Plots of the observations for the standard A versions of the model from Table 5.2 are provided in Figure 5.3. These charts show convergence in regional GDP to be stronger over the whole sample than over the two sub-periods, especially the 1980s which show a clustering of points in the centre of the chart with little evidence of convergence.

The results given in Table 5.6 relate to various sub-periods and make an attempt to incorporate allowance for business cycle effects. The results in column A are for the model without dummy variables, those in column B are with eight or nine country dummies and those in column C are for the model when all country and structural dummies are included. For ease of exposition the coefficients associated with the dummies and structural variables are again omitted from the tables.

Table 5.5. *β-convergence in GDP per capita in the EU (12) countries, 1983–90*

| | [A] | [B] | [C] | [D] |
|---|---|---|---|---|
| $\alpha$ | 0.259<br>(9.361) | 0.352<br>(7.151) | 0.049<br>(1.714) | 0.113<br>(2.476) |
| $\beta$ | -0.056<br>(-9.186) | -0.075<br>(-7.882) | -0.010<br>(-1.400) | -0.021<br>(-2.119) |
| $R^2$ | 0.581 | 0.626 | 0.894 | 0.903 |
| se | 0.020 | 0.019 | 0.010 | 0.009 |
| LR | – | 7.039<br>(5.99) | 83.891<br>(15.51) | 89.432<br>(18.31) |

*Notes*: As for Table 5.3.

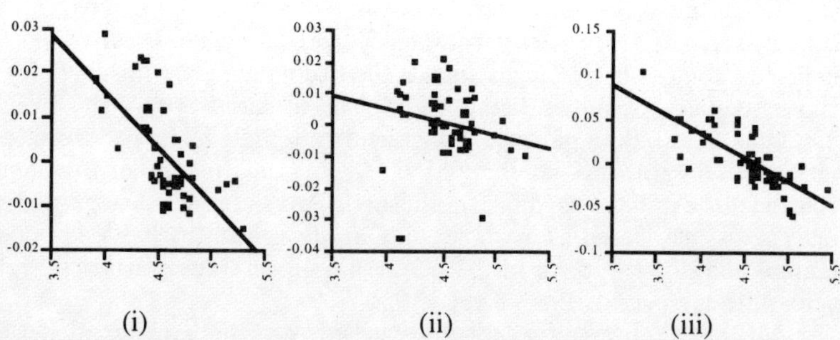


Figure 5.3 *Annual regional growth rate in GDP per capita against logarithm of regional GDP per capita covering periods (i) 1975 to 1990 for nine Members; (ii) 1980 to 1990 for ten Members; and 1983 to 1990 for twelve Members*

For the entire sample period 1975–90, and for the final sub-period 1980–90, the final column of Table 5.6 shows that specification B (including country dummies) dominates the other two specifications. This gives a rate of convergence of less than 1 per cent per annum, but greater than 0.5 per cent per annum. This rate is not only slow but, only just significant. For the period 1975–85 specification C is preferred, which yields a low, negative value of $\beta$ indicative of divergence in real per capita incomes. Too much significance should not be attributed to this result, because the coefficient is not statistically significant, but also because this decade was one of change within the EU, including the repercussions of two oil-price shocks, enlargement and the establishment of the exchange rate mechanism (ERM). Overall convergence is therefore at best weak, at less than 1 per cent per annum.

Table 5.6. *$\beta$-convergence in real GDP per capita for selected periods in the EU Regions 1975–90*

| | A | | B | | C | | LR+ |
|---|---|---|---|---|---|---|---|
| Period | $\beta$ | $R^2$ ($\sigma$) | $\beta$ | $R^2$ ($\sigma$) | $\beta$ | $R^2$ ($\sigma$) | |
| (1) 1975-90 | 0.174 | 0.504 | 0.008 | 0.965 | 0.004 | 0.966 | 132.5 |
| (0.009) | (0.018) | (0.004) | (0.003) | (0.006) | (0.005) | 1.3 | |
| (2) 1975-85 | 0.107 | 0.506 | 0.010 | 0.939 | -0.002 | 0.944 | 104.3 |
| (0.009) | (0.019) | (0.006) | (0.007) | (0.008) | (0.006) | 4.1 | |
| (3) 1980-90 | 0.034 | 0.099 | 0.006 | 0.937 | 0.013 | 0.940 | 132.8 |
| (0.012) | (0.020) | (0.004) | (0.005) | (0.007) | (0.005) | 3.0 | |
| (4) 1980-90* | 0.025 | 0.020 | 0.009 | 0.970 | 0.006 | 0.971 | 184.9 |
| (0.021) | (0.036) | (0.005) | (0.006) | (0.006) | (0.006) | 1.6 | |

*Notes:*

Values in parentheses below the $\beta$s are the standard errors, below the $R^2$s are the equation standard errors.

* includes Greece as the tenth member of the EU

+ Likelihood ratio tests for the joint significance of the dummies. For each equation the first test statistic is between specifications A and B and the second test statistic between specifications C and B. The critical value in each case is 3.84 at the 5 per cent level.

The effects of the country dummies highlight the differential growth rates within the EU over similar periods of time. Although all the dummies were not statistically significant, in every run of the equation the country dummies on the Netherlands and Germany were consistently positive and significant, while those on Ireland, Italy and Greece were always negative and significant at the 5 per cent level. This result serves to highlight the differences in per capita income levels in these regions.

Comparison of the two results for 1980–90 highlights the effect of the Greek regions on the convergence process. Specification B implies that convergence is enhanced by the inclusion of the Greek regions since the $\beta$-parameter not only rises from 0.006 to 0.009, but also becomes significant at 10 per cent. The implications of the agrarian nature of the Greek economy is also demonstrated by specification C, which includes industrial structure dummies. Since convergence is significantly enhanced by excluding the Greek regions, the conclusion is that the addition of these predominantly agrarian regions have acted to slow down the rate of overall EU growth convergence.

The issue of real economic convergence has become an important one for the European Union as moves towards greater integration are taking place. The analysis here shows that convergence of real regional incomes of the economies in the EU has not been a steady, stable process, but rather has been both a cyclical phenomenon, related to the business cycle, and a continual phenomenon despite the expansion of Union membership. This indication of a rather complicated path of convergence fits with some other studies that have been conducted.

Fagerberg *et al.* (1997), for example, examined 64 European regions of (West) Germany, France, Italy and Spain for various periods in the 1980s focusing on unemployment, migration and GDP per capita as endogenous variables within a simultaneous framework. They find that the process of convergence that earlier work had shown to end in the 1980s had become impeded by the inadequacies of the poorer regions' R&D capacity to take advantage of more advanced technologies that were being developed elsewhere. The theoretical argument is that technological knowledge is not ubiquitous and does not have the characteristics of a public good as neo-classical growth theory hypothesises.

Armstrong (1995) looks at a number of sub-periods at both the NUTS1 and NUTS2 level of spatial aggregation and again finds that, dependent on the period selected, so the pattern of convergence may vary. For example, at the NUTS1 level of aggregation he found a $\beta$-coefficient of 0.012 for the period 1950 to 1960 that rose to 0.025 in the next decade before falling again to 0.006 in 1975–93. He found even larger shifts at the NUTS2 level of spatial aggregation.

There have, therefore, been periods when convergence has been strong, as at the end of the 1970s, but also periods when the real incomes of the Union's regions have moved further apart as, for example, during the early 1980s. This is perhaps not all that surprising since it is easier to affect redistribution when the European economy is growing than when it is shrinking. In particular, this leads to the inference that real income convergence has slowed since the EU governments agreed to pursue a common monetary policy.

Monetary policy convergence may, therefore, have given rise to, or at least been associated with, a slower convergence in real regional economic performance. Further, the process of convergence has probably been slowed by the admission of predominantly agricultural countries as enlargements have taken place, but there have also been important macroeconomic shocks beyond its control.

## 5.6 WIDER COMPARISONS

While one must always be cautious when conducting comparative analysis, looking beyond the EU provides additional insights into the economic convergence question. Differing levels of aggregation – for example: some work is country rather than region based must be taken into account as must the time frames of the different pieces of work. In some instances the work has incorporated variables which have not been fully covered in EU studies or has incorporate them in different ways. In some instances this has embraced policy effect variables.[14]

Much of this work stems from studies of the US situation but there is an increasing literature from other countries. The techniques used for non-EU analysis are varied, but Table 5.7 provides a general overview summarising, where comparability is possible, the $\beta$-coefficients that have been obtained across a range of econometric convergence studies for various geographical areas, icluding those outside of the EU.

Table 5.7. *Summary of $\beta$-coefficient estimates*

| Study | Area | Period | $\beta$–value |
|---|---|---|---|
| Cashin (1995) | Australia (colonies) | 1981–1991 | 0.0121 |
| Barro & Sala-i-Martin (1992a) | USA (states) | 1880–1988 | 0.0249 |
| Barro & Sala-i-Martin (1991) | OECD Europe (countries) | 1950–1985 | 0.0178 |
| Cashin (1993) | OECD (countries) | 1971–1988 | 0.0097 |
| Coulomb & Lee (1993) | Canada (provinces) | 1961–1991 | 0.0240 |
| Barro (1991) | 98 countries | 1960–1985 | 0.0111 |
| Barro and Sala-i-Martin (1992b) | Japan (prefectures) | 1930–1987 | 0.0340 |
| Mallick & Carayannis (1994) | Mexico (states) | 1970–1980 | 0.0418 |
| | | 1980–1985 | 0.0006 |
| Shioji (1993) | Japan (prefectures) | 1960–1993 | 0.0333 |
| de la Fuente & Vives (1995) | Spain (regions) | 1981–1990 | 0.1950 |

The introduction of a system of fixed exchange rates in Europe succeeded in inducing price convergence amongst its participants, but at the same time increased the divergence between their rates of unemployment. For example, Demertzis and Hallett (1996) measure the level of the inefficiency imposed

14 A further discussion of some of this empirical work with a particular focus on regional level analysis is contained in Martin and Sunley (1998).

on the labour markets as a result of having different labour market structures under one monetary policy, and use these results to provide a new explanation for the secular rise in European unemployment based on the degree of labour market heterogeneities and the asymmetries in wage settings in each market.

The formal analysis of growth focuses on the theory of long-run economic progress. From the 1950s, the neo-classical exogenous growth model with unexplained technical progress was the dominant theoretical framework. The neoclassical growth model, as we have seen implies a tendency of convergence. If countries are similar with respect to preferences and technology, then poor countries tend to grow faster than rich countries, because of diminishing returns to reproducible capital (Barro, 1991). The question of whether a tendency for per capita product is independent of the starting level, as can be inferred from recent endogenous growth models, has led to a large literature.

Starting with Baumol (1986), most investigators use cross-country regressions to measure the impact of the initial level on the growth rate of an economy. After controlling for the quality of human capital (measured by 1960 rates of school-enrolment rates), Barro (1991) shows evidence in favour of the convergence hypothesis of neo-classical growth models. For a given quality of human capital, a poor country grows faster. Leamer (1993) re-examines Barro's finding with respect to error in variables problems and he concludes that measurements are more reliable for the developing countries.

Levine and Renelt (1992) examine whether the conclusions of existing studies are robust against changes in the information set. In accordance with Barro, they find evidence of conditional convergence (i.e. a robust negative partial correlation between per capita income and initial income as long as the regression includes secondary school enrolment rates in 1960).

Mankiw *et al.* (1992) augment the Solow growth model by including accumulation of human as well as physical capital. Their empirical results are in line with the augmented Solow model and indicate convergence. In contrast, Durlauf and Johnson (1992) report evidence in favour of local convergence. By local convergence, they refer to the case where there exist groups of countries such that convergence occurs within the group. Quah (1993) shows a tendency for divergence by examining the cross-section distribution of output per worker over time. Empirical tests of the convergence hypothesis have not yet therefore reached a consensus. Apart from measurement and estimation problems there is evidence supporting conditional convergence.

The issue of whether interregional differences in income levels within one country tend to disappear or tend to increase over time is a controversial theoretical and empirical question. Standard neo-classical growth models, models of endogenous growth and cumulative causation models disagree on whether regional income dynamics should lead to convergence or divergence.

In context of the convergence debate, Barro and Sala-i-Martin (1991, 1992) apply the cross-sectional approach to 48 US states. They exploit data on personal income since 1840 and gross state product since 1963 and find clear evidence that poor economies tend to grow faster than rich ones in per capita terms. Furthermore, Barro and Sala-i-Martin (1991) show that the process of convergence within 73 regions in Western Europe since 1950 is similar to that for the United States. In particular, the rate of convergence is about 2 per cent a year, Shioji (1993) reports a similar result for Japan. Sala-i-Martin (1996) examines the convergence hypothesis for regions in the United States (48 contiguous states), Canada, Japan, Europe total, Germany, UK, France, Italy, and Spain. Sala-i-Martin concludes, 'there is convergence both in the $\beta$ and $\sigma$ sense across regions of the US, Japan, Europe, Spain, and Canada. The speeds of $\beta$ convergence are extraordinarily similar across countries: about two per cent per year.'

Neven and Gouyette (1994) report a tendency for $\beta$ convergence for the regions of the EC in the 1980s, however at a slower pace. The process is far from stable with respect to sub-periods and sub-sets of regions. Southern Europe seemed to catch up in the early 1980s and stagnated thereafter. The convergence pattern is reversed for the North European countries. De la Fuente and Vives (1995) explore a convergence of regional per capita income in Europe since 1950. They show that a clear reduction in that convergence has stopped since the first half of the 1970s and inequality has stabilised. Moreover, within the OECD countries rates of convergence vary in time and across countries. The experience of southern Europe (Portugal, Greece, Spain) shows that the development of market mechanisms and the quality of the social and economic infrastructure is very important for the convergence process (Larre and Torres, 1991).

For the US, Bishop *et al.* (1994) present evidence that the South's income distributions moved significantly closer to the rest of the nation in the decade of the 1970s. However, the decomposition of the non-South region into Northeast, Midwest and West shows that income distributions of these regions diverged from one another. This evidence could be seen as a temporary disequilibrium accompanying structural changes and significant shocks to regional economies in the 1970s.

Hofer and Worgotter (1997) examine growth and dispersion of output per capita across nine Austrian regions and 84 districts. Time series analysis of the Austrian regions finds no evidence for cointegration between regional output and national output. Extending the empirical work by estimating a convergence-type regression for Austrian regions and districts, the rate of $\beta$-convergence is about 1 per cent a year, indicating a slow convergence pattern. Including dummy variables for types of district, $\beta$ is 2 per cent per annum, which is in line with other studies.

Hulten and Schwab (1991) investigate the unbalanced growth of US regional manufacturing industries and suggest that the main force driving differences in regional manufacturing growth over the period 1970–86 is the inter-regional flow of capital and labour, while the growth of multifactor productivity is uniform across regions. Furthermore, agglomeration economies and public capital externalities are not an important source of regional manufacturing growth. On the other hand, Berry and Kaserman (1993) support the convergence hypothesis for US state per capita income as lower-income states grow more rapidly. Moreover, low taxes and strong support for higher education foster more rapid growth. Equalising school levels and effective stock of public capital would reduce regional income disparities in Spain by one-third in the long run (de la Fuente and Vives, 1995).

In contrast, Carlino and Mills (1993) use time series techniques for analysing the development of state income in the US. This approach looks at the long-term effects of economic shocks on a region's per capita income relative to the national average. Carlino (1992), argues that the widening of regional per capita earning differentials in the last decade represents only short run adjustments to a new long-run equilibrium, induced by supply shocks in the 1970s. Carlino concludes that economic shocks have not had high persistent effects on relative per capita earnings.

Carlino and Mills (1992) examine if the pattern of relative regional per capita income in the US over the past 60 years is consistent with the hypothesis of conditional convergence. The authors allow for a compensating differential among regions. However, the hypothesis of stochastic convergence implies that shocks to relative regional per capita income had to be transitory. This hypothesis is not rejected when a break in the convergence rate $\beta$ is allowed in 1946.

## 5.7 CONCLUSIONS

In this chapter some new empirical work has been set in the context of an expanding empirical literature that has concerned itself with questions of economic convergence. The names of Barro and Sala-I-Martin are particularly associated with this work. This body of literature has grown in part as a response to a renewed intellectual interest in the question of economic growth but also reflects the availability of considerably improved data. A much clearly understanding of what is meant by convergence from an economic perspective has also helped. The empirical findings offered here regarding develops within the EU differs from the majority of the previous work in this field in being regional rather than national in its orientation.

The analysis conducted here has sought to offer some additional insights into the extent to which spatial economic convergence has been a feature of the recent history of the EU. It has made extensive use of well-tried mean reversion techniques to examine the available data on regional economic growth paths. While there remain considerable problems surrounding the quality and consistency of this data, the analysis does demonstrate the potential of modern econometric techniques to gain additional insights regarding economic convergence. Equally, however, it also shows that care must be exercised in applying these techniques.

# 6. Economic Performance and Convergence across UK Regions

## 6.1. INTRODUCTION

Since 1975 national economic performance in the UK has been marked by some profound changes and includes the deepest recession (1979–81) in the whole of the post-war period. The major impact of this recession fell on the export-oriented industries, mainly manufacturing, and, given the geographic concentration of these industries, the economic impact was also concentrated in particular regions of the UK. The subsequent period of national economic growth (1982–90) was dominated by growth in the service sector (e.g. Button and Pentecost, 1993) and averaged 4 per cent per annum yet in the early 1990s the UK economy again experienced recession. On this occasion the regions most affected were different from those most afflicted in the previous recession. In addition, regional economies have been differentially affected by the UK's membership of the EU, which gave access to EU regional assistance funds, and a change in government in 1979 which introduced a phased reform of British regional policy.

Despite the interesting recent regional history of the UK economy very little work has been undertaken which looks explicitly at UK regional divergence or convergence. Although the seminal papers of Baumol (1986), Dowrick and Nguyen (1989), Barro (1991), Barro and Sala-i-Martin (1991, 1992a) and Blanchard and Katz (1992) have given rise to a plethora of empirical work designed to test for convergence (see, for example, Button and Pentecost, 1995b; Lee *et al.*, 1996) these papers have primarily addressed the issue of convergence among large numbers of countries or regions. As a rule they purport to show that the speed of convergence is about 2 per cent per annum, but it is now acknowledged that this result arises from the particular estimation procedures used by Barro and Sala-i-Martin and adopted by most other researchers.

Papers which move away from this conditional, cross-section convergence approach are able to show that the results are much more mixed. Quah (1996), for example, says that the data can show persistence and immobility across countries, evidence of convergence clubs and some evidence showing the poor getting poorer and the rich richer, with the middle class vanishing.

This chapter differs from this vast international literature by focusing on the UK regions, which have received relatively little independent consideration. The exceptions are the papers of Martin (1993), Keil (1997) and Chatterji and Dewhurst (1996). Chatterji and Dewhurst (1996) examined movements in the gross domestic product (GDP per capita) of English and Welsh counties and Scottish regions to test whether the counties and regions are converging in terms of GDP per capita. The exercise was carried out for the period from 1977 to 1991 and for six sub-periods. Although there was no evidence of convergence over the whole period, there is some evidence of convergence within certain sub-periods. These are periods when the economy as a whole was growing slowly.

Using a shift-share accounting of 1952–89 employment data from Great Britain's sub-national planning regions, Keil (1997) presents tests of the neo-classical hypothesis that employment shares return to a set of equilibrium values after random shocks. Contrary to the neo-classical hypothesis, the tests of stationarity and cointegration strongly suggest that disturbances in shares are cumulative and permanent.

To this end the chapter employs a panel data set for the UK regions over the period 1975–93 to address two questions. First, to what extent is the economic performance of the UK regions converging or diverging and second, to what extent can this regional growth performance be explained by movements in the stock of physical and human capital within each region? Prior to this econometric analysis, however, section 6.2 gives an overview of UK regional policy.

## 6.2 UK REGIONAL POLICY

The UK has a long-standing tradition of innovative regional policy. The aim here is not to provide a history but rather to provide a few paragraphs by way of background to the empirical analysis that forms the backbone of this chapter. In particular it highlights some of the key recent developments in policy.

Generally, the history of this policy is traced back to the late 1920s and 1930s and efforts by the UK government to combat the particularly adverse effects of the Great Depression on the older industrial areas of the country.[1] At that time the unemployment rate in Scotland and Wales exceeded 30 per cent and was over 20 per cent in all other regions except southern England. In local pockets such as Saltburn (91 per cent in 1933), Jarrow (77 per cent), Cleator Moor (70 per cent) and so on the unemployment rate was considerably higher than the regional average.

The passing of a series of acts aimed at stimulating the economies of the worst affected regions (variously named Special Areas or Development Areas at different times) was, however, seen as a transient need and aimed essentially at dealing with perceived structural problems and at reducing social problems.[2] Indeed, many of the measures, such as the Industrial Transference Scheme and the Juvenile Transfer Scheme (both 1928) were explicitly aimed at assisting internal migration of unemployed workers and retraining. The amount of funds devoted to this was small and the Industrial Transference Board only helped about 40,000 people to relocate. Equally, the funds made available under such measures as the Special Areas (Development and Improvement) Act of 1934, aimed more specifically at giving grants and loans to firms in heavily depressed areas, were relatively small and could only be applied to a limited range of activities. Other measures, such as certain forms of tax exemption under the Special Areas (Amendment) Act of 1937, offered limited financial assistance. The establishment of trading estates from 1936 were equally small-scale activities and by 1939 only employed about 12,000 workers.

The Second World War removed the need for such measures and the focus of regional policy that emerged after 1945 was somewhat different. Commitments to 'full employment' combined with the need for rebuilding the economy and the acceptance of the possibility of Keynesian demand management at the macroeconomic level led to considerably more intervention in the economy.[3] It resulted in the passing of both the Distribution of Industry Act (1945) and the Town and Country Planning Act (1947) which represent the beginning of genuinely active regional

[1] Some trace the origins further back to the establishment of labour exchanges at the turn of the century as a mechanism to ease problems of structural labour imbalances.

[2] Towards the end of the 1930s additional assistance went to many depressed areas as rearmament took place; these areas both had an appropriate heavy industrial base and were distant from threats of bombing.

[3] The Barlow Report of 1940 on the *Distribution of the Industrial Population* was particularly important in this regard when it argued for a better spatial balance of economic activity in the UK for social as well as economic reasons.

policy in the UK.[4] Recovery from hostilities also required heavy industry and transport, and to a large extent this was nationalised and acquired access to public finance through this channel.

The importance of this was that much of the heavy industry was situated in areas that had been depressed in the inter-war period, allowing them a period of demand-led growth albeit with underlying and mounting structural rigidities due to public ownership. In effect, however, the late 1940s and the 1950s represented a period of buoyant macroeconomic growth and regional problems did not emerge on a large scale.

The mid-1950s saw a re-emergence of regional problems as the demand for traditional exports such as textiles was adversely hit by low-cost production in less-developed countries. The existing portfolio of policy instruments was insufficient to combat the impacts of the changes on parts of the UK and a series of new initiatives were introduced – for example, the Distribution of Industry (Industry Finance) Act (1958) and the Local Employment Act (1960).

The 1960s saw major new initiatives in regional policy. Some of these can be seen as simple extensions of what had gone before and were initiated to meet increasing problems of unemployment and low incomes in traditionally depressed areas. Other measures were more innovative. Some of these reflected efforts to be proactive in meeting foreseeable future spatial economic problems – the creation of Intermediate Areas following the Hunt Report of 1969 falls into this category – while others may in a sense be seen as experimental and test beds for new policy instruments: the introduction of the Regional Employment Premium (REP) in 1967 and of the Selective Employment Tax (SET) fall into this category.

There were also frequent changes in the areas eligible for assistance. These ranged from the large Development Areas and Special Development Areas that had their basis in the immediate post-war approach to much smaller Development Districts – the Industrial Development Act of 1966 – that it was hoped would allow for more spatial sensitivity in allocating development aid. Additionally, from 1969 there were efforts to follow the French pattern of indicative planning with strategic plans being devised for regions of the UK, setting out government objectives and policies so as to

4 The 1945 Act was important both in giving responsibility for regional policy to a single ministry, the Board of Trade, and in establishing a set of incentive measures that could be deployed to assist companies locate or develop in economically depressed regions. The 1947 legislation initiated full Industrial Development Certificates (IDCs) that could be used to prevent large manufacturing establishments locating or expanding in congested regions.

better inform the private sector and assist in its investment and production planning.[5]

The Industry Act of 1972 represented the culmination of this period of regional policy and essentially, drawing on the experiences of the preceding fifteen years or so, it brought together a package of measures that subsequently have formed the basis of regional policy. In particular, it separated out criteria for automatic aid and for selective aid and established a portfolio of policy instruments that applied in each case.

Joining the European Union in 1973 posed some problems for UK regional policy makers as well as offering new sources of regional assistance. The UK became eligible for grants, loans and other assistance from EU institutions such as the European Coal and Steel Community, the European Investment Bank and the European Social Fund. Further, it was hoped that the general economic stimulus of membership would benefit the macroeconomy with consequential positive effects for the poorer regions. Membership meant, however, that certain types of regional policy instruments posed problems. The Regional Employment Premium (REP), for example, caused difficulties since it was effectively a continuing labour subsidy and in general such subsidies were not permitted. It also meant compliance with limits on subsidies to central regions, an umbrella under which the Intermediate Regions fell. Adherence to more general economic policies, such as the EU Competition Policy, also had implications for the autonomy of UK regional policies.

Since 1973 the UK's regional policy has been closely entwined with that of the Union. New legislation has been passed, mainly to reflect the shift of economic activity from manufacturing to services (e.g. service and office subsidies were initiated in 1977), but increased harmonisation across Europe to minimise any adverse effects of beggar-thy-neighbour strategies have limited them. Where there has been a gradual shift is in terms of devolving more powers to sub-national agencies and, in particular, to Scottish and Welsh agencies. The move to establish a Scottish Parliament and a Welsh assembly reflects part of this process.

The main justification underlying UK regional policy in the 1990s, as in previous periods (Armstrong and Taylor, 1993) is to reduce the waste of resources associated with high levels of unemployment in some regions of

[5] The 1960s and early 1970s also saw a renewed academic interest in the effectiveness of regional policy. In particular; new techniques such as shift-share analysis (Moore and Rhodes, 1973; Brown, 1972) were applied in efforts both to separate systematically various elements of regional economic performance and to lay a basis for establishing counterfactuals against which trends in regional unemployment could be assessed.

the country. The fairly high levels of economic growth in the mid and latter parts of the decade have to some extent weakened this argument as the whole national economy has benefited, but areas of poor performance remain. Given this generally solid national performance, the second justification for regional aid has been the containment of inflationary pressures at a time of tight labour markets. Shifting investment to regions with relatively high unemployment takes demand-side pressures away from those with a relative shortage of labour. Added to these well-rehearsed economic arguments are the political ones that large regional disparities are simply not acceptable in a democracy.

The move towards a more integrated EU (especially since selective regional aid is an acceptable policy instrument under EU Commission rules) has given a further impetus to retaining an active regional policy.

Regional aid in the 1990s comes in four broad types, much of it going to designated Assisted Areas (Taylor and Wren, 1997):

- Regional Selective Aid is available for manufacturing and some service sector activities that invest in Assisted Areas. To obtain funding a number of criteria must be met, in particular, that jobs are created or safeguarded.
- Regional Enterprise Grants are targeted at small firms with the aim of fostering innovation and to meet investment needs.
- Expenditure on land and buildings by a variety of agencies, such as the Welsh Development Agency, to induce inward investment into the Assisted Areas.
- Rural-based financed going, for example, through The Highlands and Islands Enterprise.

The UK regional aid packages are supplemented by funds obtained from the EU (see Table 6.1). Since the mid-1980s the increase in the absolute and relative assistance coming from EU sources, which amounted to about £14 billion in Structural Fund monies or 0.3 per cent of UK GDP over the period 1989–93, has been an important element in the way regional policy has been structured. In particular, regional assistance has grown considerably to Objective 2 and Objective 5b regions of the country. The nature of the EU funds coming to the UK has also changed over time. There has in particular been a major increase in the relative amount going to the development of human resources (up from 47.3 per cent of Union spending in 1989–93 to 57.3 per cent for the period 1994–9).[6]

[6] This included such programmes as financial assistance under the Community Support Framework for training over 14,000 employees and

In terms of long-term development, a number of major infrastructure projects, and especially those located in the peripheral regions of Northern Ireland and Scotland, have received EU funding with the aim of fostering greater economic integration with other parts of the Union – for example, a high-speed rail service between Belfast and Dublin and a number of port and airport projects.

Table 6.1. *UK government expenditure on regional preferential, assistance and the allocation of the EU Structural Funds going to the UK*

| Year | Expenditure on regional preferential assistance to industry (£m at current prices) | Year | EU Structural Funds (£m at current prices) |
|---|---|---|---|
| 1989/90 | 66 | 1989 | 565 |
| 1990/91 | 629 | 1990 | 659 |
| 1991/92 | 566 | 1991 | 687 |
| 1992/93 | 470 | 1992 | 712 |
| 1993/94 | 512 | 1993 | 747 |
| 1994/95 | 502 | 1994 | 857 |
| 1995/96 | 474 | 1995 | 922 |

## 6.3 THE DATA SET AND ECONOMETRIC METHODS[7]

As we have seen, there are three principal measures of convergence in the literature (see Quah, 1996; Sala-i-Martin, 1996), called $\sigma$-convergence, $\beta$-convergence and conditional $\beta$-convergence. When considering regional economies a problem common in all the measures of convergence is that they may be influenced by the national business cycle especially over the short period. Therefore we need to take account of this effect. Here we offer three alternative approaches to this problem:

managers in Northern Ireland while 266,400 people participated in European Social Fund assisted training in Objective 2 regions.

7 For a fuller discussion of this analysis and results, see Evans and Pentecost (1998).

- The first is to measure the relative income level of the region: that is the income per capita in each region as a fraction of the income per capita in the country as a whole. Thus in the upswing a leading region will have per capita real income rising faster than national income, while in a downswing the leading region will have income below the national average.
- A second approach is to use panel data and the two-way fixed factor method (see Greene, 1993), which enables us to include time-period dummy variables to capture business cycle effects. However, a potential problem with this method is that it is short term, measuring convergence from year to year. As a result the time period dummies frequently dominate the regional dummies.
- The third approach is to measure the average annual rate of growth of income per capita over the business cycle; that is, from trough to trough or peak to peak. In this way we can better measure long-run convergence over time, although the cost is that degrees of freedom are lost such that the estimates are less efficient.

The data set is based on UK regional data as published annually in *Regional Trends*. This provides yearly data on 11 regions (including Northern Ireland), running from 1975 to 1993 inclusive. There are therefore 20 annual observations on each region, giving 220 observations in the full panel. Since we commonly use the change in real per capita GDP the available time series is reduced by one for each region, giving a full panel data set of some 209 observations (198 when Northern Ireland is excluded). To avoid the problem of the high volatility of annual growth rates of real per capita GDP in some regressions we take average changes over a number of years, which considerably reduces the number of observations. For example, comparing the growth of income over the three business cycles since 1975 reduces the number of observations to just 33 (30 excluding Northern Ireland).

There are several innovations with this data set. The first is that current price regional GDP and investment data is deflated by a regional consumer price index,[8] thus relaxing the constraint, common in this kind of work, that all regions face the same aggregate price level.

The second and more original innovation is the use of a human capital variable which is constructed from data gathered in the General Household

[8] This series was obtained from the Bank of England, although regional price indices are now commercially available.

Survey made available through the ESRC Data Archive.[9] Human capital is measured as the number of people of working age who have had, or are in current receipt of, post-compulsory education as a proportion of the number of people of working age in each region.

A third feature of the data set is the construction of a constant price regional capital stock variable.[10] This is derived from cumulating regional gross domestic fixed capital formation figures from a benchmark capital stock figure obtained from the Organisation for Economic Cooperation and Development (1976).

## 6.4. EMPIRICAL RESULTS

The results of this study fall into two categories. We begin by presenting a few visual images of the series which we wish to examine for convergence. These charts will help elucidate the nature of the problem that we attempt to explain in the econometric results. They will also constitute our evidence for rejecting both $\sigma$ and unconditional $\beta$-convergence. The econometric results, discussed in section 6.4.2, are based on the weakest notion of convergence, the conditional $\beta$-type convergence, and the two-way fixed factor method.

### 6.4.1 Empirical Results: $\sigma$ and $\beta$-convergence

Table 6.2 shows the degree of $\sigma$-convergence that has taken place in terms of the annual means, standard deviations and coefficients of variation of (the log of) real income per head for each year of the sample. These data reveal that the growth in average real income per head across the UK regions has been particularly marked since the mid-1980s, while the variation in income per head, measured by the standard deviation and coefficient of variation, has

[9] Material from the General Household Survey made available through the Office of Population Censuses and Surveys and the Economic and Social Research Council Data Archive has been used by permission of the Controller of HM Stationry Office.

[10] The benchmark capital stock figure refers to that of the UK at the end of 1975, which is £207.7 billion at 1970 prices. This stock is deflated by the gross domestic product deflator to give a stock at constant 1990 prices before it is apportioned across the UK regions according to the share of regional gross domestic product in 1975. From 1975 the series for regional gross domestic product fixed capital formation is converted to 1990 prices and cumulated. No allowance is made for depreciation.

fluctuated, but shows greatest dispersion in 1993 and the lowest dispersion in the late 1980s.

Table 6.2. *Average and dispersion of real GDP per capita per annum*

| Year | Mean GDP per capita | Standard deviation | Coefficient of variation |
|---|---|---|---|
| 1975 | 1.1137 | 0.0168 | 1.5049 |
| 1976 | 1.1083 | 0.0238 | 2.1447 |
| 1977 | 1.1124 | 0.0214 | 1.9207 |
| 1978 | 1.1319 | 0.0217 | 1.9195 |
| 1979 | 1.1234 | 0.0269 | 2.3924 |
| 1980 | 1.1283 | 0.0298 | 2.6399 |
| 1981 | 1.1300 | 0.0240 | 2.1247 |
| 1982 | 1.1485 | 0.0186 | 1.6217 |
| 1983 | 1.1707 | 0.0217 | 1.8576 |
| 1984 | 1.1658 | 0.0200 | 1.7130 |
| 1985 | 1.1851 | 0.0162 | 1.3661 |
| 1986 | 1.1941 | 0.0180 | 1.5042 |
| 1987 | 1.2101 | 0.0192 | 1.5875 |
| 1988 | 1.2255 | 0.0219 | 1.7868 |
| 1989 | 1.2370 | 0.0149 | 1.2056 |
| 1990 | 1.2334 | 0.0232 | 1.8826 |
| 1991 | 1.2301 | 0.0219 | 1.7841 |
| 1992 | 1.2392 | 0.0240 | 1.9395 |
| 1993 | 1.2515 | 0.0318 | 2.5381 |

Figure 6.1 plots the standard deviation of the log of real GDP per capita against time. This chart shows that over the sample period as a whole real regional incomes have diverged. Although incomes were more divergent from 1976 to 1988 than in 1975, there was a sharp fall in income divergence between 1988 and 1989, taking regional income divergence virtually back to the 1975 level. However, there has been a very sharp divergence in the last five years of the sample from 1989, making regional income divergence greater in 1993 than at any time over the sample period.

Figures 6.2a and 6.2b provide an impression of the levels of real GDP per capita and relative real GDP per capita in each of the regions over the sample period. Figure 6.2a shows that in every region income per head was higher in 1993 than in 1975. The region with the highest income per head in 1975 was the South-East (including London) and the same region had the highest income per head in 1993. Consistently at the other end of the income scale was Northern Ireland, with the lowest income per head in both 1975 and 1993. Figure 6.2b shows a more interesting pattern, with all regions benefiting from the late 1980s boom, but again with the South-East being the strongest and dominant region. Interestingly, in the South-East incomes rose by less than national income until the mid-1980s, when the pattern was reversed with a vengeance, until 1992. Neither Figures 6.2a nor 6.2b give much impression of the 'mobility of regions' in the income scale.

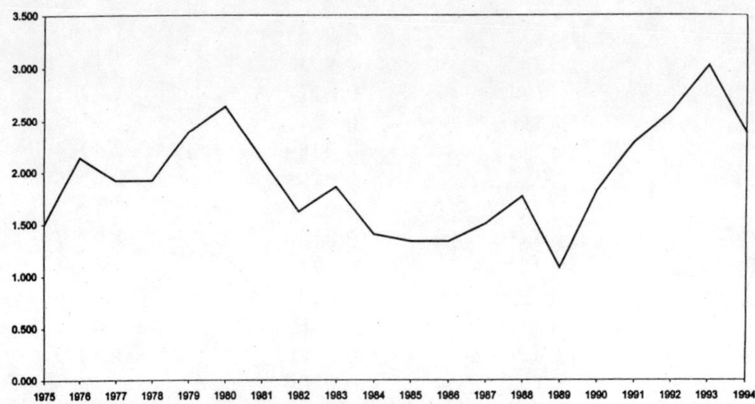


Figure 6.1 *Sigma-convergence*

The time profile suggests that there may be important differences across various phases of the business cycle. The time series is divided up into three periods, which correspond to the UK business cycle.[11] Each period runs from a trough in national economic activity to the next trough in activity. The first period runs from 1975 to 1981, the second from 1981-1985 and the third from 1985–92. The troughs of 1985 and 1992 and the intervening peaks of 1984 and 1988 were not, though, very distinct. This makes analysis problematic but cycles in the income dispersion can be found broadly consistent with the business cycle.

In the recovery phase of the first business cycle, from 1975–9, there is a clear upward trend in the coefficient of variation in Figure 6.1. From the trough of 1985 to the peak of 1988, or from 1985 to the peak of 1993, the coefficient of variation rises in the upswing of the business cycle. In the downswing from 1979 to 1981, or ignoring the mild peak of 1984–5 the coefficient of variation falls. This analysis seems to suggest that in the recession phases of these cycles income dispersion seems to decrease,

[11] As defined by the UK Office of National Statistics.

whereas in the recovery phases income dispersion seems to rise. This is consistent with the findings of Chatterji and Dewhurst (1996), but it does rely on disregarding the 'low peaks' of 1984 and 1988.[12]

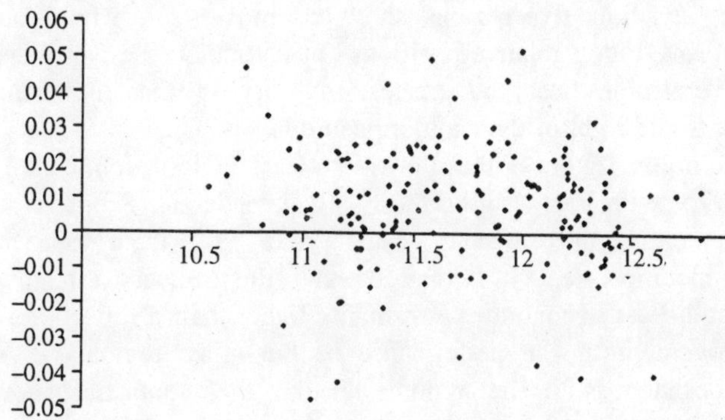


Figure 6.2a *Real GDP per head*

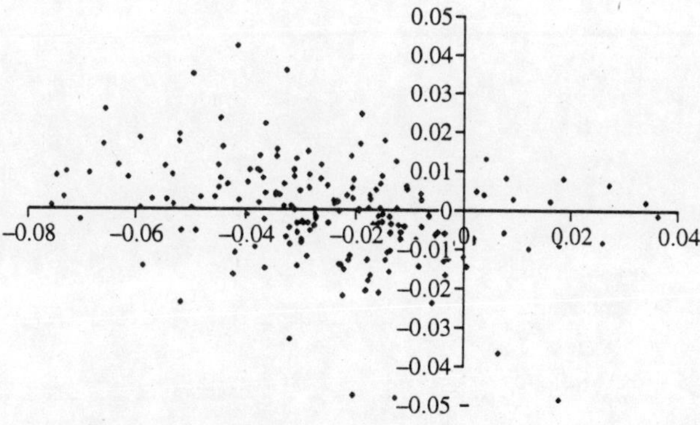


Figure 6.2b *Relative GDP per head*

Table 6.3 sheds some light on the 'mobility of regions' in the regional income distribution. Cells on the main diagonal show no relative change in

[12] It may be that the low peaks of 1984 and 1988 are a consequence of the regions not following a predicted pattern. This is consistent with the view that the nature of UK recessions has undergone significant structural change in the period since 1980 in that regional responses to the national business cycle have changed fundamentally. In particular, it seems that the South-East now appears to face the largest cyclical sensitivity to fluctuations in demand at the UK level.

the income position of the region; cells to the right of the main diagonal show an improvement in the region's relative performance over the time period in question; while the cells to the left of the main diagonal show regions that have suffered a relative decline in their positions. Over the sample period as a whole five regions show no movement, while four regions have improved their relative positions. In particular, the North and East Anglia have demonstrated the greatest mobility in that they have moved two cells to the right of their initial positions.

A second common feature is that the South-East is less dominant in 1994 than in 1975, with East Anglia, the East Midlands and Scotland all closing the gap in the 'above average' category: in 1975 there were no regions in this income category. It may be that this reflects a relative decline in the South-East's economic performance rather than a reflection of a relative improvement in the performance of the other regions – an interpretation consistent with the hypothesis that the South-East now appears to face the largest cyclical sensitivity to fluctuations in UK demand (Audas and Mackay, 1997).

Table 6.3. *Changes over time in UK regional GDP per capita, 1975–94*

| 1975 \ 1994 | Low | Below Average | Average | Above Average | High |
|---|---|---|---|---|---|
| Low | Northern Ireland | North-West<br>Yorkshire and Humberside | North | | |
| Below average | | Wales<br>West Midlands | | East Anglia | |
| Average | | | South West | East Midlands | |
| Above average | | | | | South-East |
| High | | | | | |

Figure 6.3 shows a lack of $\beta$-convergence between the UK regions over the sample period. The figure plots the log of the change in real income per head against the log of initial real income per head, following the Barro-type regression approach. Convergence would be represented by a downward pattern of the points. This may be evident, but it is extremely weak. This

negative correlation is confirmed by the Barro regression result, but the explanatory power of the regression is close to zero, although the regression coefficient suggests speed of convergence of about 9 per cent per annum, which is faster than that suggested by Barro and Sala-i-Martin (1991; 1992a).

Overall there is no clear-cut $\sigma$-convergence nor absolute $\beta$-convergence over the sample period. There is evidence of some degree of mobility across the UK regions, although this movement is not always permanent and at best is very slow. The analysis suggests that there are differences in real income levels that have persisted over the sample period. These differences may partly reflect the structural characteristics of regional economies. This raises the question of whether the regional economies converge to the same rate of growth, but to different steady state levels of income where each region has specific characteristics that define the steady state level of income (i.e. conditional $\beta$-convergence).

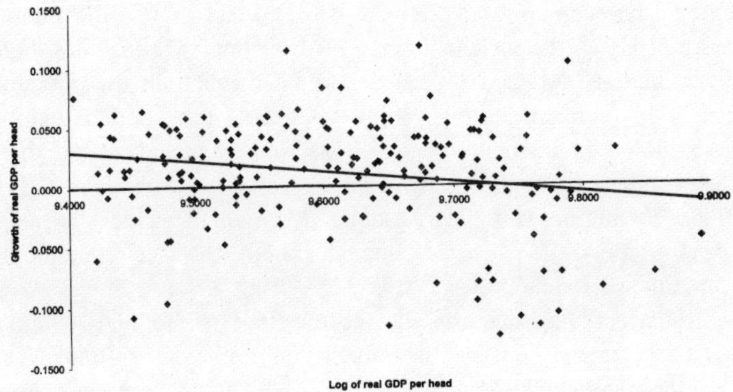


Figure 6.3 *Beta-convergence*

### 6.4.2 Conditional $\beta$-convergence

To explain the UK regional growth rates a model is set up of conditional beta-convergence.[13] This takes the usual Barro form, but includes two additional explanatory variables: physical and human capital per head. Unlike Barro, a panel data set is used and also allowance is made for different regional effects and different time period effects, by using regional and time period dummy variables to capture any cyclical effects.

[13] Levine and Renelt (1992) offer an analysis of the conditions under which there is evidence of per capita convergence in a cross-country growth regression.

The regression used is:

$$\Delta\ln(y_{it}) = a - b\ln(y_{it-1}) + c_k X_{kit-1} + d_i D_i + e_t T_t \qquad (6.1)$$

In this model X is a vector of k additional regional characteristics such as human capital, physical investment or regional aid; D is a vector of 11 regional dummy variables that provide a set of regional coefficients $d_i$, that can be interpreted as capturing specific regional characteristics; T is a vector of t time dummy variables included to capture trends in the national economy, such that coefficients $e_t$ capture the time specific nature of the rate of growth of regional income per head.

Table 6.4 shows the results of the model over the full sample period.[14] This method allows for possible structural differences across regions and for different effects over time.

The four sets of results reported in Table 6.4 refer to estimates of equation (6.1) where in (A) there are no additional economic variables, in (B) the regional real capital stock, $RKS_i$, is added and in (C) the human capital variable, $EDU_i$, is included in turn. Equation (D) includes both economic variables and for each of the four estimated equations the potential significance of 11 regional dummy variables[15] and 19 time period dummy variables is explored. In practice for each of the four estimated models three equations are estimated. The three versions are referred to as Model 1 (M1), which includes no dummy variables, Model 2 (M2) which includes regional dummies and Model 3 (M3) which includes both the set of regional dummies and time period dummies.

The various test statistics reported at the foot of Table 6.4 allow distinctions to be drawn between the models on statistical grounds. The statistics are the reported chi-squared statistics, which in every case reject both M1 and M2 in favour of model M3 at the 5 per cent level and therefore only the M3 results are reported for each form of the model.

The implied $\beta$-coefficients[16] for all versions of Model 3 are very similar at around 0.50 which show much more rapid convergence than in the absolute convergence case where the parameter is close to 0.09. Indeed, these very high values for $\beta$-effects should not be interpreted too literally for

[14] Estimation was using the two-factor, two-way method of LIMDEP version 7; see Greene (1993)

[15] Except for equations that deploy the human capital variable for which there is no data for Northern Ireland.

[16] The formula that translates the estimated coefficient, $b$, into Barro's concept of $\beta$ is: $-b = (1 - e^{-bt})/T$, where t denotes the time period and e is the base of natural logarithms (see Chapter 5).

they probably reflect the relatively similar growth rates of the UK regions and the very strong influence of the time dummy variables. The other economic explanatory variables do not perform very well and are never statistically significant. The coefficient on the physical capital variable even changes to a negative sign between equation (B) and (D), although it is marginally significant with the correct (positive) sign in (B).

Table 6.4. *Conditional β-convergence results: growth of real GDP per capita*

| Additional variables | (A) None | (B) Real capital stock | (C) Human capital stock | (D) Real and human capital stock |
|---|---|---|---|---|
| Coefficients | | | | |
| a | 0.613 | 0.158 | 0.630 | 3.474 |
| | (7.96) | (3.97) | (6.48) | (1.95) |
| b | -0.519 | -0.581 | -0.538 | -0.554 |
| | (-7.89) | (-7.64) | (-6.83) | (-7.02) |
| $c_1$ | | 0.084 | | -1.042 |
| | | (1.60) | | (-1.60) |
| $c_2$ | | | 0.026 | 0.028 |
| | | | (0.58) | (0.61) |
| $R^2$ | 0.670 | 0.675 | 0.666 | 0.672 |
| T | 209 | 209 | 160 | 160 |
| LL | 650.61 | 652.10 | 494.51 | 496.05 |
| F | F[30.178]=12.1 | F[31,177]=11.9 | F[27.132]=9.7 | F[28,131]=9.6 |
| M1vM3 | $\chi^2$[29]=220.5 | $\chi^2$[29]=220.0 | $\chi^2$[25]=151.9 | $\chi^2$[25]=220.5 |
| M2vM3 | $\chi^2$[18]=216.4 | $\chi^2$[18]=213.8 | $\chi^2$[15]=145.9 | $\chi^2$[15]=216.4 |

*Notes*: T is the number of observations in the sample; LL is the log-likelihood function; F is the test statistic for the significance of the whole equation (critical value at 5% is 1.5); $R^2$ is the coefficient of determination and the t-statistics are in parenthesis. The chi-squared statistics test the null that M1 and M3, and M2 and M3, are equivalent. Rejection of the null implies that M3 is the preferred model in each case. The critical values for $\chi^2$ at 5% are $\chi^2$[29]=42.56. $\chi^2$[22]=37.65, $\chi^2$[18]=28.87 and $\chi^2$[15]=25.00. $c_1$ is the coefficient on RKS and $c_2$ is the coefficient on EDU. Eleven regional dummy variables and 19 period dummy variables are included in specifications 4A and 4B. Specifications 4C and 4D exclude Northern Ireland, hence include only 10 regional dummies.

The goodness-of-fit statistics in all the regressions reported in Table 6.4 are all around 0.67, and are almost wholly due to the influence of the time period dummy variables. The time dummy variables are strongly significant as a group and individually show strong negative effects in the period 1976 to 1981, as the economy suffered from the oil-price induced recession. From 1983 to 1990 we have strong, positive time dummies capturing the upturn in the 1980s, following the second oil shock of the late 1970s. The dummy variables for 1991 and 1992, although not significantly different from zero at the 10 per cent level, are jointly negative, showing the ERM-induced slump, with the dummy variables for both 1993 and 1994 showing positive and significant coefficients representing the recovery. This suggests that the evolution of regional incomes in the UK has been largely driven by the business cycle.

However, this takes no account of the significance and size of the regional dummies. Most noticeably, three regions stand out as being significantly different from the rest; namely, the South-East (including London), which grows on average some 2 per cent faster than any other region, Northern Ireland and the West Midlands, which have markedly slower average rates of growth than the other UK regions, of 2 per cent and 4 per cent respectively. This result is robust across all the model specifications in Table 6.4.

## 6.5 CONCLUSIONS

The UK has a long-standing tradition of regional policies. Their motivation has almost exclusively been focused on reducing unemployment differentials and to this end a wide range of policy tools and combinations of policy instruments have been deployed. Membership of the EU has not only offered new sources of aid for economically distressed regions but has also served to stimulate the overall performance of the UK economy, with positive spillover effects into the traditionally depressed areas. At the same time it has restricted the portfolio of policy instruments the UK authorities may deploy. It is against this background that regional convergence in the country needs to be measured.

This study of UK regional real income per head has shown that UK regional incomes have exhibited some $\sigma$-divergence over the whole period and little significant absolute $\beta$-convergence. There is stronger evidence for conditional $\beta$-convergence of real GDP per capita over the past 20 years, although it is important to emphasise that conditional convergence does not imply that real regional income will converge on the same value, but rather that the regions will converge to different steady-state levels of real income.

In the strictest sense therefore conditional convergence is equivalent to sustained differences in the levels of regional real incomes per head. Furthermore, the very rapid rates of income convergence found in this chapter arise, at least in part, from the regions having fairly similar levels of income per head. In the multi-country work of Barro and Sala-i-Martin (1991), for example, it is the more diverse initial levels of regional incomes and the longer sample period that give rise to the slower estimated income convergence.

It has been found that conditional $\beta$-convergence is difficult to account for with economic variables and is found to be dominated by the national business cycle. It follows therefore that the regional problem is perhaps best tackled by reducing the amplitude of the national business cycle, rather than by specific regional policies. There is also evidence, however, that some regions have caught up with the relatively vibrant South-East region: namely Scotland and the North-East. Interestingly, these are the same regions that have had the largest regional assistance from central government since the mid-1980s, on average some 30 per cent and 18 per cent per annum, respectively, of the government's regional assistance budget. We are hesitant to suggest that regional assistance accounts for this, particularly as regional policy is known to have been inadequately funded in the UK over the period (Taylor and Wren, 1997). The literature on the effectiveness of regional policy suggests that there is a powerful economic case for regional policy; and this causal evidence suggests that the genuine convergence of real incomes per head can be influenced by governments, even if growth rates fluctuate with national business cycles.

# 7. Labour Market Convergence in the UK and Germany

## 7.1 INTRODUCTION

This chapter is concerned with developments in two European labour markets. In particular it looks at the extent to which there has been spatial convergence in service sector employment in a major EU economy, namely that of the UK.[1] It also considers more generally the relative patterns of convergence to be found in the UK as a whole and in Germany.

Whether one likes to think in terms of a 'third industrial revolution' or the coming of the 'information society', it is a fact that the last twenty years have witnessed a significant upsurge in the importance of the service sector[2]. Disregarding the question of definition, at the macroeconomic level official statistics show that the share of private and public sector services in gross domestic product now exceeds 50 per cent in industrialised countries and is above 70 per cent in some countries such as the US. The service sector accounts for between 55 per cent and 69 per cent of total employment. For instance, in Great Britain it has grown from 28 per cent of employment in 1861; 35 per cent in 1901; 46 per cent in 1951 to 69 per cent in 1988 (Marshall, 1992). One could add to these figures the work performed in tertiary occupations in the secondary sector and in the informal or 'self-service' sector (such as house work).

The objective is to look at the extent to which there has been convergence in the service sector across regions. Our underlying interest is in the potential for convergence of service sector employment across EU regions.

1 The service sector was selected for particular attention because regions with a service sector orientation are among the most successful economies in the Union with an average income per head 27 per cent above the EU average. Additionally, market services accounted for just over 50 per cent of the EU's gross value added in 1995.

2 See, for example, Fontaine (1987); Ochel and Wegner (1987); and Rodwin and Sazanami (1991)

Data for the EU as a whole, however, tend to be difficult to use for this purpose because of national variations in definitions and the lack, in many cases, of full time series covering any useful duration. Additionally, cross-national studies should ideally take into account local policy variations and this is particularly difficult to do over a range of economies as diverse as those in the EU. However, since our interest is in regional convergence it is possible to gain some insights into the factors at work by focusing on the particular pattern of convergence which has emerged in the UK. Initially, however, it is useful to review some of the previous work which has been conducted looking at the economic importance of the service sector.

The second part of the chapter is motivated less by the usefulness of looking at a key sector and more by the concern that it is often useful to look in detail at one or two specific case studies to confirm (or refute) general findings. In this case the quality of overall EU data is limited in a number of ways and it seems helpful to look at a sub-Union grouping: The UK and Germany. More general information, especially regarding causal factors and policy effects, can also be gleaned in this way.

## 7.2 THE SERVICE SECTOR AND REGIONAL DEVELOPMENT

Studies of the service sector seem especially relevant at this time and yet our understanding of the service sector is still very limited.[3] Service activities are, when compared to manufacturing industry, particularly mobile and flexible. These features come to the fore during a period of increased liberalism in factor and product markets.

Many European countries are reforming regulatory regimes which should allow greater mobility for labour employed in service activities and a greater freedom of effective choice for firms in the sector. This, of course, is being supplemented by greater international opportunities afforded by the creation of the Single European Market (and larger European Economic Space) and the political changes which have taken place in the post-communist countries of Eastern Europe. A number of individual case studies looking at the implications of these developments (for example, in the provision of professional services: Button and Fleming, 1992 and Love *et al.* 1992) highlight some of the specific implications.[4] Here we are

3 As Fuchs (1985) says, 'There is a long-standing need for more systematic, scholarly attention to the service sector. There are huge gaps in the data base, major needs for new theoretical models appropriate for the study of service firms and industries, and a large potential demand for analytical studies that use the new models and new data'.

4 There are also now a number of studies emerging that look at the factors attracting high-technology service employment in particular, e.g. Button *et al* (1999b).

concerned with services more generally and specifically with changes in employment in service industries at the regional level.

While the literature on the service sector, and in particular on its general implications for economic growth and on social change, is now extensive, it is only comparatively recently that interest has been shown in the regional implications of the growth in service sector activity (Marshall, 1992). The earlier work was either largely at the macroeconomic level and generally aspatial in its orientation – that is, it addressed questions such as the implications for public sector financing of increased service sector employment (Baumol, 1967), or was concerned with definitions and classifications useful for National Income accounting purposes (Hill, 1977).

In an economic development sense, the service economy was seen as passive and simply following trends in the manufacturing sector. This was a position heavily influenced by the arguments of Adam Smith (and supported by Karl Marx) who held that service sector employment is 'unproductive of any value' and, more recently, by the cliometric work of Fogel (1964) on the role of railways in US development.

This situation has changed in recent years according to Howells and Green (1988):

> Traditionally services have been viewed as 'passive' elements within modern industrial economies with the growth of services in regions simply following that of population and economic growth. There is, however, increasing evidence to suggest that this is no longer an adequate conceptualisation of the place of the service sector in national and regional economic development. Indeed, research suggests that in some respects the service sector is the leading rather than a lagging element in national and regional economic growth in many parts of the Community.

The explanation of the changed attitude comes in part from improved data sources which offer the opportunity to disaggregate service activities. The general finding here is the resurrection of the pre-war notion that service industries seem to have differing effects on location and development depending upon whether they are basic or non-basic. The former, which can be defined as services which are geared for national and international markets and often provide a substantial net balance of payments contribution to a region, have, until quite recently, been subjected to minimal study. They include, in particular, such services as banking, financial, computer and other information services, although in some regions tourism would also form a basic service industry. Service industries of this type can be an important driving force for regional economic growth, contributing directly to exports (Polese, 1982).

Much of the traditional work focused on the locally oriented, non-basic activities which meet the needs of local consumers and have only small multiplier effects. These include such things as policing, repair services, retailing and professional services.

Besides a better understanding of the role of service industries, political reality, combined with the scale of the service sector in all industrialised economies, means that policies toward the service sector have become important instruments in attempting to reduce regional inequalities. This is hardly surprising since services are the largest single sector in all EU economies. Perhaps of equal importance, however, is the fact that the growth in service activities has come during a period when EU regional policy has become more central to Union thinking.

As we have seen, however, since the publication of the *Thompson Report* in 1973 it has been recognised that, for equity reasons, a more active EU-based regional policy is necessary to compensate for the loss of important national discretionary powers (i.e. regarding exchange rate flexibility) which accompany any form of tighter monetary integration. In particular, therefore, policies which can lead to footloose industries being attracted to depressed areas are attractive. This is increasingly true during times when public funds for major infrastructure investments are scarce and the long term efficiency of relocating manufacturing activities is in question.

## 7.3 DEFINITIONS AND TRENDS

Of course, there are questions of exactly what is meant by service sector activities. As Kravis *et al.* (1982), pointed out, 'The nature of services, their distinction from commodities, and the question of how to value them in relation to the total production of the economy are all issues that have been debated since the beginning of modern economics and, indeed, in some respects, through the ages'.

While we, like many others, for pragmatic reasons, are used to making use of the official classifications for statistical analysis, these tend to be rather crude and questions of consistency across countries still remain. Stigler (1956), in his seminal study, made this clear over thirty-five years ago, 'there exists no authoritative consensus on either the boundaries or the classification of the service industries'.

How important it is to agree on a strict definition of what constitutes the service sector and what are service industries really depends on the question being considered. There are obvious differences between physical goods and services (Hill, 1977). The distinction between the process of production, the output and the user is clear with a good. The output can also be stored and owned. With a service, the production process and the service product are indistinguishable and the service must be consumed or it does not exist. Storage is not possible. Going beyond these sorts of generality, however, poses problems – for example, where do information and information industries fit into this categorisation?

For our purposes, and indeed for regional policy more generally, exact definitions are perhaps not that important given the ways in which data are collected and the breadth which all policy measures entail. What is perhaps more important, but often lacking, is consistency in the definitions of regional types across countries. The situation has improved in recent years as EUROSTAT has sought consistency in data collection, but historical series in particular still have problems associated with them. In practice we must make do with the best which is available and hope that distortions are minimal.

What the official data tell us is that the US led the way in service sector employment growth until the 1970s since when there has been a gradual catching up by European countries. Indeed, by 1981, Keeble *et al* (1981) reported that, 'service industries are by far the most important source of regional growth within the Community'. Even so, within the EU there are significant variations between Member States and regions as to the importance of the service sector in their economies (see Table 7.1).[5]

Table 7.1. *Employment (per cent) by sector in the EU, 1989*

| Country | Agriculture | Industry | Services |
|---|---|---|---|
| Belgium | 7.1 | 33.2 | 59.8 |
| Denmark | 5.7 | 27.4 | 66.9 |
| France | 6.9 | 30.3 | 62.8 |
| Germany | 3.9 | 40.2 | 56.0 |
| Greece | 25.3 | 25.7 | 48.9 |
| Ireland | 15.5 | 28.8 | 55.8 |
| Italy | 9.2 | 32.0 | 58.8 |
| Luxembourg | 3.8 | 29.2 | 67.0 |
| Netherlands | 4.8 | 26.7 | 68.5 |
| Portugal | 19.3 | 34.6 | 46.0 |
| Spain | 13.2 | 32.7 | 54.2 |
| UK | 2.2 | 32.6 | 65.1 |

*Source*: Statistical Office of the European Communities

In addition to national variations in the importance of service sector employment there are also significant differences between regions within individual Member States. Table 7.2 lists those EU regions that have the

5 For accounts of the developments in service sector activity within Europe, see Howells (1988), Howells and Green (1988), Illeris (1989) and Ochel and Wegner (1987). Lengellé (1980) gives a wider view of developments in industrialised countries. Gillespie and Green (1987) give a UK perspective.

highest level of service sector employment and it is clear that they are spread across a range of countries.

Table 7.2. *EU regions with high levels of service sector employment*

| NUTS 2 Region | Population ('000) | Service employment rate (%) | Unemployment rate (%) | GDP per Head (EU15=1000) |
|---|---|---|---|---|
| Ceuta Y Melilla | 131.6 | 92.6 | 26.2 | 65 |
| Brussels | 951.6 | 83.8 | 13.5 | 172 |
| Greater London | 7007.1 | 83.7 | 7.8 | 139 |
| Stockholm | 1712.1 | 82.9 | 8.1 | 123 |
| Brabant Wallon | 336.5 | 79.8 | 7.9 | 87 |
| Ile de France | 11009.1 | 79.3 | 10.7 | 165 |
| Corse | 260.2 | 78.9 | 21.0 | 81 |
| Surrey, West Sussex | 2506.7 | 77.6 | 4.1 | 95 |
| Provence-Alps-Cote d'Azur | 4429.5 | 77.5 | 16.3 | 94 |
| Wien | 1592.6 | 77.4 | 5.9 | 165 |
| Namur | 434.4 | 76.7 | 11.4 | 83 |
| Uusimaa | 1318.1 | 76.7 | 12.3 | 123 |
| Vlaams Bragbant | 995.3 | 76.4 | 4.5 | 96 |
| Hamburg | 1707.3 | 76.4 | 8.8 | 195 |
| Berlin | 3471.0 | 75.9 | 13.4 | 105 |
| Lazio | 5197.7 | 75.6 | 13.3 | 114 |
| Utrecht | 1067.0 | 75.6 | 4.1 | 120 |
| Noord-Holland | 2466.0 | 74.6 | 5.3 | 121 |

In terms of growth, the indications are that during the 1980s Portugal, Ireland, Luxembourg and Italy experienced the highest relative growth rates whilst the UK, Belgium and Spain recorded relatively low rates.[6] Further, the UK may be seen to be atypical in Europe because of the particular concentration of service employment at one centre, London. In the rest of Western Europe it is much more decentralised (Illeris, 1989). This may be a function of natural forces given the relatively *laissez-faire* approach adopted toward spatial economic policy in the UK when compared with other EU countries.

6 The importance of service sector growth to the peripheral regions of the EU during the early 1980s is discussed in more detail in Keeble *et al.* (1981) and Bartels *et al.* (1983).

It is also important to recognise that there are often major differences between the growth in consumer and public services, which tend to display a spatial distribution pattern closely aligned to the population distribution, and producer and business services, which are closely associated with the distribution of manufacturing industry. Disaggregating further and looking at the largest EU states, Elfring (1989) finds important differences in the relative importance of specific service industries between countries which can be attributed back to a variety of social, cultural and political factors.

While a number of common trends could be observed across countries there are some important distinctions (Table 7.3). For example, after a rapid expansion in the 1960s there was a deceleration in the growth of social services during the second half of the 1970s and the early 1980s, but at the same time an acceleration of employment in personal services. Germany, for example, has a relatively small proportion of employment in distributive and producer services. Breaking this down further, Elfring finds that low levels of employment in wholesale trade and business/professional services respectively largely explain this. Comparisons with service sectors outside of the EU find social service employment, for example, is considerably in excess of that in Japan (12.7 per cent).

Table 7.3. *Service employment as percentage of total employment, 1985*

| Type of service | France | Germany | Netherlands | UK |
|---|---|---|---|---|
| Producer | 8.5 | 7.2 | 10.5 | 9.5 |
| Distributive | 20.0 | 18.0 | 21.1 | 21.3 |
| Personal | 7.7 | 7.8 | 8.3 | 9.9 |
| Social | 25.7 | 21.3 | 27.6 | 24.6 |
| Total | 61.7 | 54.2 | 67.5 | 65.3 |

*Source*: Extracted from Elfring (1989)

Accepting that there exist national differences in the importance and composition of service sectors between countries, it is nevertheless interesting to look in a little more detail at trends, both over time and across regions, within a particular EU Member. The availability of a long and relatively consistent set of data on developments in the UK means that this can be done with relatively minimal adjustments to official data series and without the need for arbitrary splicing.

What we find for the UK is that in the late 1980s there was strong employment growth across all service industries but that this faltered in sub-sectors such as transport, business and other services during the recession of the early 1990s. However, as we see from Table 7.4, overall the service sector employment stood up to the recession remarkably well when contrasted to other areas of activity such as construction, manufacturing and extractive industries. While economic forecasting is never easy, there also seems to be some indication that service sector employment will continue to gain in relative terms during the late 1990s (Taylor and Lewney, 1993).

The relative importance of the factors which have lead to this expansion in service sector size are unclear. In fact, six broad forces seem to have been at work although, to date, isolating the impact of each has proved elusive. These factors are:

- the externalisation by manufacturing companies of service functions (e.g. cleaning, maintenance, catering, etc.) which were previously undertaken within the company and thus disguised as 'manufacturing' in most data sets (Howells, 1988),
- the increasing internationalisation of service activities which has come about as trade restrictions have generally been lowered, has meant that services are now more easily exported (Howells, 1988),

Table 7.4. *Employment trends (per cent changes) by sector in the UK*

| Sector | 1971-80 | 1980-85 | 1985-90 | 1990-92 |
|---|---|---|---|---|
| Agriculture | -1.5 | -1.0 | -1.4 | -3.6 |
| Mining (including oil) | -1.3 | -5.8 | -10.0 | -6.7 |
| Public utilities | -0.8 | -3.0 | -1.4 | -1.1 |
| Manufacturing | -1.6 | -4.5 | -0.6 | -4.0 |
| metal manufacturing | -3.3 | -12.2 | -2.6 | -3.8 |
| mineral products | -2.1 | -3.5 | -0.9 | -6.6 |
| chemicals | -0.6 | -4.3 | -0.6 | -4.2 |
| engineering | -1.4 | -5.4 | -0.7 | -3.7 |
| food, drink & tobacco | -1.0 | -3.6 | -1.5 | -3.8 |
| textiles, clothing & footwear | -3.8 | -4.4 | -2.5 | -4.3 |
| other manufacturing | -0.8 | -1.5 | 1.7 | -4.2 |
| Construction | 0.5 | -1.5 | 3.9 | -5.3 |
| Distribution | 1.3 | 0.5 | 2.0 | -2.8 |
| Transport & communications | -0.2 | -2.2 | 1.9 | -3.2 |
| Business services | 2.5 | 5.0 | 5.8 | -3.3 |
| Public administration & defence | 0.6 | -0.8 | -0.3 | 1.2 |
| Education and health | 2.6 | 0.1 | 1.8 | 1.1 |
| Other services | 3.0 | 4.3 | 2.9 | -3.4 |

- the increased complexity of corporate activities requires a higher level of service inputs (Noyelle and Stanback, 1984),
- the Engels' effect which means that greater affluence has resulted in increasing demands for services by final consumers as their incomes have risen (Gudgin, 1983),
- there is a lower rate of productivity increase in service industries relative to manufacturing (Baumol, 1967),

- there has been the creation of new service sector activities (e.g. in on-line information services (Howells, 1988).

Table 7.5 shows that there have been major differences in the levels of employment in the service sector between the UK regions. Equally, there are significant differences in the importance of service sector employment between the regions. Figure 7.1 provides an indication of of the trend in the share of regional employment between regions.

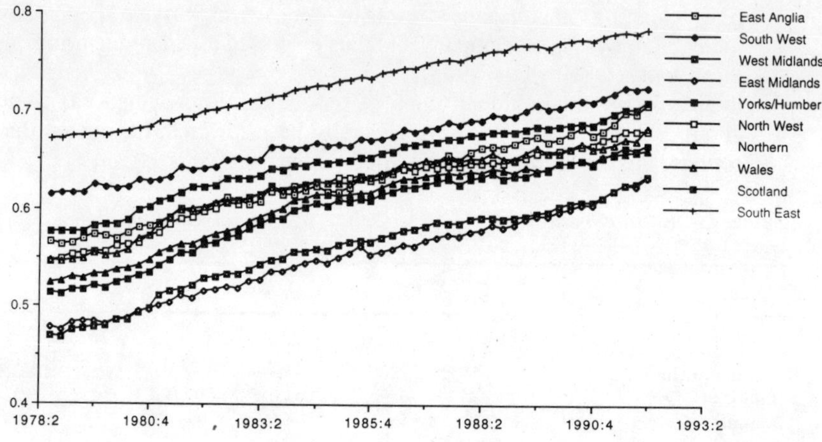


Figure 7.1 *Share of service sector employment against total employment for regions between 1978 and 1991*

Table 7.5. *UK regional employment (per cent) by sector, 1989*

| Region | Agriculture | Industry | Services |
|---|---|---|---|
| North | 2.0 | 37.0 | 61.0 |
| Yorkshire & Humberside | 1.9 | 36.7 | 61.4 |
| East Midlands | 1.8 | 39.2 | 59.0 |
| East Anglia | 4.0 | 30.5 | 65.5 |
| South East | 1.3 | 27.4 | 71.3 |
| South West | 3.4 | 30.7 | 65.0 |
| West Midlands | 2.5 | 40.5 | 57.0 |
| North West | 1.3 | 34.5 | 64.3 |
| Wales | 4.5 | 33.6 | 61.9 |
| Scotland | 3.6 | 32.6 | 63.8 |
| Northern Ireland | 5.7 | 29.3 | 65.0 |

*Source*: *Regional Trends*

In aggregate terms, and also reflecting the data in Table 7.2, the service economy is particularly important in the South-East. At a more micro level, one finds that this situation is mainly due to the concentration of business and financial services. Much of this dominance can be traced to the national pattern of service sector growth in the late 1970s and early 1980s when a rapid expansion in business services and finance was accopanied by a decline in transport and administration employment. This structural shift, most likely because of agglomeration economies, seems to have favoured the South-East and larger cities. In London, for example, employment in transport and public administration fell by 4 per cent and 19 per cent respectively between 1976 and 1981 while that in finance and business services rose by 8 per cent (Illeris, 1989).

Historically, in relative terms, starting from low base levels, regions around the South-East benefited from distributional trends and enjoyed more rapid growth rates in finance and business service employment (for example, 21 per cent in East Anglia from 1976 to 1981; 25 per cent in the East Midlands and 33 per cent in the West Midlands compared to 13 per cent in the South-East). This development, though, still left these regions well behind the South-East in overall service sector employment.

## 7.4 POLICY EFFECTS

The changes in service sector employment which have taken place have not done so entirely in a vacuum. Certainly changes in patterns of demand due to rising incomes and modifications in tastes have been extremely important. So also have technical developments which have brought about significant changes in the productivity of the manufacturing sector and have resulted in an entirely new range of service sector products emerging on the market. In addition to this, however, the institutional environment, and especially the policy environment, in which the service sector operates has changed. Some of the policy reforms have been aspatial in their nature and have led to the liberalisation of many service sector markets. Others, however, have more direct spatial implications.

The policy changes of importance have taken place at several different levels. At one level, the UK's membership of the EU means that its regions are eligible for EU regional assistance – for instance from the European Regional Development Fund. While regional assistance had traditionally been given predominantly for manufacturing and construction projects (especially infrastructure), there is now an increased amount devoted to specific forms of service sector activities, for example:

> Activities in the service sector qualifying for assistance shall be those concerning tourism or those having a choice of location. Such activities must have an impact on the development of the region and on the level of

> employment. Tourism activities must contribute to the development of tourism in the region or area in question. (EC Council Regulation 1987/84)

In addition to this the gradual opening up of the EU as it has progressed towards the Single European Market has provided opportunities for labour and capital to move more freely between Member States, for example, EU agreement on recognition of professional qualifications enhances labour mobility.

Specifically, at the national level, again the traditional emphasis of regional and industrial policy has been on the stimulation and location of manufacturing firms. Although one should perhaps modify that in the context of some past measures, especially in the 1960s and 1970s, such as the Selective Employment Tax, the Regional Employment Premium and the Office Development Permits scheme, which were specifically designed to influence the location of service sector employment albeit in a negative way. This has changed somewhat in recent years as the overall focus of policy has switched from distributional to efficiency considerations and as the importance of the service sector has grown. The changes in regional policy introduced in 1984 allowed for services of regional importance and which would not displace existing jobs (for example, value added network services, industrial R&D services, software and data processing) to be eligible for funding.[7]

More generally, the switch away from spatially related industrial policies (for example, the reduction in expenditure on regional policy from £700 million in 1983–4 to £400 million in 1987–8), the efforts to make regional policy more cost-effective and the focusing of assistance on the most disadvantaged areas (for example, through the creation of Urban Development Corporations, City Action Teams, Task Forces, etc.) can be seen as a move by government to devolve regional policy away from the centre. This, inevitably, has implications for the spatial pattern of industrial location and growth.

## 7.5 METHODOLOGY

We now turn to examine the extent to which convergence has occurred in service sector activities across the UK regions and to discuss the extent to which this has been influenced by natural market forces and the degree to which policy initiatives have been important.

There has recently been an increasing tendency in the econometric literature to favour the time-varying parameter technique to examine

7 There have also been efforts to disperse civil service employment away form London in recent years (Marshall *et al.*, 1991).

convergence.[8] Much of the justification for this comes from the argument that there has been very little formal analysis of convergence and that economists have, in the past, been rather lax in developing a rigorous method for testing for convergence between two (or more) series but have rather relied upon a number of procedures each specific to its context. Included here would be the calculation and plotting of measures of dispersion; seeking convergence of parameters in econometric relations; tests for mean reversion; cointegration of variables; and time-varying parameters.[9] In comparing the alternatives they present the case for deploying the time-varying parameter approach favoured here.

In a little more detail, the Kalman filter and time-varying methods are presented in an intuitive manner and linked to the traditional OLS regression techniques. Consider the general linear model with fixed parameters:

$$Y_t = X_t\beta + e \tag{7.1}$$

where $e$ is the error term, which is normally distributed with a zero mean and a constant variance:

$$e \sim N(0, \sigma^2 I) \tag{7.2}$$

The OLS estimator , $\beta^*$, which gives BLUE is defined as:

$$\beta^* = (X'X)^{-1}X'Y \tag{7.3}$$

with a variance-covariance matrix of

$$\mathrm{Var}(\beta^*) = P_0 = \sigma^2 (X'X)^{-1} \tag{7.4}$$

Suppose that equations (7.3) and (7.4) are estimated over a particular period. The arrival of new observations on $X$, say $X_1$, can then be used to generate new predictions of $Y$, say $Y_1$. With an unchanged structural model:

$$Y_1 = X_1\beta + e_1 \tag{7.5}$$

where $e_1$ is uncorrelated with $e$ and $e_1 \sim N(0, \sigma^2 I_1)$ or $e_1 \sim N(0, V_1)$. The predictions of $Y_1$ from (7.5), denoted as $Y_1^*$, are given as: $Y_1^* = X_1\beta^*$ with the one-step-ahead forecast error denoted as:

8 See the work of Haldane and Hall (1991) and Hall *et al.* (1992) on exchange rate convergence.

9 A useful discussion of cointegration procedures is contained in Holden and Thompson (1992).

$$v_1^* = Y^1 - Y_1^* \tag{7.6}$$

which has a covariance matrix, given by *F*, of:

$$\begin{aligned} F = \text{Cov}(v_1^*) &= E[Y_1 - E(Y_1^*)][Y_1 - E(Y_1^*)]' \\ &= E[X_1\beta + e_1 - X_1\beta^*][X_1\beta + e_1 - X_1\beta^*]' \\ &= E[X_1(\beta - \beta^*) + e_1][X_1(\beta - \beta^*) + e_1]' \\ &= E[X_1(\beta - \beta^*)(\beta - \beta^*)'X_1' + e_1e_1'] \\ &= E[X_1\text{Cov}(\beta^*)X_1' + e_1e_1'] \\ &= \sigma^2[X_1(X'X)^{-1}X_1' + e_1e_1'] \\ &= [X_1P_0X_1' + V_1] \end{aligned} \tag{7.7}$$

Hence the variance of *Y* around *Y** depends upon the uncertainty in estimating the parameters in $\beta$, denoted by $\text{Cov}(\beta^*) = P_0$, and also the intrinsic uncertainty in equation (7.1), given by $V_1$.

The general form of the Kalman filter consists of a measurement equation, a transition equation, prediction equations and updating equations. The measurement equation at time t is:

$$y_t = X_t\beta_t + e_t \qquad e_t \sim N(0, \Omega_t) \tag{7.8}$$

where *X* is a known matrix and $e_t$ is an *n* x 1 vector of error terms with zero mean and covariance $W_t$. The $\beta_t$ is unobservable, but it can be estimated using the transition equation, which is:

$$\beta_t = T_t\beta_{t+1} + R_t\eta_t \qquad \eta_t \sim N(0, Q_t) \tag{7.9}$$

where, $T_t$ and $R_t$ are assumed to be known (*m* x *m*) matrices and $\eta_t$ is an (*m* x 1) vector of error terms with zero means and covariance matrix $Q_t$. It is assumed that $\eta_t$ and $\varepsilon_t$ are uncorrelated for all t, that $\beta_{t-1}$ is independent of the error term in the transition equation and that $b_t$ is uncorrelated with the measurement error.

Starting with an initial estimate of $\beta_{t-1}$, namely $\beta^*_{t-1}$ (at time t-1), and an initial estimate of its covariance matrix, $P_{t-1}$ the unbiased predictor of $\beta_t$, based on information available at t–1, is $\beta^*_{t/t-1}$, which is given by the transition equation:

$$\beta_{t/t-1} = T_t\beta_{t-1} \tag{7.10}$$

The estimate of the covariance matrix takes the form given above, based on information available at t–1:

$$\mathrm{Cov}(\beta_{t/t-1}) = P_{t/t-1} = (T_t P_{t-1} T'_t + R_t Q_t R'_t) \tag{7.11}$$

Equations (7.10) and (7.11) are the prediction equations for the state vector $\beta_t$ and its covariance which may be calculated without any reference to the observations $y_t$. This information, at t–1, can be used to predict $\psi_t$ at time t and its covariance matrix of the one-step-ahead prediction errors $F_t$:

$$y_{t/t-1} = X_t \beta_{t/t-1}$$

The one-step-ahead prediction error, $v_t^*$, is $v_t^* = y_t - y_{t/t-1}$ with covariance matrix:

$$\begin{aligned} F_t &= \mathrm{Cov}(v_t^*) \\ &= [X_t P_{t/t-1} X'_t + \Omega_t] \end{aligned} \tag{7.12}$$

The updating equations for $P_t$ and $\beta_t$ are now:

$$P_T = P_{t/t-1} - P_t X'_t (F_t)^{-1} X_t P_{t/t-1} \tag{7.13}$$

and

$$\beta_t = \beta_{t/t-1} + P_{t/t-1} X'_t (F_t)^{-1} \{y_t - X_t \beta_{t/t-1}\} \tag{7.14}$$

Equations (7.13) and (7.14) are the updating equations of the Kalman filter which work recursively through time.

The smoothed estimates reported below are the best estimates of $\beta_t$, given all information, t = 1, 2, ...T in the sample. That is, smoothing is a process where we can look back from t = T, to obtain best estimates of T–1, T–2, etc.

On the last round of the Kalman filter we obtain $\beta_T$ and its covariance matrix $P_T$. The smoothing equations are recursive equations that work backwards from $\beta_T$, and $\Pi_T$. If $\beta^*_{t/T}$ and $P_{t/T}$ denote the smoothed estimator and its covariance then the smoothing equations are:

$$\beta^*_{t/T} = \beta^*_t + P^*_t(\beta^*_{t+1/T}\, T_{t+1}\, \beta^*_t) \tag{7.15}$$

$$P_{t/T} = P_T + P^*_t(P_{t+1/T} - P_{t+1/t}) P^{*'}_t \tag{7.16}$$

and where $P^*_t = (P_t T'_{t+1/t}) P'_{t+1/t}$

There is in fact little intuitive feel one can give to these smoothing recursions. In the case of time-varying parameters the smoothed estimates may be interpreted as the best estimates obtainable with all the data available, even though the parameters are still assumed to vary over time.

## 7.6 THE MODEL

Two versions of the time-varying parameter model are deployed here. The first approach is to look at the share of service sector employment as a proportion of employees in employment – i.e. $(SE/EE)_i$ for each region. In this case the appropriate specification is:

$$\left\{\left[\frac{(SE)}{(EE)}\right]_{GB} - \left[\frac{(SE)}{(EE)}\right]_i\right\} = a'(t) + \beta(t)\left\{\left[\frac{(SE)}{(EE)}\right]_{GB}\left[\frac{(SE)}{(EE)}\right]_{01}\right\} + u_t \qquad \text{(Model 1)}$$

(7.17)

Since we are not dealing with rates of change here, both the $\alpha'(t)$ and $\beta(t)$ parameters are of interest (Hall *et al.*, 1992). In this version of the model if $\beta(t) = >1$ then the share of service sector employment in region i moves towards that of the South-East; if $\beta(t) => 0$ then the share of service sector employment converges on the British average. In this case we do not want to impose any prior value on $\alpha'$, which may be regarded as our general alternative hypothesis. If the difference between service sector employment in Great Britain and region i is not led by the South-East region, then $\alpha'$ will be a non-stationary process reflecting the non-convergence of our series. Hence, the dual requirement for convergence is that both $\alpha'(t)$ tends to a constant and that $\beta(t)$ tends to zero.

An alternative hypothesis takes the form:

$$(E_{GB} - E_i) = \alpha(t) + \beta(t)[E_{GB} - E_{01}] + e_t \qquad \text{(Model 2)} \qquad (7.18)$$

where: E is the percentage change in service sector employment; i denotes the regions; and t denotes the quarters

The base region, 01, is taken to be London and the South-East. The conclusions derived from time-varying parameter techniques are not dependent on the base chosen although this does affect the arithmetic nature of the numbers produced.

Since in this case the data used represent percentage changes in employment, $\alpha(t)=0$ in all cases and can, therefore, be omitted. For confirmation, all the models were run with a stochastic constant, in addition to those presented here. In terms of interpretation, convergence takes place if the $\beta$ coefficients move towards a common constant, i.e. from the model if:

$\beta(t) => 0$ then $E_{GB} => E_i$

$\beta(t) => 1$ then $E_{GB} => E_{01}$

In other words, if $\beta(t) => 0$ then region i's service sector employment grows in line with the British average growth in service sector employment. Alternatively, if $\beta(t) =>1$ then it grows at the same rate as the South-East. Further, if $\beta(t) => (<0)$ then the convergence is towards a growth rate less than the national average. The process means, in a sense, that two alternative hypotheses are being explored. First, that regional service sector employment growth is being drawn along by growth in the lead region. Second, that convergence (if found) in employment growth is due to more general trends in the economy.

## 7.7 EMPIRICAL ESTIMATES

In many cases it does not matter which technique is deployed as they will all give similar indications of the level of convergence. But, equally, there is no automatic reason why this should be the case. As suggested above, one can attempt to look at possible convergence by examining trends in some key parameters. The data used for the convergence testing covers the ten British regions and comprises quarterly employment statistics for the period second quarter 1978 to fourth quarter 1991 – a total of 55 observations for each region.[10]

At the regional level the most basic of these would be to consider trends in such things as the mean, standard deviation and coefficient of variations across regions. As can be seen from Figure 7.2, which uses data on the share of service sector employment against total employment for regions between 1978 and 1991, there is little indication of convergence. The mean relative importance of service sector employment has risen but at almost an identical rate as the standard deviation across regions. It does not, though, tell us about the pattern of the trends within this overall picture. The rate of growth of service sector employment also showed no evidence of convergence using the standard deviation and coefficient of variation measures.

On the basis of the Dickey–Fuller and Augmented Dickey–Fuller tests for stationarity, reported in Table 7.6, the share of service sector employment in total employment in each of the ten regions of Great Britain is shown to be non-stationary, with the possible exceptions of East Anglia and the South-West regions. These two regions seem to show some convergence around a deterministic trend.

10 The data are taken from the *National On-line Manpower Information System* (NOMIS).

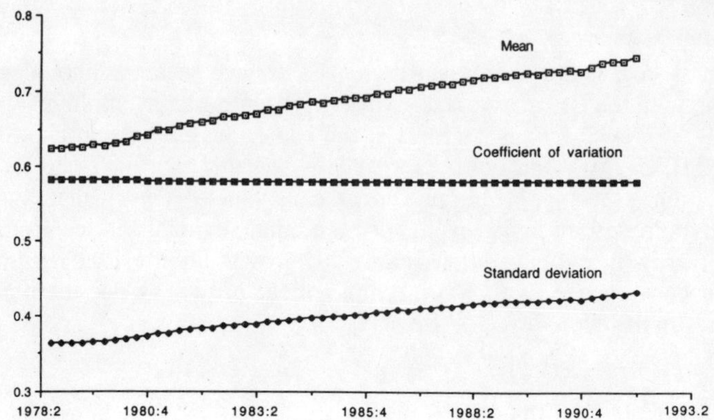


Figure 7.2 *Mean, standard deviations and coefficients of variation of the share of service sector employment for British regions, 1978–91*

Table 7.6. *Integrability tests for share of service employment*

| | Dickey-Fuller* | | Augmented Dickey-Fuller* | |
|---|---|---|---|---|
| | [A] | [B] | [A] | [B] |
| South East | –0.6538 | –1.8807 | –1.2533 | –0.6356 |
| East Anglia | 0.0291 | –4.4470 | –0.1172 | –4.2297 |
| South West | –0.3812 | –5.0417 | –0.2875 | –4.1192 |
| West Midlands | –1.7244 | –1.5072 | –2.3886 | –1.9288 |
| East Midlands | 0.2023 | –2.8535 | –0.0584 | –1.8926 |
| Yorks/Humber | –1.5799 | –1.0246 | –2.7147 | –0.7596 |
| North West | –2.4800 | –1.4994 | –2.9298 | –1.5042 |
| Northern | –2.5225 | –0.6079 | –2.8552 | –0.5578 |
| Wales | –1.4859 | –1.5053 | –2.0292 | –1.7339 |
| Scotland | –1.3426 | –1.5102 | –1.7135 | –1.5425 |
| Great Britain | –1.4279 | –1.2897 | –2.5071 | –0.9284 |
| Critical Values† | –2.9157 | –3.4935 | –2.9167 | –3.4952 |

*Notes*:

* The null hypothesis is that the variable is I(1), against the alternative that it is stationary, I(0). The statistics in the A columns do not include a time trend, but those in columns B do.

† Critical values at the 5 per cent level.

If the non-stationary regional series are cointegrated, however, they could still be convergent. In this case it would be expected that a maximum of nine cointegrating vectors would emerge between the ten regional series. Table 7.7 indicates that there are four cointegrating vectors, indicative of non-convergence of service sector employment as a proportion of total employment for most regions, since if all regions converged there would be just a single cointegrating vector.

Table 7.7. *Test statistics for the number of cointegrating vectors for the British regions*

| Number of cointegrating vectors | Test statistics | 5% critical values |
|---|---|---|
| 0 | none | 244.1 |
| 1 | 373.0 | 202.9 |
| 2 | 179.0 | 165.6 |
| 3 | 135.3 | 131.7 |
| 4 | 99.9 | 102.1 |
| 5 | 77.0 | 76.1 |
| 6 | 48.7 | 53.1 |
| 7 | 28.1 | 34.9 |
| 8 | 17.3 | 20.0 |
| 9 | 6.9 | 9.2 |

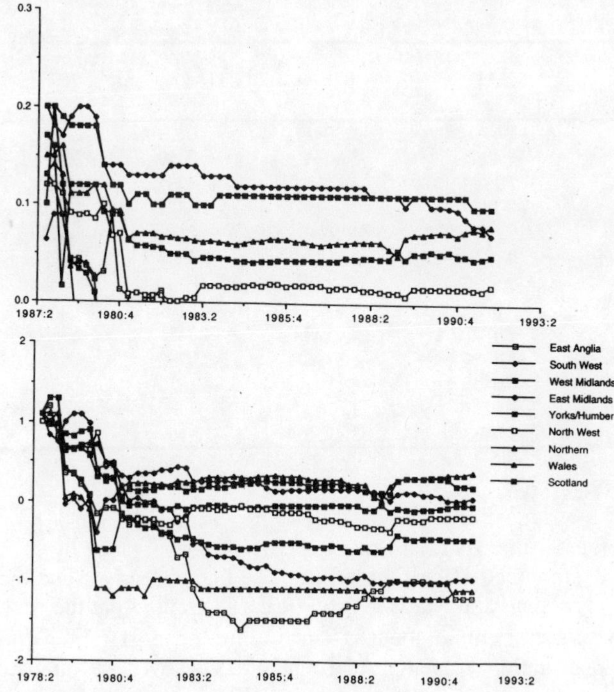


Figure 7.3 *Values (α and β) for service sector employment share*

Finally, the time-varying parameter method (Cuthbertson, 1988) was applied to Model 1 as in equation (7.17). This method produces results indicating little convergence in the proportion of service sector employment between the regions as a whole. Closer inspection of Figure 7.3 provides some evidence of convergence between the South-West and East Anglia, which is consistent with using the Dickey–Fuller tests, although little convergence between the northern regions and the southern regions of the country.

An alternative hypothesis, reflected in the specification of Model 2 – equation (7.18) – is that it is the rate of growth of service sector employment that may converge rather than the share of service sector employment in total employment. Table 7.8 shows that the Dickey–Fuller test statistics all reject the null hypothesis of non-stationarity, implying that there may be convergence in service sector employment growth rates. Figure 7.4 demonstrates, after smoothing, this convergence of the $\beta$ coefficients.

Table 7.8. *Dickey-Fuller tests for the rate of change in service sector employment levels*

| | Dickey-Fuller* | | Augmented Dickey-Fuller* | |
|---|---|---|---|---|
| | [A] | [B] | [A] | [B] |
| South East | –7.5460 | –7.5091 | –3.0309 | –2.9685 |
| East Anglia | –8.4863 | –8.6044 | –7.5269 | –7.9256 |
| South West | –7.7844 | –7.8050 | –8.4752 | –8.7594 |
| West Midlands | –7.1314 | –7.0649 | –3.6891 | –3.6836 |
| East Midlands | –10.6187 | –11.4870 | –4.2169 | –5.0349 |
| Yorks/Humber | –8.9001 | –8.9806 | –4.0836 | –4.1750 |
| North West | –8.6928 | –9.0219 | –3.9381 | –4.4646 |
| Northern | –7.8735 | –8.0129 | –4.3451 | –4.4646 |
| Wales | –7.8735 | –8.0129 | –4.3451 | –4.5653 |
| Scotland | –8.2929 | –8.5196 | –5.0287 | –5.3113 |
| Great Britain | –8.5439 | –8.8991 | –6.3856 | –6.9172 |
| Critical Values† | –2.9167 | –3.4935 | –2.9167 | –3.4952 |

*Notes:* As for Table 7.6

What emerges is that there are strong signs of convergence by the late 1980s and the smoothed data highlight this most clearly. The actual convergence is in general towards $\beta(t) \Rightarrow (<0)$ this implies that the regional growth in service sector employment is converging for most regions but at a rate below the national average.[11] There are, however, a number of

[11] For example, simple arithmetic tells us that, if the $\beta$ coefficient converges on –0.6 for region i, then with a national growth rate in service sector

exceptions to this general picture. The Northern region, for example, exhibits a gradual convergence on the national growth rate in service sector employment. Further, Yorkshire and Humberside, while exhibiting a degree of convergence consistent with most of the other regions also traces out a much more erratic path over time.

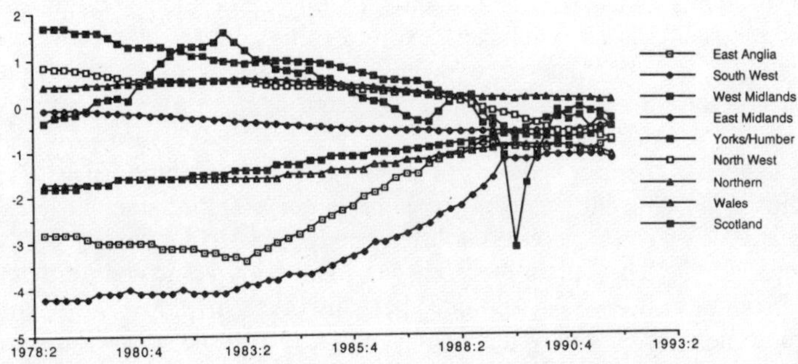


Figure 7.4 *Smoothed β values for service sector employment growth*

These results provide some support for the Central Place type of model of economic growth which emphasises the importance and dominance, because of the overlaying network of economic markets, of a key region – in the UK case London and the South-East. In this sense it offers rather more rigorous support for the more general European findings of people such as Howells (1988), who talk about, 'core regions (such as Madrid in Spain, the South-East (London) region of the UK, or Lazio (Rome) in Italy'. What unfortunately the data do not enable us to do is to decompose service sector employment into its various sub-components. This may be of longer-term importance as high-technology jobs play an increasingly important role in the national economy.

## 7.8 REGIONAL ECONOMIC CONVERGENCE IN GREAT BRITAIN AND GERMANY

The notion of β-convergence and the associated mean reversion techniques for testing, and the use of the initial value regressions, are not without their

employment of 0.4 per quarter and growth in the South-East of 0.6 per quarter, then region i will have a growth rate of 0.28 per quarter.

theoretical limitations.[12] Further, the empirical findings of Quah, using Markov chain methods, and Durhauf and Johnson, using regression tests and Quandt tests, have produced results contradictory to their studies found using mean reversion procedures. Durhauf and Johnson, for instance, concluding that there are convergence clubs.

Hence, while mean reversion techniques offer an indication of the degree to which less-wealthy regions are catching up with faster growing ones, it provides little by way of an account of how individual regions are performing. Techniques that can explore this latter question are, unfortunately, data intensive, expecially in terms of time series requirements, and suitable data for the EU area as a whole are currently lacking.

This analysis, therefore, does not attempt to look at the EU in its entirety but rather concentrates on two of the larger Member states, the UK and Germany.[13] These two countries offer good, long-term quarterly data at the regional level. They also represent nations with somewhat different regional problems. Both have certainly been involved in industrial renewal and restructuring but Germany has been integrated into the wider European market longer than Britain and its transition has, in consequence, been smoothed somewhat. It has, however, been limited in its regional policy by particular factors, such as the situation of West Berlin and its separation of several regions from their natural markets to the east.

The British regional problem has centred around the need to switch from a world market approach to trade to one focused more directly on Europe. This has placed particular strains on regions in the north and west of the country which are peripheral to the main European markets.

Equally important, Great Britain and Germany represent countries with differing approaches to regional policy in terms of the philosophies adopted and the institutions responsible for carrying the policies through.

Regional policy in Germany operates within a federal structure with considerable power devolved to the Länder which also operate, in many instances, as the executive arm for federal-directed regional policy. Great Britain, with the exception of separate Scottish and Welsh Offices, does not

12 De Long (1988), Durlauf and Johnson (1992) and Quah (1993) offer comment on some of the procedures employed. In particular, they have pointed out that aggregate convergence does not represent conclusive evidence favouring global convergence as predicted by neo-classical theory with constant returns and exogenous technical progress. A negative coefficient of the variable defining the initial condition is compatible with local convergence in a context of multiple equilibria and endogenous growth.

13 Strictly, for reasons of consistency, it is only the set of regions which made up the former Federal Republic of Germany plus West Berlin which are considered. Equally, Northern Ireland is, because of its particular circumstances, excluded from the UK estimations, leaving the regions of Great Britain.

have anything resembling a federal structure but rather functions through central government and very localised lower-tier governments.

The differences, though, go deeper than this. Germany has a tradition of pursuing a very active regional policy,[14] not least in the recent past because the division of the country in the post-1945 period isolated many areas from their natural markets. While this was tempered in the cost-conscious years of the late 1980s it has still remained relatively strong. Molle (1990) offers a useful overview of the European regional situation and sets the differing policy stances in context.

In contrast, the approach in Great Britain, certainly for most of the period reviewed, has been one involving less concern with explicitly equalising spatial disparities and more with general industrial efficiency, including the attraction of significant foreign investments, and, in specific areas, urban regeneration. The former can be explained both in terms of the poorer national economic record of Britain generall, and the perceived need to emphasise national income growth and in terms of the general political tenor of the governments for much of this time.

The evolution of the EU's regional policy should theoretically help to bring together these divergent national approaches. In terms of this study, and despite the establishment of the ERDF in 1975 and other initiatives, the importance of active EU policies over the period analysed is extremely limited. The main structural funds (ERDF, European Social Fund and the Guidance Section of the European Agricultural Guidance and Guarantee Fund) were revamped in 1989, but major injections of money only emerged in 1993 when increases in structural funds to ECU 27.4 billion by 1999 were agreed to. Equally, the recent freeing up in intra-Union trade, which may be seen as assisting regions exploit more completely their comparative advantages, only began to take effect from 1993.

## 7.9 UNEMPLOYMENT CONVERGENCE RESULTS

To provide more detail of the approach adopted here, the method of time-varying parameters is presented in an intuitive manner and linked to the traditional ordinary least squares (OLS) regression method.

The specific model of convergence to be estimated using time-varying parameters is:

$$(u_C - u_i)_t = \alpha(t) + \beta(t)[u_C - u_{01}]_t + \varepsilon_t \tag{7.19}$$

where: $u$ is the regional unemployment measured as a percentage; i denotes the regions; t denotes the quarters; C denotes the country of study; and 01 is

14 See Owen Smith (1994) for details of German regional policy.

the base region (Table 7.9) and is taken to be the region with the lowest unemployment.[15]

The data used in this study covers 78 quarters from the first quarter of 1974 to the second quarter of 1993 for NUTS level 1 regions in Britain and the pre-unified Federal Republic of Germany. This is the most aggregated level of regional classification in the EU. It provides consistent data over a reasonable period but suffers from the extent of averaging which is inevitable with broad geographical classifications. Further, the boundaries of these regions are defined in political terms and, therefore, often bear little resemblance to either the homogenous or the nodal regions which form the basis of most regional economic theory. The regions are listed in Table 7.9 along with the coding used in the subsequent estimations. The data consist of time series observations on unemployment, which in the British case are seasonally adjusted but which in the German case are seasonally unadjusted.

Table 7.9. *Definitions of regions*

| | | | |
|---|---|---|---|
| North | GB01 | Schlewig-Holstein-Hamburg | G01 |
| Yorkshire and Humberside | GB02 | Niders-Bremen | G02 |
| East Midlands | GB03 | Nordhien-Westphalia | G03 |
| East Anglia | GB04 | Hessen | G04 |
| South East* | GB05 | Rhine-Palatinate-Saarland | G05 |
| South West | GB06 | Baden-Wurtemberg* | G06 |
| West Midlands | GB07 | Nordbayern | G07 |
| North West | GB08 | Sudbayern | G08 |
| Wales | GB09 | Berlin (West) | G09 |
| Scotland | GB10 | | |

* Base region for calculations

The application of time-varying parameter techniques to the model outlined in equation (7.19) provides the estimates of both $\alpha(t)$ and $\beta(t)$ for Great Britain and Germany set out in Figures 7.5 and 7.6. With regard to the specific alternative, it is apparent that the $\beta$s do not tend to unity either for Great Britain or Germany. Indeed, for many regions the $\beta s$ change very little over time and are often close to zero. There is, therefore, little support for the hypothesis of regional unemployment convergence whereby regional unemployment rates converge to those of the low-unemployment base regions.

15 The conclusions derived from time-varying parameter techniques are not dependent on the base chosen although this does affect the arithmetic nature of the numbers produced. For a discussion of the implications of this specification see section 7.6.

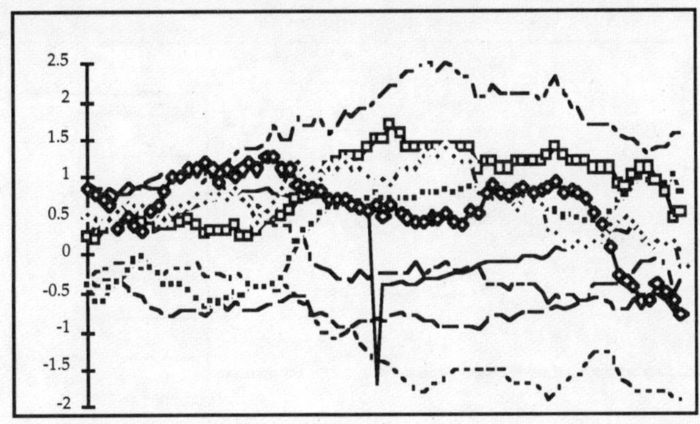


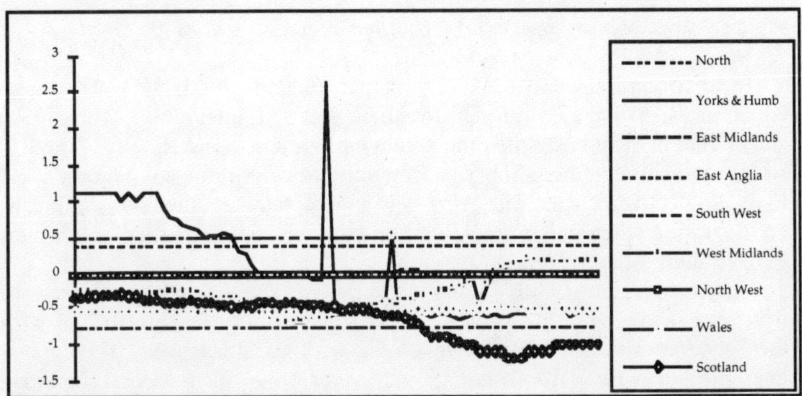


Figure 7.5 $\alpha$ *(top segment) and* $\beta$ *(bottom segment) values for Great Britain*

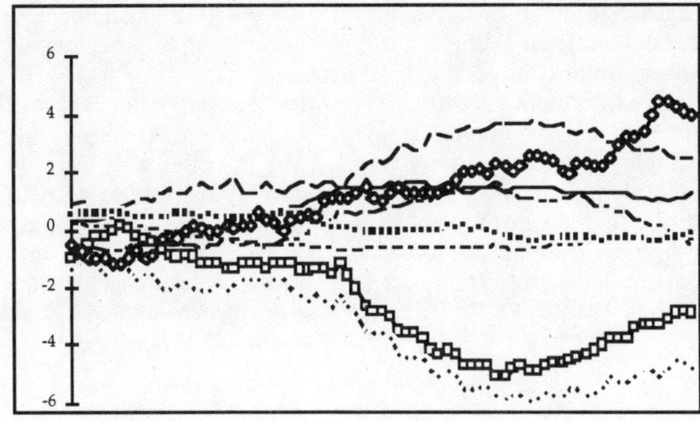

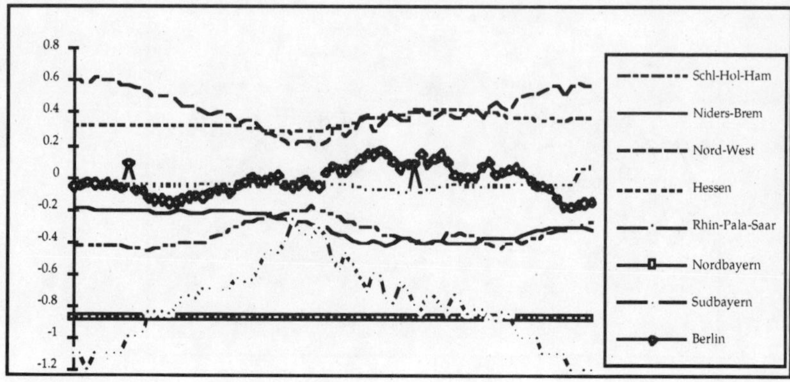


Figure 7.6 $\alpha$ *(top segment) and* $\beta$ *(bottom segment) values for Germany*

Prior to applying the time-varying parameter method, the variables in equation (7.19) were each tested for their order of integration. Table 7.10 shows that in most cases the relative unemployment variables were found to be I(1) indicating non-stationarity although not ruling out cointegration and long-run convergence. The time-varying parameter method dominates cointegration when one is assessing convergence and, in particular, changes in the pattern of convergence over time.

The top panels of both Figures 7.5 and 7.6 show that the $\alpha$s do vary over time, showing in most cases a divergence from zero. This, in line with the general alternative, is consistent with a divergence of regional unemployment rates from the national average rate, for reasons other than movement in the base rate of unemployment, in both Great Britain and Germany.

Moreover, the size of the $\alpha$ coefficients in these figures suggest that this divergence has been much larger in Germany than in Great Britain. This greater divergence seems to be due largely to the differing unemployment performance between West Berlin and the Nordrhein-Westphalia regions on the one hand and Nordbayern and Sudbayern regions on the other.

In the shorter term, until the early 1980s when regional policy was still highly active, there is, however, some indication from Germany that regional unemployment rates were converging. The $\alpha$ values were virtually constant and close to zero while the $\beta$s were arguably converging towards unity with the exception of Nordrhein-Westphalia. This subsequently changed to divergence during the second half of the series with $\alpha$ values showing a marked divergence from zero and several $\beta$ values changing the direction of trend. The picture for Britain is less pronounced although there are indications that the *a* coefficients began exploding only in the early years of the 1980s.[16]

Table 7.10. *Orders of integration of the British and German regions*

| Great Britain | $H_0$:I(1) | Germany | $H_0$:I(1) |
|---|---|---|---|
| $u_{01} - u_{GB}$ | -1.67(3) | $u_{01} - u_{G}$ | -1.46(8) |
| $u_{02} - u_{GB}$ | -2.99*(3) | $u_{02} - u_{G}$ | -1.82(8) |
| $u_{03} - u_{GB}$ | -4.11*(3) | $u_{03} - u_{G}$ | -2.06(8) |
| $u_{04} - u_{GB}$ | -2.27(0) | $u_{04} - u_{G}$ | -1.84(8) |
| $u_{05} - u_{GB}$ | -1.77(5) | $u_{05} - u_{G}$ | -1.12(8) |
| $u_{06} - u_{GB}$ | -1.13(2) | $u_{06} - u_{G}$ | -1.70(8) |
| $u_{07} - u_{GB}$ | -2.09(2) | $u_{07} - u_{G}$ | -1.64(8) |
| $u_{08} - u_{GB}$ | -0.25(0) | $u_{08} - u_{G}$ | -1.55(8) |
| $u_{09} - u_{GB}$ | -0.63(2) | $u_{09} - u_{G}$ | -0.71(4) |
| $u_{10} - u_{GB}$ | -1.69(3) | | |
| $u_{01} - u_{05}$ | -2.26(5) | $u_{01} - u_{06}$ | -1.82(8) |
| $u_{02} - u_{05}$ | -2.04(2) | $u_{02} - u_{06}$ | -1.99(8) |
| $u_{03} - u_{05}$ | -0.49(2) | $u_{03} - u_{06}$ | -1.56(4) |
| $u_{04} - u_{05}$ | 0.61(2) | $u_{04} - u_{06}$ | -1.20(4) |
| $u_{06} - u_{05}$ | 0.44(0) | $u_{05} - u_{06}$ | -1.44(8) |
| $u_{07} - u_{05}$ | -1.69(3) | $u_{07} - u_{06}$ | -0.65(8) |
| $u_{08} - u_{05}$ | -1.72(5) | $u_{08} - u_{06}$ | 0.22(8) |
| $u_{09} - u_{05}$ | -1.11(7) | $u_{09} - u_{06}$ | -1.65(8) |
| $u_{10} - u_{05}$ | -2.19(4) | | |

*Notes*: Critical value -2.57 at 10% significance level denoted by *.
Numbers in parenthesis indicate lags included to give white noise residuals for augmented Dickey-Fuller test (Dickey and Fuller, 1979).

Regional economic policy has come to the fore of political debate as moves towards a more unified Europe take place. One of the difficulties, however, is that relatively little rigorous analysis has been completed looking at the relative economic performance of regions over time and, in particular, whether that performance is converging or not. This study has sought to explore the extent of any convergence within both Great Britain and Germany at the mesoeconomic level, with specific reference to rates of unemployment.

The period studied is an extensive one but the time-varying parameter procedures employed reveal no consistent pattern of convergence. Where there is some indication of convergence it is with respect to the period of

16 A number of studies in the early 1970s suggested that UK regional policy, certainly up until that time, had been helpful in improving the employment situation in the least prosperous parts of Britain, for example Moore and Rhodes (1973).

active German regional policy, until the early 1980s with a somewhat weaker pattern also emerging with respect to Britain. Whether this was in fact due to the strength and nature of regional policy during this period is open to reflection. There has, however, since the early 1980s been a clear and continuous divergence between regional unemployment rates in both Britain and Germany.

The causes of this divergence are not explicitly considered here although structural changes in regional labour markets and differing macroeconomic circumstances are competing explanations together with the decline in intensity of regional policy.

## 7.10 CONCLUSIONS

The scale of service sector employment inevitably means that it is economically important to most regions in Europe. The specific characteristics of many of the sub-sectors, especially its relatively footloose nature, also means that it is in many ways more amenable to policy incentives aimed at reducing disparities in such things as regional unemployment rates. At the theoretical level, however, there is comparatively little understanding as to the actual forces leading to locations of service sector activities. Indeed, at a more basic level, measures of convergence have, in the past tended to be rather superficial and offered the potential for producing conflicting results. In this chapter we have tried to look at the degree to which there has been convergence in employment in service sector activities across regions, using a number of alternative procedures and regional time series data. The different methodologies do produce broadly consistent results for the UK.

The share of service sector employment in total employment does not exhibit convergence on any of the three measures employed. This suggests that the rising number of service sector employees over our sample period has been partly offset in some regions by an increase in total numbers employed. In terms of the rate of growth of service sector employment, the time-varying parameter technique shows that this has exhibited some convergence over the sample period. This is at a rate below the national average due to the dominance of the faster, growing London and South-East region in the British average. Clearly, it would be helpful to examine the situation at a sub-regional, or even urban, level and to explore convergence for individual service industries, but the statistical procedures necessary require considerable data inputs to see if convergence is or is not occurring. Unfortunately, quarterly data at this level of spatial aggregation not available for a sufficiently long period.

In terms of comparing the UK and Germany at the mesoeconomic level and making use of time-varying parameter techniques, the period of the study (1974 to 1993) shows no consistent pattern of convergence. Where there is some sign of convergence this corresponds to a period of active German regional policy with somewhat weaker patterns emerging for the UK. Since the early part of the 1980s there has been a clear and continuous divergence between the regional employment rates of the two countries. This may be due to structural changes in the regional labour market and to differing macroeconomic circumstances as much as being related to declines in the intensity of regional policy.

# 8. Infrastructure and Regional Economic Development

## 8.1 INTRODUCTION

The link between infrastructure provision and economic growth is far from fully understood.[1] Nevertheless, efforts to improve and expand the infrastructure of regions, and to extend the physical infrastructure linking regions, have been important components of regional policies in Europe. The arguments supporting this are diverse but in recent years have been stimulated by empirical work suggesting a positive link between the quantity of infrastructure investment and rates of productivity change. These claims have subsequently been examined in a series of studies and, to date, the results are inconclusive.

Debates over the role of infrastructure in economic development certainly date back to Adam Smith and experts on economic history could probably find a longer pedigree. The intensity of the debates has waxed and waned over the years but there are few signs of a consensus emerging. The recent upsurge of academic analyses of this topic, which as with many of these things coincided with adjustments in broader economic policy strategies, is generally traced back to work on the US economy by Aschauer (1989, 1990). Since then the literature and debates surrounding Aschauer's findings that, at the macroeconomic level, there exists evidence of a positive link between infrastructure investment and aggregate productivity have mushroomed.

Interest in the role of infrastructure has also been stimulated by findings at the more microlevel, especially by geographers, local planners and management scientists. This work has been less technical in its orientation and has sought through questionnaires and interviews to elicit from

1 Rietveld and Bruinsma (1998) provide an up-to-date assessment as well as new empirical findings. The emphasis of this chapter is on the link between infrastructure provision and economic change at the regional level. There is a large and growing effort to understand how infrastructure influences land-use at the intra-urban level but this is not part of our concern.

businessmen the reasons influencing their location choices.[2] Table 8.1, which provides results involving large European firms, offers a set of fairly typical findings from this non-modelling approach. As can be seen, many of the key location factors (notably transport and communications) are closely tied to the availability of high quality infrastructure.[3]

One reason that EU policy makers have recently become so interested in the role of infrastructure in regional development, irrespective of the certainty of its economic impact, is that there are manifest differences in the scale and quality of the infrastructure provided both nationally amongst Members States and between regions within them.[4] Such inequalities can pose political as well as economic problems.

Measuring the level of long-lived, specific and diverse assets such as infrastructure is far from easy. Biehl (1996) has developed one index that offers practical guidance and this provides some insights for 1985–6 (Table 8.2). As we see below, there are problems in defining what constitutes

2 Such studies generally suffer from respondents trying to provide ex post justifications for their actions or giving answers designed to sway future public policy.

3 Ignoring multiplier and similar effects, whether improved infrastructure will act as a net attraction for firms is traditionally seen as dependent upon a range of considerations of which infrastructure is but one. Consider the case of two regions, A and B with their base costs of production of a homogeneous product being $\$C_A$ and $\$C_B$ respectively. Their central points are M miles apart and the only infrastructure involved is transport which at the outset costs \$t per ton mile. The situation depicted below illustrates this

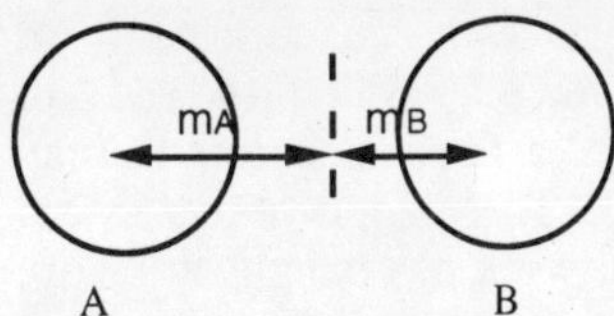


Initially the market is divided with producers in A serving an area out to $m_A$ and producers in B serving to $m_B$. The market share for A being determined as: $m_A = 0.5\{M+(C_B - C_{BA})/t$.

If transport infrastructure is improved between the two regions reducing transport costs then this will affect the relative economic positions of A and B. Essentially low-cost producers gain and high-cost producers lose. If, at the extreme, $(C_B - C_{BA}) > Mt$ then B will be forced from the market entirely. More recently Krugman's (1991) extension of the cumulative causation approach to economic growth with its inclusion of transport considerations and focus on urban concentrations would also indicate that improved infrastructure could be harmful to less-developed areas. What these approaches do not consider is the trade creation effects of improved infrastructure and this is largely what the more macro studies have focused on.

4 For the period 1994–9, some ECU 45 billion (41 per cent) of total EU spending in Objective 1 regions went on infrastructure.

infrastructure and many would neither agree with the definitions adopted here nor the measurement criteria, but the table does offer a guide to the concerns of the Commission.[5]

Table 8.1. *Percentage of firms that consider the location factors concerned as absolutely essential for locating their business*

| Factor | Per cent |
|---|---|
| Easy access to markets, clients or customers | 63 |
| Transport links with other cities and international centres | 52 |
| Quality of telecommunications | 46 |
| Cost and availability of staff | 43 |
| Business climate and availability of financial incentives | 36 |
| Value for money of office space | 26 |
| Availability of office space | 22 |
| Ease of travelling around within the city | 22 |
| Languages spoken | 18 |
| High quality of the environment | 11 |
| Quality of life for employees | 10 |

*Source*: Healy and Baker (1996)

We are not strictly concerned with the theoretical dimensions of the debate but rather with a somewhat different aspect of the revived interest in the role of infrastructure in the economic development process. A particular feature of recent work has been the heavy reliance on quantification and econometrics. Availability of data coupled with the widespread use of computers and standardised software have produced a flood of papers testing, refining and modifying the Aschauer framework. These applications extend across a large number of countries.[6] This body of work has sought to clarify

5 In addition to simple issues of a political feeling that there is a need to assist regions with poor infrastructure develop their assets, the *Sixth Periodic Report on the Social and Economic Situation and Development of the Regions of the European Union* highlights the two reasons that the EU economists have pressed for more focus to be put on gaining more knowledge about the role infrastructure (1) public sector budgetary constraints are forcing a larger private sector involvement in infrastructure provision and appraisal requires improved information; and (2) infrastructure has positive externalities in that once provided it is available at zero cost and hence improves the productivity of private business, and especially small firms, and this effect needs quantification (Commission of the European Communities, 1999).

6 Indeed, the material has become extensive enough for at least two major literature reviews to have appeared in recent years (Munnell, 1990; Gramlich,

and categorise the various empirical studies which have been completed and to offer some guidance as to why their results sometimes differ. In his paper, Gramlich (1994), for instance, discusses a range of factors including the definition of variables used, the problems of missing variables, issues of causality and simultaneous equation bias.

Table 8.2. *Relative infrastructure levels in EU countries, 1985 (EU=100)*

| Country | Transport | Telecoms | Energy | Education | Aggregate |
|---|---|---|---|---|---|
| Germany | 143 | 108 | 88 | 135 | 116 |
| France | 110 | 128 | 179 | 91 | 123 |
| Italy | 81 | 74 | 84 | 107 | 85 |
| Netherlands | 259 | 128 | 180 | 74 | 145 |
| Belgium | 302 | 128 | 263 | 101 | 179 |
| Luxembourg | 266 | 189 | 335 | 93 | 199 |
| UK | 135 | 108 | 112 | 74 | 195 |
| Denmark | 194 | 149 | 62 | 117 | 124 |
| Ireland | 104 | 63 | 42 | 73 | 67 |
| Spain | 78 | 70 | 49 | 114 | 74 |
| Greece | 63 | 93 | 33 | 52 | 56 |
| Portugal | 51 | 34 | 37 | 35 | 38 |

It is difficult to fault the quality of these various reviews and the types of conclusions which they arrive at. They are, however, traditional literary reviews and this, in itself, has its limitations. The surveys of this body of work on infrastructure, which has involved quite sophisticated econometric analysis, have tended to report findings in tabular fashion with verbal comment and discussion of the strengths and weaknesses of each study included. This approach is obviously valuable and important, and this should certainly not be forgotten, but with respect to empirical work such qualitative assessments inevitably do not include important quantitative consideration. A complementary approach is to supplement the traditional literary methodology with that of the statistician. This is in essence what meta-analysis does; it provides a quantitative summary or assessment of research domains.

Given the scale of the effort which has gone into producing work on the role of infrastructure at the macro- and mesoeconomic levels and the nature of the resultant output, there seems scope for applying statistical procedures

1994) and for several major conferences to focus on the subject (e.g. Organisation for Economic Co-operation and Development, 1994, and Mintz and Preston, 1993).

in an attempt to provide more quantification of the importance of some of the differentiating features highlighted by Gramlich, Munnell and others. This chapter, therefore, proceeds by initially offering a very brief account of the background to the debate. It then moves to describe the philosophy of meta-analysis and to provide guidance as to its potential role in complementing traditional review procedures, before developing a framework for conducting a meta-analysis of a collection of econometric studies in the field of infrastructure investment. Finally, some results are presented and discussed.

## 8.2 LINKING ENDOGENOUS GROWTH AND INFRA-STRUCTURE ENDOWMENTS

The recent work of Romer, Lucas and others on endogenous economic growth, as was seen in Chapter 4, draws upon longer-established concepts of circular-and-cumulative causation associated initially with the ideas of Myrdal and which were implicitly embodied in meso-level work of Kaldor (1970) in the UK.[7] The contemporary academic literature in the field focuses on the importance of economies of scale, agglomeration and knowledge spillover effects and indicates that economic growth tends to be faster in areas that have a relatively large stock of capital, a highly educated population and an economic environment favourable to the accumulation of knowledge.

At around the same time as these recent studies focusing on endogenous growth emerged, another strand of intellectual curiosity was also reawakened concerning the role of social overhead capital, and in particular publicly supplied infrastructure, in the economic growth process. This strand of the literature has a long pedigree, but was particularly rich in the context of development economics in the 1950s and 1960s with the publication of seminal works by economists such as Hirschman (1958) on unbalanced growth theories. The appearance of a provocative empirical study by Aschauer (1989) rekindled old fires and led to a major reassessment of the inter-relationship between infrastructure investment and economic efficiency.

The recent work on endogenous growth and that on the importance of infrastructure in the growth process may be seen as linked in several ways. The preliminary literature appeared at a time when most of the world's economies were in recession and governments were seeking ways to stimulate economic growth. This was also occurring at a time when efforts were being made to free up trade and when a number of major geographical groupings of countries were developing closer economic ties (for example, the creation of the North America Free Trade Area (NAFTA) and the Single

7 See the survey papers by Nijkamp and Poot (1998) and Durlauf and Quah (1998).

European Market initiative). Intellectually, Keynesian ideas had been replaced by neo-classical economic policies with their much greater emphasis on efficiency, supply-side constraints and sectoral importance. Endogenous growth theory breaks with this approach and puts a focus on cumulative processes. Equally, an emphasis on the role of infrastructure reflects the importance of stimuli in the development process.

This chapter sets out to examine the empirical and theoretical work, reflecting on some of the underpinnings of the endogenous growth debate and the usefulness of public capital in stimulating economic development. Initially, it puts a little more flesh on why there are linkages between these two often separately viewed bodies of research. To pre-empt the conclusions, the jury is still out on the validity of both schools of thought and the verdict is not looking promising for either.

To explore in a little more detail where the debates on endogenous growth and infrastructure availability interact it is useful to review again briefly exactly what the recent empirical evidence shows regarding the extent to which regional economies are actually converging or, as in accord with the endogenous growth theory, diverging.

Barro and Sala-i-Martin's studies of Japanese, US and European regions are, as we have seen, perhaps the most cited contemporary studies in the economic convergence field. They conclude that there is conditional convergence whereby regions are converging towards their national steady-state at an annual rate of about 2 per cent. Conditional convergence is relevant when economies are not structurally similar and GDP per capita does not converge to the same levels but differences between countries become stationary so that growth rates are the same in the long run. Aggregate convergence, in contrast, is consistent with a neo-classical framework whereby each region, while having differing initial positions, converge to a common per capita level of income determined by exogenous technical progress.

This work is not, however, without its problems. While Barro and Sala–i-Martin's work on European regions, for example, offers interesting insights into economic convergence it is forced to rely for its empirical analysis on several disparate data sets and to use a number of alternative proxies for variables such as industrial composition in different time frames as explanatory variables.

Adopting a more consistent and more extensive set of data, coupled with some policy shock variables, Button and Pentecost (1995b) find that convergence of real regional incomes economies in the European Union has not been a steady, stable process, but rather has been both a cyclical phenomenon, related to the business cycle, and a continual phenomenon despite the expansion of Union' membership. There have been periods when convergence has been strong, as at the end of the 1970s, but also periods when the real incomes of the Union's regions have moved further apart as, for example, during the early 1980s. Equally, work on regional unemployment rates in the regions of Germany and Great Britain (Button and Pentecost, 1995a) deploying time-varying parameter techniques reveals little, if any, convergence in recent times.

In simply eye-balling a list of the results from a number of the key studies that have explored economic convergence there is confirmation that there is, as of yet, no consensus as to the strength of any automatic convergence process.

While an overview of results is hardly conclusive, not least because the underlying analyses are of varying quality, the range of results does pose a practical problem for policy makers. If there is no or, at the very least, very little regional convergence in economic performance then this can result in political difficulties emerging for efforts such as those of the EU and NAFTA to bring about freer trade and greater economic integration. Acceptance of such policies usually involves resolving distribution as well as efficiency questions. The inconclusive nature of the results also implies that proactive policies may be necessary if the aim is to overcome continuing economic differences between regions. This is in line with much of the reasoning behind the endogenous growth theorising.[8] The importance of the contributions of Aschauer and others in this context is in raising the issue of the potential role that infrastructure investment can play in this regard.

One way of looking at the issue is to use a simplified version of a diagram used in Biehl (1991) – Figure 8.1. This diagram takes it as given that both the productivity of a region (P) and its labour costs (W) rise with regions' infrastructure endowments although, the latter at a slower pace.[9] In the diagram, regions to the right of point A have labour cost/productivity ratios of less than 1 while the opposite holds for regions to the left of A. As these ratios are indicative of each region's competitive position, this implies lower income and fewer jobs to regions to the left of A. The opposite is true for regions to the right of A. Factor mobility theory tells us that out-migration will take place from regions to the left of A alongside net capital exports. This means that actual GDP and actual employment may not be proportional to a region's infrastructure endowment. Regions to the right of A will tend to enjoy an actual GDP per capita in excess of their potential GDP with the reverse true of regions to the left of the cross-over point.

Aschauer's (1989, 1990, 1994) empirical analysis effectively provided arguments supporting the idea that enhanced infrastructure provision will permit those regions to the left of A to more completely realise their full economic potential by helping them retain their more mobile factors of

8 Romer (1986), for instance, puts an emphasis on improving the capacity of a region to develop its endogenous growth potential by investing in engineering and similar training.

9 Biehl spells out a number of reasons why this is a reasonable assumption for brevity they are not repeated here.

production. This analysis itself raises a number of key questions concerning not only definitions of infrastructure and measurement questions but also important intellectual concerns over causality – and especially the extent to which infrastructure provision is itself part of an endogenous growth process.

Much of the debate over public expenditure's productivity relates to the role of infrastructure. What exactly, however, is meant by infrastructure? The provision of adequate infrastructure is often seen as a necessary prerequisite for economic advancement but, while economists are generally rather particular in the ways in which specific goods are categorised, the definition of infrastructure – sometimes equally opaquely referred to as 'social overhead capital' – tends to be vague and imprecise. Lakshmanan (1989) talks of the term as 'often employed in a loose impressionistic manner'.

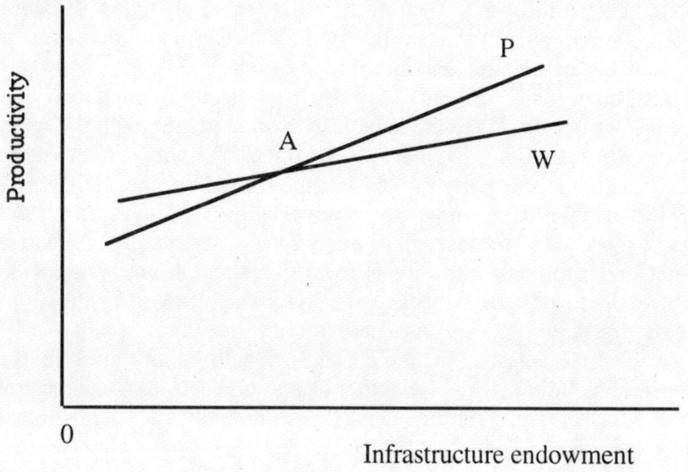


Figure 8.1 *Productivity and labour cost ties to infrastructure endowments*

Where there have been efforts at delineation, the tendency is frequently to look at particular physical features and to offer lists of such characteristics: Nurske (1953), for instance, lists features such as: 'provide services basic to any production capacity'; 'cannot be imported from abroad' and 'large and costly installations'. Hirschman (1958) lists sectors, *viz.*, 'In its widest sense, it includes all public services from law and order through education and public health to transportation, communications, power and water supply as well as such agricultural overhead capital as irrigation and drainage systems. The hard core of the concept can probably be restricted to transportation and power.'

More recently, these characteristics have tended to be outlined in rather more technical terms and, in particular, the possible relevance of notions such as information flows (Youngson, 1967) and, as a particular case of externalities, of public goods, have been examined.[10]

While definitions are very important, here we have tended to shy away from getting too deeply involved in the issue and to adopt the easy way out by following the spirit of Jacob Viner's wisecrack that 'Economics is what economists do' and simply treat infrastructure as 'what most people consider it to be'. From a strict definition perspective this may be seen as a form of passing the buck but in practical terms and given the nature of the chapter, it seems unlikely that it will lead to any substantive degree of confusion.

There has recently been something of an up surge of interest by European policy makers in the role which transport, communications and other infrastructure plays in stimulating economic development. From an intellectual perspective this can, looking back over the literature of the past century or so, be seen to fit in with a cyclical pattern of changing academic interests. More pragmatically, a number of key factors can, perhaps, be highlighted as being of specific relevance for the 1990s.

There have been major technical advances in telecommunications that require new infrastructure if they are to be fully exploited, although the exact nature of this infrastructure is not always agreed upon. With more conventional forms of transport, rapidly rising demand in the 1970s and, especially, the 1980s at a time of relatively limited investment and replacement expenditure means that many existing facilities require refurbishment and additional capacity is needed under current policies to match forecast demand. Bottlenecks already exist and pressures for improvements for key links in the network are already a reality. The expansion of the European Union, its closer ties with other states in the wider European Economic Space and the changes in eastern and central Europe have added pressure for reviewing both national and pan-national approaches to infrastructure provision.

As part of this increased interest, by both policy makers and academics, the whole questioning of the mechanisms of supply and control have also come under review. In many European countries the role of the state in providing infrastructure has been the subject of detailed debate. There has, for instance, been increased interest in embracing private sector undertakings in the provision of new infrastructure such as roads and railways and there has been privatisation of existing infrastructure.

The exact importance of infrastructure as an element in the economic development process has long been disputed.[11] Much seems to depend upon

10 For example, Andersson (1993) and Andersson and Kobayashi (1989) take the public good line

11 There is also a literature at a more micro level, and in particular work has been undertaken at the regional or local project level on the impact of individual

the degree to which supply considerations are thought important. The Keynesian approach, epitomised by the Harrod–Domar framework, indicates that causality runs from economic exploitation to income and infrastructure generation. In contrast, neo-classical economics is essentially supply-driven and transport and other infrastructure are generally seen as important elements in the production function. Much of the recent work follows the neo-classical mode in looking at the links between infrastructure provision and economic development through some form of aggregate production function analysis. It has sought to see how well it, and its individual elements, explain economic performance.[12]

The usual format is to take a production function of the standard form

$$Y = f(L,K,J) \tag{8.1}$$

with Y indicating output; L labour; K the stock of private capital and J the stock of public capital.[13] The relevant parameters are then estimated – often employing a Cobb-Douglas specification (Rietveld and Bruinsma, 1998) – using either time series data for a particular area – such as Aschauer's (1989) work in the USA – or by cross-sectional analysis across regions – such as Biehl's (1986; 1991) work on the European Union.[14]

These models were used to estimate the output elasticities of public infrastructure investments but the results generated have not been highly robust, as can be seen in the summary of some of the main studies set out in Table 8.3.

pieces of infrastructure. This is an extremely important topic but largely outside of the scope of this chapter. What should be said is that the empirical evidence to date on the link between infrastructure investment and industrial location can at best be described as ambiguous.

12 A separate, more theoretical approach is to use duality theory applied to a restricted profit function to determine the net benefits which private manufacturing firms obtain from public services. Seitz (1993), for instance, uses this approach to look at the benefits of the German public road network. Munnell (1992) offers some comment on the limitations of this methodology.

13 There are variations on this and Prud'homme (1993), for instance, favours $Y = f(L,K,J,F)$ where F stands for the functionaries (those employed in the public sector).

14 In some cases – e.g. Dalenberg (1987); Keeler and Ying (1988); Berdt and Hansson (1991), and Lynde and Richmond (1992a) - a cost function has been employed rather than the production function. The aim is to see if costs of production fall with increased public capital. This approach takes the general form: $C = f(IP, Q, PK)$; where, C is the cost of production; IP is the vector of input prices; Q is the output level and PK is public capital. The main limitation of the model is that input prices are taken as exogenous to the system.

Many of the early studies, especially from the US, at the national and state levels, provided statistically significant and apparently robust evidence that well-designed and -operated infrastructure can expand the economic productivity of an area. Aschauer, for example, looking at data covering the period 1949 to 1985, concluded that a 1 per cent increase in the public capital stock could raise total factor productivity by 0.39 per cent while Munnell (1990) tabulates output elasticities of public capital derived from US studies in the 0.03 to 0.39 range although with a preponderance of results toward the upper end of the range. Similar positive findings are recorded by Biehl (1991) regarding the European Union.

Table 8.3. *Summary of estimated output elasticities of public infrastructure investments from selected studies*

| Author | Aggregation | Output elasticity of public capital |
|---|---|---|
| Aschauer (1990) | Mational | 0.39 |
| Holtz-Eakin (1992) | National | 0.39 |
| Munnell (1990) | National | 0.34 |
| Costa *et al.* (1987) | States | 0.20 |
| Eiser (1991) | States | 0.17 |
| Munnell (1990) | State | 0.15 |
| Mera (1973) | Regions | 0.20 |
| Duffy-Deno and Eberts (1991) | Urban Areas | 0.08 |
| Eberts and Fogarty (1987) | Urban Areas | 0.03 |

More recently, these studies have been subjected to a variety of criticisms. Gramlich (1994) and Button (1998b) offer summaries but, very briefly, the key points include the following:

- First, while econometric studies may throw up positive correlation between economic performance and the state of infrastructure, the direction of causation is not immediately clear. Wealthier areas may simply have more resources for infrastructure provision. The efforts at testing for causality are, as yet, minimal.[15]

15 The study of public expenditure by US cities by Eberts and Fogarty (1987) explores this issue and produces inconclusive results about causality. Duffy-Deno and Eberts (1991) develop a simultaneous model for 28 US metropolitan areas in which personal income is a function of, among other things, the public capital stock which is, in turn, partly related to income. The importance of the

- Second, as seen above, the term infrastructure is a flexible one with no agreed definition, and simply taking official accountancy data may disguise important measurement, qualitative and definition factors. In US work, for instance, while Aschauer (1989) and Munnell (1990) used a 4 category 'core' sub-set of the nine US Bureau of Labor Statistics infrastructure categories, others have employed the full set.
- Third, the way in which infrastructure is managed and priced may be as important as the provision of infrastructure *per se* (Winston, 1991; Button, 1996). In terms of policy, therefore, account must be taken of the short-term levels of utilisation, maintenance and so on in addition to the stock of, and investment in, infrastructure.
- Fourth, even within the very vague notion we have regarding what constitutes infrastructure, there are numerous sectors and elements.[16] From a policy perspective it is, therefore, important to isolate the roles of, say, transport, energy and softer infrastructure such as law, education, business services and defence in influencing macroeconomic performance.
- There are similar issues on the output side and Nadiria and Manuenias (1996) have pointed to closer links between infrastructure investment and particular industrial sectors.[17]
- Sixth, as more studies emerge they are producing much wider ranges of results as Morrison (1993) puts it, 'A clear consensus about the impacts of infrastructure investment has as yet been elusive, at least partly because different methodologies generate varying results and implications.' In a study by Sturm and Haan (1995), deploying US and Netherlands data, for instance, point to the fact that the data series in most studies looking at the economic effects of public capital are neither stationary nor co-integrated and, thus, conclusions that public capital has a positive effect on private sector productivity are not well founded. Equally, Jorgensen (1991) has questioned the basic premise underlying the use of a production function approach. This sensitivity may, of course, go beyond simple matters of technique if there is, in fact, no underlying relationship.
- The studies that have been completed frequently indicate rates of returns on public capital investments – Aschauer's (1989) calculations give

public capital stock on income remain significant but is found to be about half that of a single-equation, unidirectional model. Talley (1996) provides a more complete specification of the theoretical framework that links productivity and transport infrastructure which transcends any of the empirical work that has been completed to date.

16 While the vast majority of these macro studies look at public infrastructure as a whole a small number have focused on particular elements, such as Keeler and Ying's (1988) work on the productivity of the US highway system.

17 For instance, high-technology activities would seem to require high quality transport and comunications infrastructure (Button *et al.*, 1999b).

returns of 38 to 56 per cent – in excess either of levels outside the range of any *a priori* expectation or of those found in individual micro-project appraisals.

In addition to the theme of productivity, another issue which has received much attention, especially in the European context, is the potential impact of investment of public capital on employment. There are potentially two major ways in which infrastructure may affect employment. The first concerns the substitution/complementarity effects that may occur between production factors due to infrastructure availability. The second relates to the differentiated impacts infrastructure investments may have on the competitive position of regions or countries.

According to the standard theory of the firm, an improvement in an external input, such as infrastructure, can be seen as a shift in the production function with the effect that fewer private inputs are needed to produce a given volume of production. In the standard case of a Cobb–Douglas production technology, this would lead to a decrease in both private capital and employment. With other technologies one may arrive at situations whereby a reallocation takes place between private capital and employment. With respect to the transport sector, there often seems to be a tendency for infrastructure investments to result in more capital-intensive methods of production. Investments in seaports, for instance, facilitate the use of large container ships, implying greater capital intensity in the way transport services are supplied. Similar arguments can be applied to links in transport networks such as wider canals or higher railway tunnels.

This is not the entire story, however, because higher productivity in a competitive environment, through a lowering of prices, will also stimulate demand, in addition to the substitution effect away from labour; therefore, there will also be a demand effect generating an increase in overall production and a higher demand for labour services. The price elasticity of demand is an important parameter in determining the overall impact of these forces – if it is high then one may anticipate a large increase in production volumes and thus also potentially in employment. Since different sectors make use of infrastructure with differing intensities so production costs will change at different rates. Shifts will take place between sectors, leading to employment growth in those with high price elasticities and higher intensities of infrastructure use, and decline of employment in other types of sectors. Nothing can be said *a priori* about the sizes of these effects but there is no automatic reason to anticipate that overall employment effects would be positive.

Another perspective concerns inter-regional or international competition. Transport infrastructure improvements can lead to decreases in transport costs and hence stimulate inter-regional trade. The intensity of competition increases because sectors in regions which were formerly sheltered are now confronted by relatively cheap imports. The result is that, while consumers in these regions may be able to buy at lower prices, employment in these sectors and in such regions declines. In exporting regions an increase in employment may be anticipated. The theory of trade, therefore, predicts that in each region employment in some sectors will expand while in others it will contract as a result of the infrastructure improvement. The overall impact on a region will depend on, amongst other things, its sectoral structure. The flexibility of the labour force is also important and a rigidity can mean that employment loss in one sector cannot be completely compensated for in others (Rietveld, 1995).

These conclusions contradict the widely held belief in Europe, not only in the EU but also with respect to the restructuring of the former state-controlled economies of central and eastern Europe, that infrastructure investments have a large impact on employment. The possible reason is that in many cases new infrastructure does lead to high growth rates of economic activity in its immediate surroundings. Closer inspection, however, usually reveals that such growth is mainly a matter of differential growth within regions. Locations near access points to roads, for example, grow at a faster rate than the regional average whereas locations further away grow at lower rates.

It should be noted that the majority of firms that relocate move a very short distance. Relocation of firms in response to infrastructure improvements mainly occurs on a local scale and is not a major cause of differences in regional growth rates. A study of the location behaviour of firms with more than 10 employees in the eastern part of the Netherlands, for example, found that 75 per cent of those that relocated did so to places in the same municipality (Bruinsma *et al.*, 1997). A closer inspection reveals that in the relocation process, 42 per cent of the firms remained at approximately the same distance from the nearest ramp of a highway, 41 per cent moved to a closer location and 16 per cent moved further away. Such findings underline that the rapid growth in the number of firms that is sometimes observed at particular places near newly improved highways is to a considerable extent the consequence of relocation within regions. These relocation processes are, of course, quite relevant at a local level, but from a broader regional or national perspective they are less important.

As seen above, the original findings produced by Aschauer regarding the role of infrastructure as a stimulus to economic productivity have been the subject of a substantial number of follow-up studies which have sought to refine his basic methodology and to examine the validity of his empirical findings.

The up surge of interest in the role of public infrastructure investment in helping to realise economic growth potential was initially empirically driven – and largely came from findings on the macro size of the output elasticities of public capital. Certainly there has been a long-standing debate about how infrastructure may help regional development. Some of the support for more public sector investment was along the lines suggested by

Biehl but equally there are more conventional Keynesian arguments centred around demand management.

Intellectually, the difficulty with the work linking infrastructure to economic development at the macro level is that public capital is diverse by nature, impacts on economies in a variety of ways and is the subject of decision-making that can be efficient or not.[18]

Some of these problems can easily be seen by taking the example of transport infrastructure (Figure 8.2). While it is true that the act of investment itself may have primary multiplier implications combined with some secondary effects in terms of longer-term maintenance, if the facility principally serves transit traffic there is unlikely to be a great deal of value added. Equally, if it serves trade flows into and from the region then the implications for the area's local GDP will depend on the region's comparative and competitive advantages (Sharp, 1980). There is no reason to suppose that automatically these would be positive.

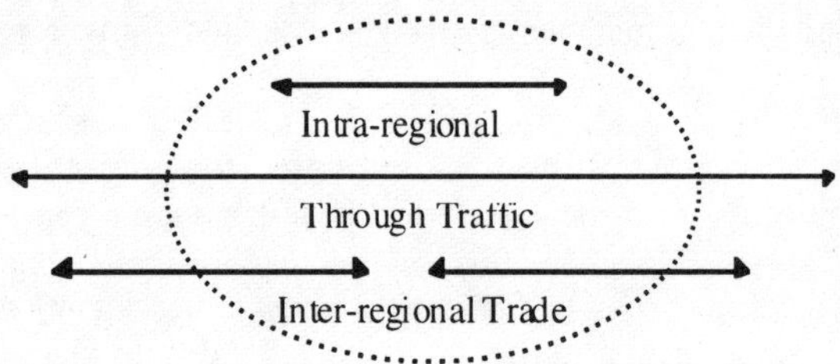


Figure 8.2 *Influence of transport infrastructure on a region*

Given the diversity of regional economies in most countries, some being much more open by nature while others are transit areas, and accepting that it is unlikely that they will all have the same initial endowment of infrastructure, it is difficult to see why automatically one would anticipate that expanding the public capital base would lead to improved economic performance. This is particularly true if the opportunity costs of investments are not fully considered.

## 8.3 INFRASTRUCTURE POLICY

Infrastructure provision has formed an explicit part of UK regional policy since the initiation of policies in the 1930s to develop trading estates to

18 It would be interesting, for instance, to see the results of a retrospective Aschauer-style analysis conducted for the former USSR.

stimulate industrial rejuvenation in economically depressed areas of northern England. In a sense this was a measure which ran counter to the neo-classical orthodoxy of the time with its focus on facilitating greater labour mobility (for instance through the creation of labour exchanges and the provision of various mobility allowances). Other countries took a somewhat different position and, in particular, many continental European nations have long sought to influence the location of industrial development via a proactive approach to infrastructure provision.

More recently, developments both within the EU and with regard to the policies of such institutions as the European Bank for Economic Reconstruction and Development (EBRD) towards the post-communist societies of central and eastern Europe, have led to renewed interest in ensuring that infrastructure policy should at least not hinder economic developments.[19] In particular, while the Common Transport Policy of the EU has traditionally been concerned with the harmonisation and liberalisation of transport operations within the Union, the Treaty of Maastricht explicitly brings up the issue of transport networks (Title XII) and master plans for high-speed rail, combined transport, motorways and inland waterways have been developed.

Since one of the justifications for this wider European interest in transport infrastructure at all levels is to meet social and regional objectives, and in particular to assist in the integration of peripheral areas into the Community, there is an acceptance of a need to understand more fully the importance of such infrastructure for industrial location. In fact, solid evidence of the nature of the links involved and their quantification is still missing – indeed much of the EU policy in this regard stems from belief rather than from analysis. This is not to say that there has been no work done on the overall importance of transport and other public infrastructure for economic development. Aschauer (1989) and Biehl (1986) offer, for instance, examples of macro studies of the importance of infrastructure and there is a body of more micro analysis although much of this is contained in grey literature such as consultants' reports.

Meta-analysis, while certainly not circumventing all of the limitations associated with traditional reviewing procedures, would seem to offer at least a partial way forward. It is, in simple terms, the use of formal statistical techniques to sum up a body of separate but similar studies. Glass (1976) offers a formal definition:

> Meta-analysis refers to the analysis of analysis... the statistical analysis of a large collection of analysis results from individual studies for the purpose of integrating the findings. In connotes a rigorous alternative to the casual, narrative discussions of research studies which typify our attempts to make sense of the rapidly expanding research literature.

19 See Vickerman (1991) and McQuaid *et al.* (1993) for discussions of recent developments in EU transport infrastructure policy.

It provides a series of techniques that allow the cumulative results of a set of individual studies to be pulled together.[20] In doing this it can not only help to provide more accurate evaluations of quantitative parameters but may also offer insights into phenomena for which no specific study currently exists. It can also, in certain circumstances, help to pinpoint political bias and to provide more clearly defined valuations of the economic costs and benefits from the plethora of data that exist. It can act as a supplement to more common literary type approaches when reviewing the usefulness of parameters derived from prior studies and help direct new research to areas where there is greatest need.

The idea of meta-analysis has a relatively extensive history, especially with respect to replicated physical experiments and it has been widely employed in psychology and medical research, but its application to micro-economic issues has until now been extremely limited. Some of the few recent examples include the examination of causes of X-inefficiencies[21] across a range of different industrial studies and studies of absenteeism[22].It offers several advantages over conventional procedures – by conventional reviewing techniques we mean studies which list results of previous work and debate their pros and cons in a literary fashion with the aim of isolating superior work or analysis which may be used as the basis for further analysis or decision-making.

There is the problem that the output of most traditional reviews tends to be in the form of taxonomies of findings without any specific attempt to relate these to the review's purpose. In consequence such reviews seldom meet the needs of those engaged in quantitative forecasting. Added to this is the subjectivity that tends to accompany a basically literary type approach. Further, the result of any statistical verification procedure can be a greater degree of conflict in the outcome that exists in the base studies themselves. Although disagreements amongst findings is itself not bad – it suggests a need to seek an explanation for the diversity – traditional methods do not normally attempt more than a description of the problem.

Second, there is the problem that traditional reviewing, because it does not necessarily embrace sound statistical practice, is usually scientifically unsound. A common problem is that if a majority of studies come up with similar conclusions these are accepted on a sort of voting basis irrespective of the quality of the data used or reliability of techniques employed. Meta-analysis, while not entirely solving this problem, can, at least, indicate the

20 It represents one of a number of broad methods for synthesising quantitative findings, see Button (1998a).

21 X-inefficiency reflects a situation where production is not on the lowest possible cost curve. The situation arises because of inadequate incentive structures for management to be cost-minimisers

22 For a survey of the applications of meta-analysis in economics; see Button *et al.* (1999a).

sensitivity of results to the type of data used and methodology employed. Finally, the traditional review process is frequently inefficient because of the difficulties of mentally handling a large number of different findings.

The meta analysis conducted here makes use of 28 estimates of the output elasticity of public infrastructure investment.[23] These studies cover a range of countries, employed a variety of techniques, involved various levels of spatial aggregation and were conducted at different times. The sources embrace both published and unpublished findings.

The selection process was one of scanning the literature and taking those studies that provide comparable results. This procedure clearly suffers from several of the defects which can be levelled against meta analysis – for example, lack of comprehensive coverage and an excessive focus on just one output measure (Button, 1998a) – but the aim is to offer supplementary analysis to conventional literary reviews and to concentrate on exploring quantitatively some of the assertions which previous reviews have made.

The analysis employs a standard least squares regression procedure.[24] The variables included are selected to elicit some quantification of the types of effect that may influence the values of public sector infrastructure investment output elasticities derived in econometric studies. To do this involves estimating the following equation:

$$E_i = a + b_1X_{i1} + b_2X_{i2} + b_3X_{i3}+b_4X_{i4} + b_5X_{i5} + b_6X_{i6} + b_7X_{i7} + b_8X_{i8} + \varepsilon \tag{8.2}$$

where:

$E_i$ is the estimated elasticity for area derived in study i;

$X_1$ takes the value of 0 for US studies and 1 otherwise;

$X_2$ takes the value of 0 for national studies and 1 otherwise (regional, urban);

$X_3$ takes the value of 1 for cross section data and 0 otherwise;

$X_4$ takes the value of 1 if pooled time series-cross sectional data is used and 0 otherwise;

$X_5$ takes the value of 1 if the study is in first differences and 0 otherwise;

23 These estimates were taken from the following studies (in some instances studies offer more than one estimate derived, for example, using alternative techniques): Aschauer (1989; 1990; 1994), Bajo-Rubio and Sosvilla (1993); Berdt and Hansson (1991); Christodoulakis (1993); Costa *et al.* (1987); Evans and Karras (1994); Ford and Poret (1991); Fukuchi (1978); Hakfoort *et al.* (1993); Holz-Eakin (1992); Hulten and Schwab (1991); Kelijian and Robinson (1995); Lynche (1994); Lynde and Richmond (1992); Mera (1973); Merriman (1990); Pinnoi (1994); Prud'homme (1996); Ratner, (1983); Sarafoglou *et al.* (1994); Seitz (1994); Tatom (1991; 1993); and Toen-Gout and Jongeling (1993).

24 A more complete desciption of this analysis is contained in Button and Rietveld (1999).

$X_6$ takes the value of 0 if publication was prior to 1991 and 1 otherwise;
$X_7$ takes the value of 0 if a Cobb–Douglas specification was used and 0 otherwise.
$X_8$ is gross national product per capita.

The equation provides a relatively good overall fit to the data (see the results presented in Table 8.4) although the significance of individual variables is often low. It also provides confirmation for some of the conclusions reached in a rather more intuitive manner in a number of the recent literary reviews. The magnitude of the constant coefficient is broadly in line with the general level of national output elasticity found in Munnell (1992) and the negative sign and scale (albeit only at a low level of statistical significance) of the $X_2$ variable provides confirmation of the importance of the level of aggregation when assessing the magnitude of output elasticities.

Table 8.4. *Regression results*

| Variable | Estimate | Standard error | t-value | Prob > \| t \| | Standardised estimate | Correlation with dependent variable |
|---|---|---|---|---|---|---|
| a | 0.343 | 0.230 | 1.488 | 0.153 | | |
| X1 | 0.240 | 0.108 | 2.219 | 0.039 | 0.517 | 0.547 |
| X2 | -0.140 | 0.127 | -1.106 | 0.282 | -0.315 | -0.260 |
| X3 | -0.104 | 0.158 | -0.660 | 0.517 | -0.163 | -0.091 |
| X4 | -0.033 | 0.117 | -0.283 | 0.780 | -0.074 | -0.050 |
| X5 | -0.076 | 0.095 | -0.796 | 0.436 | -0.169 | -0.181 |
| X6 | -0.124 | 0.080 | -1.552 | 0.137 | -0.278 | -0.226 |
| X7 | 0.095 | 0.114 | 0.832 | 0.416 | 0.163 | 0.027 |
| X8 | -0.003 | 0.009 | -0.322 | 0.751 | -0.075 | -0.417 |

$R^2 = 0.513$ Total sum of squares = 1.388
$F(8, 19) = 2.498$ Residual sum of squares = 0.676

There is considerable debate in the literature about the desirability of estimating elasticities in terms of differences in order to deal with the problem of common trends (Hulten and Schwab, 1991). It is still debatable whether this transformation is statistically desirable (Munnell, 1992), but what does emerge from the meta analysis is that elasticities derived from equations involving differences (variable $X_5$) seem to produce lower estimates than those calculated directly. This transformation, for example, has a much greater potential impact on the elasticity than consideration of whether the underlying model is of a Cobb–Douglas or of a more flexible form (cf. the result for variable $X_7$). There is also an indication that there has been something of a decline in the elasticity values which have been calculated over time (the $X_6$ variable) which may be a reflection of improved data sources or of more careful econometric analysis not captured in the other variables included in equation (8.2).

Interestingly the dummy variable indicating whether a study was of US origin or not is highly significant and suggestive of the fact that US studies, other things being equal, tend to produce lower elasticities than do studies conducted elsewhere. There is correlation between $X_1$ and $X_8$ and omission of the nationality dummy results in the $X_8$ coefficient taking a positive and significant sign. Since the US is a high-income country it may be that countries with high GDP per capita do have lower elasticities rather than that there is an explicit nationality effect in play.

Theoretically this can be explained in terms of the substantial base level and quality of infrastructure found in high-income countries and the scale, scope and density economies which accompany this. Additional infrastructure in this context may provide little additional potential stimulus especially if the economy enjoys flexible labour and private capital markets. What it does imply, however, is that previous surveys which have, in the main, tended to concentrate on the North American literature may, assuming the direction of causation is from infrastructure investment to economic stimulus, have been under-estimating output elasticities in many parts of the world.

Public sector infrastructure investment has re-emerged as a major political concern both within major economies such as the US and amongst co-ordinating economies such as those in the European Union. This meta-analysis has brought together the results of a number of studies which have sought to calculate the output elasticity of public sector infrastructure investment. It has not been concerned with matters such as direction of causality but has focused more narrowly on the extent to which it is possible to explain relatively rigorously why studies have produced quite wide variations in their results.

The results suggest that variations in results stem from a variety of sources, some of which can be explained by the nature of the economies under review but others are more closely linked to the study methodology employed. In particular, the attention paid in many surveys to the situation in North America may be misleading if findings are extended elsewhere.

Given these problems, perhaps the most objective position is to say that the role of adequate transport and other infrastructure is now seen by many as being a necessary but not sufficient condition for economic development. In this sense one can think of transport and similar infrastructure not as exerting a primary effect on development but rather as a facilitator which assists and reinforces other, more immediate instruments such as the release of land for construction and the direct provision of new buildings. Similarly, Breheny and McQuaid (1987) have argued that transport infrastructure was one of a number of 'layers of cumulative advantage' in the development of England's M4 highway corridor.

What these aggregate studies, and criticisms of them, also seem to imply is that micro sectoral studies are necessary to isolate the role of specific types of infrastructure if high levels of intra-public infrastructure efficiency are to be attained. This, of course, poses particular problems since most infrastructure-based policies involve the use of a portfolio of instruments rather than a single policy tool.

As with recent debates at the national level in many industrialised countries, so at the micro level a link between infrastructure provision and the economic development of local economies has become an oft-cited reason for the provision of new premises, transport facilities and other elements of infrastructure. Equally, though, the empirical evidence supporting such a link is not altogether solid. Table 8.5 provides details of some of the previous studies which have been undertaken of specific transport infrastructure developments in the UK and the US.

Table 8.5. *Summary of studies examining links between transport infrastructure and local economic development* [25]

| *Author* | *Geographical scale* | *Infrastructure* | *Conclusions* |
|---|---|---|---|
| Botham (1980) | 28 Zones (UK) | Changing nature of highway | Small centralising effect on employment |
| Briggs (1981) | Non-metropolitan counties (US) | Provision of highways | Presence of interstate highway is no guarantee of county development |
| Cleary & Thomas (1973) | Regional level (UK) | New estuarial crossing | Little relocation but changes in firm's operations |
| Dodgson (1974) | Zones in North (UK) | New motorway | Small effect on employment |
| Eagle et al (1987) | 87 counties (US) | New highway expenditure | No increase in employment |
| Evers et al (1987) | Regional level (Netherlands) | High-speed rail | Some effect on employment |
| Forrest et al (1987) | Metropolitan areas (US) | Light rapid transit | Property blight - good for urban renewal |
| Judge (1983) | Regional level (UK) | New motorway | Small economic impact |
| Langley (1981) | Highway corridor (US) | Highway | Devalued property in area |
| Mackie et al (1986) | Regional level (UK) | New estuarial crossing | Small overall effect |
| Mills (1981) | Metropolitan areas (US) | Interstate highways | No significant effect on location patterns |
| Moon (1986) | Metropolitan areas (US) | Highway interchanges | Existence of interchange villages |
| Pickett (1984) | Local districts (UK) | Light rapid transit | Properties close to the line benefit |
| Stephandes (1990) | 87 counties (US) | New highway expenditure | Could affect employment - depends on county's economy |
| Stephandes et al (1986) | 87 counties (US) | New highway expenditure | Some positive association with employment |
| Watterson (1986) | Metropolitan area (UK) | Light rapid transit | Modest growth in land use |
| Wilson et al (1982) | Regional level (US) | Existing highways | Transport affects location decisions but not development |

*Source*: Extracted from Leitham (1993) which contains a more comprehensive description of each of the studies.

25 A further survey is contained in Giuliano (1989), which throws up very similar results to Leitham's, and a good discussion of the recent developments relating to the theoretical side of the debate is contained in Rietveld (1989).

A variety of techniques have been used in these studies, and there is always the question of the suitability of the design of any individual scheme to meet the objectives set, but despite this there is certainly no indication that transport infrastructure in itself has a major impact on local economic development. A number of possible explanations for this have been forthcoming.

From a narrow empirical perspective it is sometimes claimed that given the relatively small proportion of industrial costs which are expended on transport in the UK – estimated at about 5.7 per cent of total operating costs by Diamond and Spence (1989) – it is unlikely that a strong link between economic performance and transport provision will exist. There may, however, be quite significant differences in transport costs by location even when, on average, they constitute only a relatively small part of costs. Also, as Gwilliam (1979) pointed out, these types of statistics could be relating to the wrong question and the more important issue is the importance of costs in profit determination. There are also the non-monetary aspects of transport to consider – speed, reliability and the like – which are increasingly important in sectors where just-in-time production management has been adopted. Finally, reliable inter-urban transport, good international transport links and high-quality local transport are often found in empirical studies to be necessary to attract the type of labour required by high-technology industries (Button, 1987; Herzog *et al.* 1986).

The emerging view can be seen as one of satisficing rather than maximising. There is a base level of transport infrastructure which is important if undertakings are to be attracted to an area and additions beyond this are of little relevance. Indeed, given the scale of potential search costs involved and the range of site options available, there is an intuitive logic in the notion of bounded rationality and the meeting of threshold objectives rather than looking for transport cost minimising locations.[26]

Finally, most of the empirical studies cited also tend to use revealed preference approaches in their analysis and are typified by regression models relating location choices to a set of explanatory variables. This approach, while shedding useful insights, can, because of specification problems and interactive effects, sometimes prove a rather blunt instrument. While alternative methods also have their limitations, actually asking firms what has influenced location choices does provide a viable alternative approach especially when the sample is large enough to limit potential biases in responses.

If one accepts both that transport infrastructure at least serves a facilitating role and that most local development initiatives embrace a portfolio of policy instruments, often with land-use policies playing a

26 A more complete discussion of satisficing and notions of bounded rationality are to be found in Simon (1978).

dominant role, then one can couch questions concerning the part played by transport in terms of the degree to which transport contributes to this portfolio and, in particular, to strengthening the power of the dominant policy instrument. In order to do this, data were gathered regarding the reasons why firms elected to take up new premises. Since local agencies have the power to both provide such premises themselves and, through planning controls, to influence strongly the private sector, the availability of new premises has long been seen as a primary tool in stimulating local economic activities.[27]

In 1991, the Department of Physical Planning at Strathclyde Regional Council (SRC) in Scotland undertook one of a series of surveys considering the scope and nature of firms occupying premises within the Region of Strathclyde. This survey was concerned with all new build industrial and business premises on industrial/business park zoned land which had been completed in the period 1981–91.[28] These premises were identified through the annual monitoring of the take-up of industrial land. Strathclyde Region itself has a population of 2.2 million and is centred on the urban conurbation of Glasgow in the west of Scotland. A total of 2076 completed, validated questionnaires were received from 939 premises. Of those visited, 498 were either vacant or used for storage, the return rate was therefore 59 per cent for occupied premises. On the basis of the sample, it was estimated that new development in the Region accounted for some 42,000 jobs and 1.7 million square metres of floorspace.[29]

Analyses of this survey enables relationships between transport and location decisions for different types of firms to be examined in several ways (throughout the discussion, the term firm has been used to denote a plant irrespective of ownership):

- the overall level of importance given to transport-related factors by occupiers of new-build industrial and business developments in the context of a range of location factors,
- selected hypotheses that different types of firms targeted by regional policies may have different preference functions for both transport generally and for different modes of transport. In particular, possible differences between: inter-regional and intra-regional or new-start firms; inward investment firms of different nationalities; type of industry; size of firm; and age of firm,
- the role of transport in the firms' decision to leave their previous location,

27 For a discussion of UK policy on property development, see Fothergill *et al.* (1987).

28 See McQuaid *et al.* (1993) for further details.

29 To set the study in the broader context of transport provision and costs in Scotland as a whole, see Chisholm (1986).

- the reasons behind preferences for different modes of transport.

The importance of transport in the location decisions of firms when they are exploring the desirability of new premises can be examined at several levels. Policy makers, especially when seeking to solve short-term unemployment difficulties, may, for example, be interested simply in the overall number of firms that land-use strategies can attract. Longer-term policy, however, is likely to be more concerned with robust linkages and networks and thus with the types of firm which fit most efficiently into the dynamics of the local economy. Transport itself is also not homogeneous in its attributes and so modal preferences may also be relevant.

The firms were asked to assess the importance of factors which they may have considered to be of importance to their company in the choice of their new premises. Table 8.6 summarises the overall responses to the location factors respondents were invited to assess. It gives mean scores derived from a one to four coding: [30] 1 - Very important; 2 – Importance; 3 – Minor importance; 4 – Not important

Table 8.6. *Overall mean scores of factors in the choice of location*

| Rank | Location factor | Mean Score | No. of Firms |
|---|---|---|---|
| 1 | Road links | 3.287 | 885 |
| 2 | Lease/rental costs | 3.241 | 801 |
| 3 | Building layout | 3.021 | 859 |
| 4 | Car parking | 2.882 | 891 |
| 5 | Access to markets | 2.820 | 723 |
| 6 | Site amenity | 2.804 | 859 |
| 7 | Access to required staff | 2.745 | 835 |
| 8 | Image of area | 2.701 | 857 |
| 9 | Access to suppliers | 2.643 | 820 |
| 10 | Government assistance | 2.619 | 554 |
| 11 | Access to support services | 2.393 | 765 |
| 12 | Access to public | 2.229 | 628 |
| 13 | Bus links | 2.074 | 705 |
| 14 | Air links | 1.950 | 598 |
| 15 | Rail links | 1.670 | 610 |
| 16 | Acess to education facilities | 1.614 | 498 |
| 17 | Access to executive housing | 1.560 | 509 |
| 18 | Access to recreation facilities | 1.421 | 501. |

30 'Not applicable' responses are excluded.

In the analysis of all firms, road linkages emerge as the most highly rated location factor. A range of general accessibility factors (such as markets, access to staff, suppliers and support services) take precedence over the other transport-specific factors (such as bus linkages and air linkages) with rail linkages apparently the least significant transport factor. Factors specific to premises (such as lease/rental costs, building layout, car parking and site amenity) are all rated higher than geographical factors, such, as for example, image of area and the availability of government assistanc[31]

The data were disaggregated to enable the identification of key sub-groups which appear to be significantly more or less sensitive to transport issues and, therefore, more likely to be influenced by infrastructure provision when making a location decision. Such considerations would then clearly have implications for the policies of providing improved transport infrastructure in order to attract development and companies to regions and sub-regions.

A model is tested with $T_X = f(O,L,I,A,S)$ where T is the importance to a firm's location choice of transport infrastructure for mode *x*; and is related to *O*: which is the origin of the firm (i.e. whether it moved from within the region or from elsewhere, or was it a start-up firm); *L*, the relationship of the firm to other parts of its organisation (i.e. whether it has a parent company and if so, where it is located); *I* is the industry (nature of business); *A* and *S* are other firm characteristics (age of firm and size of firm respectively). Aspects of this model are tested using analysis of variance (ANOVA) and multivariate analysis.

The disaggregations shown in Table 8.7 are some that it was thought may display different response profiles for the location factors. The disaggregated categories and sub-groups are shown with the percentage of the respondents who answered either 'very important' or 'important' to each factor. These figures provide an overview of the relative numbers of the nature and scope of the firms occupying new industrial and business premises in the survey.

The percentages of those responding 'very important' or 'important' to the transport factors give an indication of differences in the sub-groups' perceptions of these factors. To investigate if these differences are of statistical significance, each disaggregated category and its sub-groups were

31 A more detailed breakdown of the responses of firms to the transport specific and general accessibility location factors indicates the dominant influence of those answering 'very important'. Access to markets, however, was more important than access to staff or suppliers of road links in the location decisions of all firms, with 81 per cent rating it very important or important in the choice of their current location. Only 10 per cent rate rail links similarly with air links 18 per cent and bus links 24 per cent. In terms of the more general accessibility factors, the access to staff was considered most important, followed by access to suppliers and access to markets.

then analysed utilising ANOVA procedures.[32] The base test was whether there exists a significant difference in the mean values of the sub-groups in relation to the transport factors. The relevant F values, and associated probability or p values, are shown in Table 8.8.

Table 8.7. *Structure of the database and disaggregations*

| | | | Percentage of Respondents Stating Very Important/Important | | | |
|---|---|---|---|---|---|---|
| Disaggregated Categories | SubGroups | n* | Road Links | Rail Links | Air Links | Bus Links |
| (i) Origin of firm | 1. New start | 304 | 75 | 10 | 16 | 24 |
| | 2. Intra-Regional moves | 393 | 80 | 9 | 14 | 25 |
| | 3. Inward Investment | 214 | 91 | 14 | 30 | 22 |
| (ii) Location of parent company | 1. Same Region (Strathclyde) | 59 | 71 | 15 | 14 | 37 |
| | 2. Rest of Country (UK) | 228 | 92 | 12 | 25 | 23 |
| | 3. Rest of World | 48 | 79 | 17 | 62 | 19 |
| | 4. No parent company | 597 | 78 | 9 | 13 | 23 |
| (iii) Nature of business | 1. Primary | 12 | 92 | 25 | 33 | 25 |
| | 2. Manufacturing | 364 | 80 | 12 | 30 | 25 |
| | 3. Construction | 88 | 82 | 6 | 10 | 17 |
| | 4. Distribution | 201 | 87 | 11 | 18 | 22 |
| | 5. Other services | 274 | 78 | 11 | 7 | 26 |
| (iv) Age of firm | 1. Less than one year | 55 | 85 | 11 | 11 | 20 |
| | 2. 1-5 years | 263 | 76 | 10 | 18 | 22 |
| | 3. 6-10 years | 202 | 85 | 12 | 17 | 27 |
| | 4. >10 years | 407 | 84 | 10 | 20 | 24 |
| (v) Size of firm | 1. <10 employees | 562 | 78 | 10 | 13 | 20 |
| | 2. 11-50 employees | 297 | 84 | 11 | 24 | 26 |
| | 3. >50 employees | 88 | 91 | 19 | 40 | 42 |
| (vi) Part of a larger organization | 1. Yes | 341 | 86 | 14 | 28 | 25 |
| | 2. No | 597 | 78 | 9 | 12 | 24 |

* Some of the above disaggregations do not add up to the total of 939 data records due to non-responses.

The influence of the characteristics of firms on the importance attached to transport mode location factors can be examined by exploring several hypotheses. The first is that inward investing firms (i.e. inter-regional moves by firms into their premises from outside the region) consider transport links more important than either existing indigenous firms (intra-regional moves by firms within the region) or new starts (firms with this as their first location). Results in Table 8.7 support the hypothesis that there are significant differences between such firms for road and air travel modes, but not for bus or rail modes. Table 8.6 indicated that 91 per cent of inward investment, 80 per cent of indigenous firms and 75 per cent of new starts

32 The 1 to 4 response coding described earlier was employed in order to assess differences in the means of the sub-categories.

consider road links to be very important or important. For air transport, the differences are more marked with 30 per cent of inward investors rating it as important or very important, compared to 14 per cent and 16 per cent for the other groups. Although not significantly different, inward investors also rate rail as very important/important more often than the others, but buses less often. These results may reflect the relative importance of the different modes of transport for inter-regional and intra-regional travel, with buses primarily used by the localwork force, air for movements of goods, services and people between regions, and roads for inter-and intra-regional travel.

Table 8.8. *Analysis of disaggregated categories*

| Disaggregated Categories (1) | Road Links | | Rail Links | | Air Links | | Bus Links | |
|---|---|---|---|---|---|---|---|---|
| | 'F' | 'p' | 'F' | 'p' | 'F' | 'p' | 'F' | 'p' |
| (i) Origin of firm | 17.56 | .00** | 0.30 | .74 | 6.85 | .00** | 1.84 | .16 |
| (ii) Location of parent company | 10.44 | .00** | 2.21 | .09 | 15.86 | .00** | 0.85 | .46 |
| (iii) Nature of business | 2.07 | .08 | 0.88 | .47 | 1.34 | .25 | 0.77 | .55 |
| (iv) Age of firm | 2.95 | .01* | 1.14 | .33 | 2.05 | .07 | 0.57 | .72 |
| (v) Size of firm | 6.16 | .00** | 4.35 | .01* | 23.30 | .00** | 7.75 | .00** |
| (vi) Part of larger organization | 10.62 | .00** | 5.00 | .03* | 10.16 | .00** | 2.22 | .11 |

* Significant at 5 per cent
** Significant at 1 per cent
(1) See Table 8.6 for details.

A second hypothesis is that branch plants place greater emphasis on inter-regional modes. Schmenner (1982), for example, found that for branch plant moves in the US at site level emphasis was placed on transport facilities and utilities. Here, significant differences emerge between branch and non-branch plants for road and air and rail, with the former citing transport as being more important in each case.[33] Further disaggregation reveals significant differences (for roads) between branch plants created by inward investment (91 per cent) and branches moving within the region (74 per cent). For plant relocations, those moving into the region consider roads of more importance (93 per cent stating very important/important), than those that have moved from another part of the region (80 per cent).

33 For instance, 86 per cent of branch plants cited road links as being very important or important compared to 78 per cent of non-branch plants.

A third hypothesis is that the location of a firm's parent company influences the importance attached to road and air transport links, but not rail or bus links, due to the need for intra-organisational communications. Table 8.7 reveals differences for road and air between those with head offices outside the region, either abroad or elsewhere in the country, those based in the region (either parents or branches of other regional, i.e. Strathclyde firms) and those with no parent company.[34] Rail and bus differences are not significant, perhaps reflecting their limited use for long-distance communication. Some 92 per cent of branch plants with the parent located elsewhere in the country indicated road links as very important/important.

There are a number of differences for branch firms with head offices outside the UK. Firms are separated into those with head offices in the Strathclyde region, the rest of the country (UK) and the rest of the world (ROW). Disaggregating the ROW firms into EU and non-European firms provides additional insights. Road links are considerably more important for branches of other UK based firms (92 per cent) than for branch regional firms (71 per cent), regional single plant firms (78 per cent) or ROW firms (79 per cent). Of this latter group, only 67 per cent of European firms rate roads very important or important, compared to 83 per cent of non-European world firms. Similarly, European firms cite rail links (8 per cent), as being of less important than do UK firms (12 per cent)[35] while other international firms indicate rail as more important (19 per cent). European and non-European firms rate bus links as slightly less important than do UK firms. Air transport is most important to branches of non-European parents (67 per cent), compared to European branches (50 per cent).

Overall, road links seem to be crucial for all types of firm, while air links are also important for firms with foreign parents. Several factors may explain this such as a perceptual difference between areas, the possibility that some European parent firms may not require good communications or the likelihood that some firms are particularly interested in locating near their market in Scotland. In terms of improved European integration and attractiveness for non-European inward investment, road and air links seem important, but for indigenous firms road links are perceived as being far more relevant.

The fourth hypothesis is that although all firms are located in industrial areas, it is likely that different industries place different importance upon different modes of transport. There is no evidence to support this for any mode. The sample size for primary industries is small, but they and distribution industries place greatest importance on roads, while, together

34 Similar results were obtained when single plant firms (i.e. no parent company) were excluded from the analysis.

35 This may in large part be due to the difficulties in linking into the European rail network.

with manufacturing, they place the greatest emphasis upon air. Such relationships, however, are not significant.[36]

The fifth hypothesis is that the age of a firm is not related to the importance given to each mode of transport infrastructure. The evidence in Table 8.7 supports this save in the case of roads, upon which younger firms place more emphasis. For air, the importance rises with the age of firms, but this is not significant. Transport infrastructure does not, thus, appear to be more important for younger firms.

The sixth hypothesis is that the size of a firm will influence the importance it gives to transport because larger firms have greater numbers of employees travelling, since they may locate further from residential areas, and will have stronger links with suppliers and customers outside the local area. The results support this.

In addition to assessing factors considered in the choice of current location, respondents offering a previous address were asked to respond to a set of factors relating to the move from their prior location. The main reasons are found to be expansion (82 per cent citing this as very important or important), layout restrictions (58 per cent), poor image (48 per cent), and car parking and new markets (both 43 per cent). Poor road links are cited as very important or important in 33 per cent of cases with other transport factors appearing less significant (rail with 11 per cent, air 9 per cent, and bus links 11 per cent).

Overall the results suggest that transport infrastructure plays a relatively minor role in causing firms to leave their previous location. While transport links emerge as important in attracting firms to their current location (i.e. in the search process), they are not usually crucial in causing them to leave their previous location. What this analysis omits, however, is adequate consideration of interactive effects.

Categorical multivariate data expressed in the form of a contingency table can be examined using sets of hierarchical log-linear models.[37] A multinomial sampling distribution is assumed with each of the cells in the table having an unknown probability. The structure of the table is examined in order to explain the variations in cell probabilities in terms of the classificatory variables and their interactions. This can be undertaken with or without a distinction between response and explanatory variables. The most parsimonious and useful models from the set which give a satisfactory fit to the data are then selected and estimates of cell frequencies obtained.

In applications where a factor-response relationship is assumed or under investigation, the interactions between the explanatory variables are taken as

36 This may partly be explained by the specific function of the plant and the type of premises required being more important than the general type of industry.

37 Wrigley (1985) and Upton (1980) offer theoretical background material and prior examples of the use of this approach.

fixed and all models considered include the interactions between these defined explanatory variables. It is only the effects of the interactions between explanatory and response variables which are assessed in the modelling process in this case. If no explanatory-response relationship is assumed, all the terms and interactions in the table are considered in order to explain the structure of the contingency table. Both of these methods were employed in the analysis but only the latter is reported as it was found on the whole to give a better fit to the data.[38]

From the ANOVA analysis of disaggregated categories (Tables 8.6 and 8.7), the following disaggregations were identified for multivariate analysis, in the form of a 4-way contingency table (ABCD) where: A – Origin of firm; B – size of firm; C – location of parent company (if any); D – attitude to transport links by mode.

Although 'larger organisation' was also a significant factor in the analysis, it was excluded on the grounds of parsimony as it is implicitly incorporated in the 'location of parent company' disaggregation. Nature of business and age of firm were also excluded following the earlier analysis. In addition, each transport mode factor (road links, rail links, air links, bus links) was transformed into binary form:[39] with Y indicating 'very important' or 'important' and N indicating 'minor importance' or 'not important'

Four-way contingency tables are constructed for each transport mode[40]. The majority of respondents are new-start firms with fewer than ten employees, and have no parent company. In terms of the influence of transport modes in the choice of location, they generally rate roads as most important.

A number of log-linear models are fitted to the observations to determine the estimated cell frequencies. Those specified below include those factors and interactions between factors which add significantly to the explanatory power of the model. Goodness of fit measures for the models are given in Table 8.9. All the specification shown have a satisfactory fit to the observed data at the 5 per cent significance level:

$$\log_e m_{ijkl} = \lambda_i^A + \lambda_j^B + \lambda_k^C + \lambda_l^D + \lambda_{ij}^{AB} + \lambda_{ik}^{AC} + \lambda_{jk}^{BC} + \lambda_{kl}^{CD} \qquad \text{Road}$$

$$\log_e m_{ijkl} = \lambda_i^A + \lambda_j^B + \lambda_k^C + \lambda_l^D + \lambda_{ij}^{AB} + \lambda_{ik}^{AC} + \lambda_{jk}^{BC} \qquad \text{Rail}$$

$$\log_e m_{ijkl} = \lambda_i^A + \lambda_j^B + \lambda_k^C + \lambda_l^D + \lambda_{ij}^{AB} + \lambda_{ik}^{AC} + \lambda_{il}^{AD} + \lambda_{jk}^{BC} + \lambda_{jl}^{BD} + \lambda_{kl}^{CD} + \lambda_{ikl}^{ACD} + \lambda_{jkl}^{BCD} \qquad \text{Air}$$

$$\log_e m_{ijkl} = \lambda_i^A + \lambda_j^B + \lambda_k^C + \lambda_l^D + \lambda_{ij}^{AB} + \lambda_{ik}^{AC} + \lambda_{jk}^{BC} + \lambda_{jl}^{BD} + \lambda_{kl}^{CD} \qquad \text{Bus}$$

38 The models were selected using forward and backward stepwise selection processes choosing from a large set of estimated models.

39 Respondents answering 'not applicable' to the transport factors or not answering at all are excluded.

40 The full tables are to be found in Button *et al.* (1995).

The inclusion of a single factor (e.g. A or B) indicates that this factor is required to describe the $n$-way contingency table.[41] Two-way interaction factors (e.g. AB) imply that there is an association between the two variables that is independent of the level of the other variables. In the same way, three way interaction factors (e.g. ABC) imply a three way association regardless of the value of the fourth variable. Likewise, the categories of variable D are conditionally equiprobable given the level of the joint variable ABC.

Table 8.9. *Goodness of fit*

| Model | $G^2$ | d.f. | 'p' |
|---|---|---|---|
| 1: Road | 43.28 | 44 | .503 |
| 2: Rail | 58.10 | 47 | .129 |
| 3: Air | 40.59 | 28 | .059 |
| 4: Bus | 57.46 | 42 | .056 |

*Note*: $G^2$ is the likelihood ratio $\chi^2$ statistic and is defined as the sum over all the cells of $n\log_e(n/e)$. It has an approximate $\chi^2$ distribution with the appropriate degrees of freedom.

The models for each of the four transport modes has seven factors in common (A, B, C, D, AB, AC, BC), indicating that for each model all four variables (A, B, C, D) should be included. The relationships between variables show strong associations between origin and firm size, origin and location of parent company, and firm size and location of parent company regardless of transport mode. This may be expected because they represent some easily assumed relationships, for example, that small firms will be new starts and not have a parent company.

The road model indicates that the location of parent company and the importance of road links are associated. From Table 8.6 it can be seen that firms with parent companies in the rest of the UK consider roads to be of greater importance than firms with parents located elsewhere or no parent company. Interestingly, the association between road links and origin and between road links and firm size do not add significantly to the explanatory power of the model and are excluded. The results also indicate that firms from outside the region do place greater importance upon road links than that of regional firms (either branches of regional firms or single plant firms). Roads appear to have a greater significance for inward investment than for the growth of endogenously controlled firms. This may reflect the larger road transport needs of exogenously controlled firms in terms of the

41 That is, the table cannot legitimately be collapsed over this variable to form a $(n-1)$-way contingency table.

market and supplier networks often determined from head office as well as the need for links to the head office and other branches.

The structural variables, origin, size of firm and location of parent company, in addition to the rail links term, are sufficient to describe the rail links contingency table. The association between firm size and rail links found in Table 8.7 was not supported as no association between them (that was independent of origin of firm or location of parent company) was found in the multivariate analysis.

The air transport model indicates that aviation is associated with each of the other variables (origin of firm, firm size and location of parent company) individually. Additionally there are two three-way interactions, first between origin of firm, location of parent company and air links, and second between size of firm, location of parent company and air links. This implies that the assessment of air links is associated jointly with origin of firm and location of parent company, in addition to size of firm and location of parent company. Equally, the categories of 'firm size' are conditionally equiprobable given the levels of the joint variable origin by location of parent company by air links and the categories of 'origin' are conditionally equiprobable given the levels of the joint variable firm size by location of parent company by air links. This again emphasises the relative importance of air transport links for exogeously controlled firms.

An association between size of firm and bus links was expected from Table 8.7. It is also seen in Table 8.6 that the importance of bus links increases with the size of the firm. An additional interaction between location of parent company and bus links that emerged from the multivariate analysis was perhaps less expected and may be due to correlation with the size of firm variable.

What emerges from the multivariate analysis are distinct variations between the modes of transport as influences on choice of firms' locations. Also, exogenously controlled firms give greater importance to transport, especially to road and air, than endogenously controlled firms (both single plant and branch plant firms).

## 8.4 CONCLUSIONS

At a practical level the EU has directed considerable resources into upgrading the infrastructure of Europe and considerable administrative effort into improving the coherency with which infrastructure policies are pursued by Member States. This has been deemed important as part of the political and social integration process as well as being seen as an element in the regional economic policy of the Union. In this sense it can be considered on a par with the policies pursued by countries such as the US and Canada during their early phases of integration.

This has been taking place at a time when academics have shown a renewed interest in the way infrastructure can influence economic development. Interest in the role which infrastructure can constructively play in stimulating development at the regional, meso-level has grown as economic integration has become a focus of attention in Europe and North America. Complete knowledge of the importance of infrastructure in affecting regional economic performance or of the roles which different forms of infrastructure may play, is, however, still lacking. The evidence of aggregate studies suggests that infrastructure investment is important but technical limitations prevent complete confidence being placed on the parameters generated by empirical work.

While such analysis is important for resolving macroeconomic policy debates concerning public/private resource allocation, at the micro level it is the implication of sectoral infrastructure policy and project-specific impacts which are of greatest relevance. The empirical results reported here focus on a case study of the role transport plays in facilitating successful development initiatives, most notably regarding policies relating to the availability of new premises, at the local and regional level. What emerges is that there are important differences between the types of transport infrastructure that complement policies for new premises which depend on the types of firm involved.[42] Further, poor or inappropriate transport does not seem to stimulate firm migration but quality and the nature of local transport infrastructure is an element in the search criteria once a decision to relocate has been reached. The importance of these findings from a wider policy perspective is that it may well be important to focus on the microeconomic analysis of individual investment schemes, and to trace through the implications, rather than to pursue extensive analysis on a large spatial scale.

42 This finding supports the essentially Dutch empirical work of Rietveld and Bruinsma (1998) who, when it comes to the spatial economic implications of infrastructure enhancement, point to the importance of the existing infrastructure networks, the structures of the regional economies involved and the overall state of the macro-economy when the infrastructure comes on line.

# 9. Conclusions

## 9.1 INTRODUCTION

In this book we have explored the issue of regional economic development and the effectiveness of regional economic policies with a specific focus. The geographical domain has been that of the European Union. The extent of the regional problem has implicitly been defined in terms of variations in the economic performance of different areas within the Union. Our framework for theoretical analysis and subsequent policy appraisal has been that of the New Economic Growth theories and the new methods of empirics that has tended to emerge with it..

This not the only approach that could have been pursued. The EU serves a number of key economic functions, not least of which is the fostering of political cohesion. This political dimension, and indeed other issues of social and nationality considerations, are largely ignored in this study.

The justification for looking almost entirely at traditional economic indicators is their dominance in much of the current debate within the EU. If for no other reason than the periodic enlargements of the Union which bring with them more spatial diversity, the scale of the EUs regional economic problems have grown with time. Moves towards greater economic and political integration, and especially those related to monetary policy, have further stimulated concern about the longer-term needs for an effective EU regional policy.

The objective of this concluding chapter is not simply to summarise the findings that have gone before but rather to reflect on the types of regional economic problems that are likely to be important within the EU over the next two decades or so. In part these issues will depend on what has gone before. There will inevitably have been a learning process but also underlying future concerns will be the way the present is viewed. If it is felt that economic convergence is a natural force and has been moving forward, then this will lead to a different perception to that formed if policy makers take hold of ideas of cumulative divergence. There are also matters of an institutional nature and in particular the importance of movements towards fiscal reforms and monetary integration.

## 9.2 THE EXTENT OF ECONOMIC CONVERGENCE

Looking at the simple data the EU Commission has tended to the conclusion that there is a degree of convergence in the performance of regional economies across the Union (Commission of the European Communities, 1999). Some econometric work, notably by Barro and Sala-i-Martin (1995), has given support to this view albeit in terms of a slightly different definition of convergence. The topic, as has been demonstrated, however, is not yet closed.

Defining and then measuring economic convergence is not a simple matter. There are several ways in which one can look at convergence, even within the narrower notion of economic convergence. The recent application of powerful economic theorising and of heavy-duty econometric analysis has provided some insights as to the nature of economic convergence but the initial hopes that the work of Barro, Sala-i-Martin and others would prove definitive have proved incorrect. What we do know is that measuring economic convergence is trickier than was initially suspected and that even if the form of measurement is agreed upon, assessing it poses another level of problems.

The issue of economic convergence is also one that transcends the borders of the EU. It is a subject of renewed interest in a number of larger countries and within several major trading blocks. The amount of work that has been conducted on the topic, and it has only been partly surveyed in this volume, is considerable and yet there is still no consensus as to the best methodology. This does not mean that the work has no value, but rather it can be interpreted that there is no simple answer. In looking at the findings of the various studies, what seems to suggest itself is the need to ensure that the question being posed is germane to the problem being addressed. Many regional issues concerning the EU are political rather than economic in their origin and conventional measures of (sigma) convergence probably meet the needs of decision makers. From a longer term, strategic perspective in the context of the larger integration of the EU economies, however, more sophisticated indicators may well be needed.

## 9.3 SHAPING THE FUTURE OF EU REGIONAL POLICY

It is certain that the future EU regional policy will deviate quite markedly from the experiences of the past. Learning from previous experiences will itself lead to new thinking and approaches but the forces for change range well beyond this. There are a number of traditional forces that will continue to play their part in the way the regions of the EU evolve but in addition there are a number of factors that will result in trend breaks and new trends emerging. Foreseeing all of these is impossible but some are beginning to become apparent already.

### 9.3.1 New members

What is the optimal size for the EU? There are strong pressures for a continual enlargement that would involve, in particular, bringing in former communist countries (an issue dealt with specifically below). From a regional perspective, the continual enlargement of the Union, be it with the remaining western states or the post-communist states of central and eastern Europe, will inevitably bring with it increased problems. In the past, although the admission of Finland, Austria and Sweden posed few problems, the incorporation of the southern European economies such as Spain and Portugal increased the number of poorer regions and added, in particular, to the difficulties associated with predominantly agricultural areas.

The idea of geographically widening the EU, whilst at the same time engaging in an institutional deepening, has the appeal of opening a larger market area for trade and of furthering the cause of European political integration. From a regional policy perspective, however, it poses major fiscal problems in terms of generating adequate aid for disadvantaged regions. In previous enlargements, notably that of 1986, the need to divert regional aid to the depressed regions of new members diluted that available for poorer regions within the existing membership. There are serious issues concerning the ability of the Structural Funds to cope with a significant enlargement that would involve a large number of poorer regions (Baldwin, 1994).[1] Under-funding of regional policy is likely to become an even more important issue as the structural impacts of the EU adopting a Single Currency begins to be realised.

### 9.3.2 Post-communist Europe

The entry of post-communist states is, in many ways, a special case of enlargement that extends historic political considerations. The economic situation in central and eastern European poses two fundamental types of challenge to the EU. At the macro level, the bringing in of central and eastern European countries into the EU promises to pose particular problems because of their generally poor economic state[2]. In one sense many of these economies have performed well in recent years, with economic growth rates over twice (5.5 per cent) that of the EU (2.4 per cent) in 1995. But even so the gap for all countries has only closed from 29 per cent in 1993 to 31 per cent in 1995. The performance of the central and

[1] This issue is to be considered in a review of the Structural Funds in 1999.

[2] Thare are also problems associated with their different fiscal and monetray systems (Budd, 1997).

eastern European states, however, has been anything but uniform and whilst countries such as Poland, Estonia and the Slovak Republic have done especially well, at the other extreme Bulgaria, Romania and the Czech Republic have experienced slower growth.[3]

At a meso level this issue is more one of diversity that makes developing a common approach to enlargement difficult. There are important differences at the regional and structural level within the various central and eastern European nations. Most traditional forms of industry in these countries is highly X-inefficient[4] and the service sector was at an early stage of development prior to transition. The latter has grown quite noticeably, although unevenly, in recent years, with it now representing 65 per cent of GDP in Estonia and Hungary in 1995. It still is only 35 per cent, however, in Romania. Equally there has been a move away from agricultural production as privatisation has taken place and subsidies reduced.

Spatially, the available data highlights the imbalances within the central and eastern economies to be largely in terms of an urban-rural divide. In particular, the large urban centre areas close to borders with western economies have done relatively well and have attracted good flows of foreign direct investment. These regions also tend to enjoy higher-quality infrastructure. Other areas are generally characterised by declining manufacturing activities and agriculture. Exceptions to this are the Czech Republic which has a relatively even geographical spread of economic activity although the Prague region is somewhat more affluent than the rest of the country. In Romania there are differences in the extent of industrial decline between regions, while in Poland, while regional differences are relatively small, there are pockets of severe economic depression, often immediately adjacent to the most prosperous part of the country.

### 9.3.3 International trade factors

The institutional framework within which international trade is conducted has changed considerably since the end of the Second World War. Major trading blocs such as the EU and, to a much lesser extent, NAFTA, are only one manifestation of this. The General Agreement on Tariffs and Trade (GATT) and, more recently, the General Agreement on Trade in Services (GATS) represent rather larger-scale developments while bringing in the central and eastern European states to the free market structure can be seen as another.

In one way these institutional changes can be perceived as a movement favouring freer trade and the reduction in trade barriers. In another way, the

[3] The gap in GDP between the EU average and Bulgaria and Romania has actually been widening.

[4] This has had serious implications as they have been thrown into world markets but nevertheless industrial production in countries such as the Czech Republic still represents a significantly larger part of their GDP than in the EU.

growth of free trade areas in particular can be taken as a move towards the oligopolisation of trade. Freer trade may take place within blocs but the creation of 'fortress blocs' can act to limit trade between them[5].

One important issue that will inevitably grow in importance is how the EU is going to treat other trading blocs. There has been a recent history of friction over trade in agricultural products with the US with the latter complaining that EU agricultural support has enabled European farmers to placed subsidised crops on the world market. Equally the EU has complained of a similar practice in the US. Support for disadvantaged agricultural regions is a politically sensitive topic on both sides of the Atlantic and it seems probable that friction will inevitably continue.[6]

Wider measures to free trade are also likely to have long-term implications for regional policy. The line between a trade subsidy and regional aid is a thin one as has been seen in the past as new members of the EU have found that what they had traditionally deemed regional assistance was in the EU Commission's eyes a subsidy (for example, the UK's Regional Employment Premium). With industry becoming increasingly footloose and having to commit fewer sunk costs to a particular location, the overall comparative advantage of the EU may decline and disadvantaged regions within it become even more uncompetitive. To some extent this has already happened as poorer regions have found themselves competing globally with newly industrialising countriess (NICs) and Third World economies to produce less-sophisticated, labour-intensive goods.

Through its Research and Technical Development (RTD) programme, the Union is already putting funds into trying to boost the overall performance of EU industry; with a considerable amount of the resources going to disadvantaged regions.[7] The latter, however, still lag considerably behind the wealthier regions of the Union.

### 9.3.4 Changing industrial structure

The last 20 years has seen a major shift in the economic structure of virtually all developed countries. A long-term decline in the importance of agriculture has been accompanied by a relative decline in the importance of industrial production. Service sector employment and output has, at the

[5] One could also argue that this problem of fortress blocs was a characteristic of the period when the economies of central and eastern Europe were formed together as the Comecon bloc with intra-member trade taking priority over trade with outside countries. The growth of trade since 1989 reflects the barriers that such insular attitudes can produce.

[6] The creation of a Transatlantic Free Trade Agreement has been suggested but seems a remote possibility.

[7] The regional dimension of RTD activities of the EU have essentially been an attempt to make up for some of the shortfall in private sector expenditure on these activities (Commission of the European Communities, 1999).

same time, generally grown at a prodigious rate, even allowing for any problems involved in National Income Accounting measures. This employment offers high incomes and is recognised from a regional policy point of view as being attractive in that it is relatively geographically mobile.

The regional policy required to attract and maintain service sector employment is somewhat different to that associated with developing manufacturing industry. They are generally less dependent on traditional forms of infrastructure and look at such things as the 'generalised costs' of alternative locations and at levels of accessibility (Button *et al*, 1999). The experience of the EU has been rather more with up-grading the industrial bases of areas that have suffered economic decline or have a large and inefficient agricultural sector.

## 9.4 FISCAL AND REGIONAL POLICIES UNDER EMU

Regional economic performance in the EU depends to a considerable extent on the interaction between fiscal policy, which remains primarily a national policy instrument, and regional policy, which has a more centralist aspect, through the Cohesion and Structural budgets. There are circumstances in which these two policies are likely to be in conflict to the detriment of the regional economies. In particular, there are two specific aspects of fiscal policy that are also important for regional policy: redistribution policy and stabilisation policy.

The Single European Act stresses the idea of harmonious development and of social cohesion among member countries. In this context inter-regional redistribution to reinforce cohesion within the union, a goal that was officially adopted in Article 130a of the Single European Act, is important. This goes beyond the notion of equity and is closely linked to efficiency in that it aims to provide instruments to level the competitive playing field as far as structural endowments are concerned through investment programmes to upgrade infrastructure and human skills (European Economy, 1993). Inter-regional redistribution is effected through the structural funds budget of the Union. Regional redistribution remains limited by the overall size of the Union budget (about 1 per cent of Union GDP). Moreover, these funds are directed mainly towards specific policy areas and regions, in that they foster public infrastructure and the formation of human capital and are conditional and subsidiary in nature (i.e. the programmes are established at the regional level and are only co-financed by the EU).

The scope for inter-regional transfers among member countries is likely to remain limited, despite recent moves to increase the size of the structural funds. Some economists have argued that grants are unnecessary and may even be counterproductive as the very process of economic integration should narrow the income differentials within and among the nations of the European Union. This is as a consequence of greater scope for market arbitrage after the formation of the Monetary Union. Much of the evidence in this book, however, does not support this non-interventionist, automatic market-clearing view of regional adjustment.

With regards to the stabilisation function of fiscal policy, the traditional literature suggests that it should be centralised. There is, however, little support for this in the EU and hence the Union is unlikely to centralise income tax or unemployment insurance arrangements in the foreseeable future. The income tax, nevertheless, retains some of its stabilising features even when decentralised, provided that the Union is confronted with symmetric external shocks. Thus if the Union as a whole is subject to a symmetrical external shock, the automatic built-in stabilising properties of the set of national fiscal arrangements could be effective and co-ordinated national policy actions may not be needed.

The case is, of course, rather more difficult for regionally asymmetric shocks. Where these occur, markets should be allowed to react whenever such shocks are permanent. Labour migration and capital flows must then operate to change relative prices in order to restore macroeconomic equilibrium. If, however, due to a lack of labour mobility, these flows are slow to take place and hence relative prices slow to adjust, then there will be a temporary regional problem. In this case, an active regional policy is required to bring about or speed the adjustment. In this case however, regional stabilisation policies would be unsustainable because government spending would run counter to the change in long-run taxable capacity, which declines as income falls. Increased budget deficits could only be contemplated within the strict rules of the Maastricht Treaty and the Stability Pact. These agreements constrain budget deficits to be less than 3 per cent of GDP and suggest that over the cycle the national governments should operate a balanced budget. In this case there is a conflict between fiscal policy and regional policy.

Where these asymmetric shocks are only temporary, rather than permanent, a case can be made in favour of central intervention through, for example, a central unemployment insurance scheme or even direct grants. Such policies need not require a large central budget (Goodhart and Smith, 1993) and avoid the potential moral hazard problems.[8] On the other hand, Majocchi and Rey (1993) have argued that a temporary shock is more effectively dealt with by regional policy rather than by Union-wide, fiscal policy, although this does again raise the issue of how this regional policy is to be financed.

[8] These occur where the national authorities, knowing of the existence of such contracts, deliberately exaggerate the regional problem to secure more insurance funds from the Union.

The conflict between regional and fiscal policy is essentially due to the restrictive criteria set for fiscal policy in the Maastricht Treaty.[9] In this sense the Treaty also serves to restrict the operation of national regional policy, while at the same time the funds available for a centrally operated regional policy are very limited. This inherent deflationary bias in EMU and lack of significant central funding for an EU-wide regional policy may well result in more divergent regional economic performance.

[9] The Maastricht Treaty is asymmetric in that it does not restrict fiscal surpluses. Thus governments, to avoid being fined for fiscal laxity, may tend to err on the side of caution and hence attempt to balance the budget, rather than operate a strongly discretionary fiscal policy.

# References


Anderson, B. (1993) Factors affecting European privatisation and deregulation policies in local public transport: the evidence from Scandinavia, *Transportation Research* 26A: 179–91.

Andersson, A.E. and Kobayashi, K (1989) Some theoretical aspects of spatial equilibria with public goods, in Andersson, A.E., Batten, D.F., Johansson, B. and Nijkamp, P. (eds), *Advances in Spatial Theory and Dynamics*, Amsterdam: North-Holland.

Ardeni, P.G. (1992) On the way to the EMU: testing convergence of the European economies, *Economic Notes by Monte dei Paschi di Siena*, 21: 238–57.

Armstrong, H.W. (1978) Community regional policy: a survey and critique, *Regional Studies*, 12: 511–28.

Armstrong, H.W. (1992) The role and evolution of European Community regional policy, in Keating, M. and Jones, J.B. (eds), *Regions in the European Community*, Oxford: Oxford University Press.

Armstrong, H.W. (1995) *Trends and Disparities in Regional GDP per Capita in the European Union, United States and Australia*, Brussels: European Commission Report 94/00/74/017.

Armstrong, H.W. and King, J.E. (1994) Regional income disparities in Australia and the European union, University of La Trobe, Economics Department, Discussion Paper.

Armstrong, H.W. and Taylor, J. (1993) *Regional Economics and Policy*, 2nd Edn., London: Harvester Wheatsheaf.

Arrow, K.J. (1962) The economic implications of learning by doing, *Review of Economic Studies*, 29: 155-173.

Aschauer, D.A. (1989) Is public expenditure productive?, *Journal of Monetary Economics* 23: 177–200.

Aschauer, D.A. (1990) Why is infrastructure important?, in Munnell, P. (ed), *Is There a Shortfall in Public Capital Investment?*, Boston: Conference Series, 34, Federal Reserve Bank of Boston.

Aschauer, D.A. (1994) Infrastructure and macroeconomic performance: direct and indirect effects, paper to *OECD Conference on Capital Formation and Employment*, Amsterdam.

Audas, R.P. and Mackay, R.R. (1997) A tale of two recessions, *Regional Studies* 31: 867–74.

Bajo-Rubio, O. and Sosvilla-Rivero, S. (1993) Does public capital affect private sector performance? An analysis of the Spanish case, 1964–88, *Economic Modelling* 10: 179–85.

Balassa, B. (1961) *The Theory of Economic Integration,* New York: Richard Irwin.

Balwin, R.E. (1994) *Towards an Integrated Europe*, London: Centre for Economic Policy Research.

Barro, R.J. (1991) Economic growth in a cross section of countries, *Quarterly Journal of Economics* 106: 407–43.

Barro, R.J. and Becker, G.S. (1989) Fertility choice in a model of economic growth, *Econometrica* 57: 481–501.

Barro, R.J. and Sala-i-Martin, X. (1991) Convergence across states and regions, *Brookings Papers on Economic Activity* 1: 107–82.

Barro, R.J. and Sala-i-Martin, X. (1992a) Convergence, *Journal of Political Economy* 100: 223–51.

Barro, R.J. and Sala-i-Martin, X. (1992b) Regional growth and migration: a Japanese–US comparison, *Journal of the Japanese and the International Economies* 6: 256–78.

Barro, R.J. and Sala-i-Martin, X. (1995) *Economic Growth*, New York: McGraw-Hill.

Barros, P.P. and Garoupa, N. (1995) Portugal–EU convergence: some evidence, mimeo

Bartels, C.P.A., Boonstra, D. and Vlessert, H.H. (1983) *Prospects for the Regional Development of the Tertiary Sector,* Oudmelon: Buro Bartels.

Baumol, W.J. (1967) Macroeconomics of unbalanced growth: the anatomy of the urban crisis, *American Economic Review* 57: 415–26.

Baumol, W.J. (1986) Productivity growth, convergence and welfare: what the long run data show, *American Economic Review* 76: 1075–85.

Becker, G.S. and Barro, R.J. (1988) A reformulation of the economic theory of fertility, *Quarterly Journal of Economics* 103:1–25.

Becker, G.S., Murphy, K.M. and Tamura, R.F. (1990) Human capital, fertility and economic growth, *Journal of Political Economy* 98: S12–S37.

Begg, I. (1989) European integration and regional policy, *Oxford Review of Economic Policy* 5: 90–104.

Berdt, E.R. and Hansson, B. (1991) Measuring the contribution of public infrastructure capital in Sweden, *National Bureau of Economic Research Working Paper* 3842.

Bernard, A.B. and Durlauf, S.N. (1991), Interpreting tests of the convergence hypothesis, Working Paper, Stanford University.

Berry, D.M. and Kaserman, D.L. (1993) A diffusion model of long-run state economic development, *Atlantic Economic Journal* 21: 39–54.

Biehl, D. (1986) *The Contribution of Infrastructure to Regional Development,* Regional Policy Division, European Communities, Brussels.

Biehl, D. (1991) The role of infrastructure in regional development, in Vickerman, R.W. (ed), *Infrastructure and Regional Development*, London, Pion.

Bishop, J.A., Formby, J.P and Thistle, P.D. (1994) Convergence and divergence of regional income distributions and welfare, *Review of Economics and Statistics* 79: 228–34.

Blanchard, J.B. and Katz, L.F. (1992) Regional evolutions, *Brookings Papers on Economic Activity* 1:1992: 1–75.

Borjas, G.J. (1989) Economic theory and international migration, *International Migration Review* 23: 457–85.

Borts, G. (1960) The equalisation of returns and regional economic growth, *American Economic Review* 50: 319–47.

Botham, R.W. (1980) The regional development effects of road investment, *Transportation Planning and Technology* 6: 97–108.

Breheny, M. and McQuaid, R.W. (1987) High-tech UK – the development of the United Kingdom's major centre in high technology industries, in Breheny, M. and McQuaid, R.W. (eds), *The Development of High Technology Industries: an International Survey*, Croom Helm, London.

Breusch, T. and Pagan, A. (1980) The LM test and its application to model specification in econometrics, *Review of Economic Studies* 47: 239–54.

Briggs, R. (1981) Interstate highway system and development in non-metropolitan areas, *Transportation Research Record* 812: 9–12.

Brown, A.J. (1992) *The Framework of Regional Economics in the United Kingdom,* Cambridge, Cambridge University Press.

Bruinsma, F.R., Rienstra, S.A. and Rietveld, P. (1997) Economic impacts of the construction of a transport corridor: a multi-level and multi-approach case study for the construction of the A1 highway in the Netherlands, *Regional Studies* 31: 391–403.

Budd, L. (1997) Regional integration and convergence and the problems of fiscal and monetary systems: some lessons from Eastern Europe, *Regional Studies* 31: 559–70.

Button, K.J. (1996) Ownership, investment and pricing of transport and communications infrastructure in France by means of regionally estimated production functions, in Batten, D.F. and Karlsson, C. (eds), *Infrastructure and the Complexity of Economic Development,* Berlin: Springer-Verlag. .

Button, K.J. (1998a) The three faces of synthesis: bringing together quantitative findings in the field of transport and environmental policy, *Environment and Planning C, Government and Policy* 16: 516–28

Button, K.J. (1998b) Infrastructure investment, endogenous growth and economic convergence, *Annals of Regional Science* 32: 145–63.

Button, K.J. and Fleming, M.C., (1992) The professions in the Single European Market: a case study of architects in the UK, *Journal of Common Market Studies* 30: 403–18.

Button, K.J. and Pentecost, E.J. (1993a) Regional service sector convergence, *Regional Studies* 27: 623–36.

Button, K.J. and Pentecost, E.J. (1993b) Measuring convergence of the EC regional economies, paper to the Royal Economics Society Annual Conference, York.

Button, K.J. and Pentecost, E.J. (1993c) EC regional economic development, paper presented at the Annual Conference of the Regional Science International, Nottingham.

Button, K.J. and Pentecost, E.J. (1995a) Regional economic convergence in Great Britain and Germany, in Armstrong, H. and Vickerman, R. (eds), *Convergence and Divergence among European Regions*, London: Pion.

Button, K.J. and Pentecost, E.J. (1995b) Testing for convergence of the EU regional economies' *Economic Inquiry* 33: 664–71

Button, K.J. and Rietveld, P. (1999) A meta-analysis of the impact of infrastructure policy on regional development, in H. Kohno, P. Nijkamp and J. Poot (eds.) *Regional Cohesion and Competition in the Process of Globalisation: Vol. 2, General Trends and Policies*, Berlin: Spinger-Verlag.

Button, K.J., Jongma, S. and Kerr, J. (1999a) Meta-analysis approaches and applied microeconomics, in S.B. Dahiya (ed), *The Current State of Economic Science*, Rohtak: Spellbound Publications.

Button, K.J., Lall, S., Stough, R. and Trice, M. (1999b) High-technology employment and hub airports, *Journal of Air Transport Management* (forthcoming)

Cappellin, R. (1989) The diffusion of producer services in the urban system, in Cappellin, R. and Nijkamp, P. (eds), *Theories and Policies of Technological Developments at the Local Level*, Aldershot: Gower.

Cardoso, A.R. (1993) Regional inequalities in Europe – have they really been decreasing?, *Applied Economics* 25: 1093–100.

Carlino, G.A. (1992) Are regional per capita earning diverging? *Business Review* (Federal Reserve Bank of Philadelphia) 1–12.

Cashin, P. A. (1993) *Essays on Economic Growth: the Effect of Government on Growth and an Analysis of Growth in, and Convergence Across, the Seven Colonies of Australia*, PhD thesis, Yale University.

Cashin, P.A. (1995) Economic growth and convergence across the seven colonies of Australia: 1861–1991, *Economic Record* 71: 132–44.

Cashin, P.A.and Loayza, N. (1995) 'Paradise Lost'? Growth, convergence and migration in the South Pacific, *IMF Staff Papers*, 42: 608–41.

Cecchini, P. (1988) *The European Challenge: 1992, The Benefits of the Single European Market*, Aldershot: Wildwood.

Chatterji, M. and Dewhurst, J.H.L. (1996) Convergence clubs and relative economic performance in Great Britain: 1977–1991, *Regional Studies* 30: 31–40.

Cheshire, P., Camagi, R., de Gaudemar, J.-P. and Cuadrado Roura, J.R. (1991) 1957 to 1992: moving towards a Europe of regions and regional policy, in Rodwin, L. and Sazanami, H. (eds), *Industrial Change and Regional Economic Transformation: The Experience of Western Europe*, London: Harper Collins.

Chisholm, M. (1989) Regional variations in transport costs in Britain, with special reference to Scotland, *Transactions of the Institute of British Geographers* 12: 303–14.

Christodoulakis. N. (1993)*Public Infrastructure and Private Productivity: A Discussion of Empirical Studies and an Application to Greece*, Athens: Athens University of Economics and Business.

Cingolani, M. (1993) Disparités regionales de produit par téte dans la Communauté Européenne, *EIB Papers* 19: 7–41.

Cleary, W.J. and Thomas, R.E. (1973) The economic consequences of the Severn Bridge and its associated motorways, Bath: University of Bath.

Commission of the European Communities (1988) *Peripheral Regions in a Community of Twelve Member States*, Luxembourg: OOPEC.

Commission of the European Communities (1989) *Guide to the Reform of the Community's Structural Funds,* Luxembourg: OOPEC.

Commission of the European Communities (1991) *As regiões na década de 1990 – quarto relarório periódico relativo à situação sócio-económica e ao desenvolvimento das regiõs da Comunidade*, Luxembourg: OOPEC.

Commission of the European Communities (1992)*Transport Infrastructure*, Document COM(92) 231 Final, Brussels: European Commission

Commission of the European Communities (1994) *Competitiveness and Cohesion Trends in the Regions: Fifth Periodic Report on the Social and Economic Situation and Development of the Regions of the Community*. Luxembourg: OOPEC.

Commission of the European Communities (1999) *Sixth Periodic Report on the Social and Economic Situation and Development of the Regions of the European Union,* Luxembourg : European Commission.

Costa, J., da Silva Ellson, R.W. and Martin, R.C. (1987) Public capital, regional output and development: some empirical evidence, *Journal of Regional Science* 27: 419–37.

Coulomb, S. and Lee, F. (1993) Regional economic disparities in Canada mimeo.

Cuadrado Roura, J.R. and Suárez-Villa, L. (1992) Regional economic integration and the evolution of disparities, paper to the World Congress of the Regional Science Association, Palma de Mallorca.

Curlino, G.A. and Mills, L.O. (1993) Are US regional incomes converging? *Journal of Monetary Economics* 32:335–46.

Cuthbertson, K. (1988) Expectations, learning and the Kalman filter, *Manchester School* 56: 233–46.

Dalenberg, D. (1989) *Estimates of Elasticities of Substitution between Public and Private Inputs in the Manufacturing Sector of Metropolitan Areas*, PhD thesis, University of Oregon.

Davis, S. (1979) *The Diffusion of Process Innovations*, Cambridge: Cambridge University Press.

De Grauwe, P. (1997) *The Economics of Monetary Integration*, 3rd. Edn Oxford: Oxford University Press.

De La Fuente, A. and Vives, X. (1995) Infrastructure and education as instruments of regional policy: evidence from Spain, *Economic Policy* 11–51.

De Long, J.B. (1988) Productivity growth, convergence, and welfare: comment, *American Economic Review* 78: 1138–54

Demertzis, M. and Hallett, A.H. (1996) Regional regularities and the business cycle: an exploration of the rise in European unemployment, *Regional Studies* 30: 15–29.

Despicht, N.S. and Flockton, C. (1970) Regional policy in the European Communities: the shadow of integration, *Loughborough Journal of Social Sciences*, 9: 24–41.

Diamond, D. and Spence, N. (1989) *Infrastructure and Industrial Costs in British Industry*, London: HMSO.

Dickey, D.A. and Fuller, W.A. (1979) Distribution of the estimators for autoregressive time series with a unit root, *Journal of the American Statistical Association* 74: 427–31.

Di Liberto, A. (1994) Convergence across Italian regions, *Nota di Lavora*, 68.94, Fondazione Eni Enrico Matteri.

Dixon, R. and Thirlwall, A.P. (1975) A model of regional growth-rate differences on Kaldorian lines, *Oxford Economic Papers* 27: 201–14.

Dodgson, J..S. (1974) Motorway investment, industrial transport costs and subregional growth: the M62 case-study, *Regional Studies* 8: 75–91.

Dowrick, S. and Nguyen, D.-T. (1989) OECD comparative economic growth 1950–85: catch-up and convergence, *American Economic Review* 79: 1010–30.

Duffy-Deno, K. and Eberts, R.W. (1991) Public infrastructure and regional economic development: a simultaneous approach, *Journal of Urban Economics* 30: 329–43.

Durlauf, S.N. and Johnson, P.A. (1992) Local versus global convergence across national economies, LSE Financial Markets Group Discussion Papers Series, no.131.

Durlauf, S.N. and Quah, D.T. (1998) The new empirics of economic growth, *National Bureau of Economic Research Working Paper* 6422.

Eagle, D. and Stephanedes, Y.J. (1987) Dynamic highway impacts on economic development, *Transportation Research Record* 1116: 56–62.

Eberts, R.W. and Fogarty, M.S. (1987) *Estimating the Relationship between Local Public and Private Investment.* Working Paper 8703. Federal Reserve Bank of Cleveland.

Elfring, T. (1989) New evidence on the expansion of service employment in advanced economies, *Review of Income and Wealth* 35: 409–40.

Emerson, M., Gros, D., Italianer, A., Pisani-Ferry, J. and Reichenbach, H. (1992) *One Market, One Money*, Oxford: Oxford University Press.

European Commission (1973) *Report on the Regional Problems in the Enlarged Community,* COM (73)550, Brussels: EEC.

European Commission (1977) *Report of the Study Group on the Role of Public Finance in European Integration*, Brussels: EEC.

European Economy (1993), *Stable Money and Sound Finances: Community Public Finance in the Perspective of EMU, Report of an Independent Group of Economists*, Brussels: Commission of the European Communities, Directorate-General for Economic and Financial Affairs, no. 53.

Eurostat (1990) *Regions Statistical Yearbook 1989*, Luxembourg: OOPEC.

Evans, J.L. and Pentecost, E.J. (1998) Economic performance of UK regions: convergence or divergence?, *Environment and Planning C, Government and Policy* 16: 649–658

Evans, P. and Karras, G. (1994) Is government capital productive? Evidence from a panel of seven countries, *Journal of Macroeconomics* 16: 271–9

Evers, G.H.M., van der Meer, P.H., Oosterhaven, J. and Polak, J.B. (1987) Regional impacts of new transport infrastructure: a multi-sector potentials approach, *Transportation* 14: 113–26.

Fagerberg, J. and Verspagen, B. (1995) Convergence or divergence in the European Union: theory and fact, paper presented at the 2nd Conference on Economic Integration and Regional Gaps, Cagliari.

Fagerberg, J., Verspagen, B. and Caniels, M. (1997) Technology, growth and unemployment across European regions, *Regional Studies* 31: 457–66.

Fogel, R.W. (1964) *Railroads and American Economic Growth: Essays in Econometric History*, Baltimore: Johns Hopkins University Press.

Fontaine, C. (1987) *L'expansion des services. Un quart de siècle en France et dans le monde,* Paris,I-III. Rexervices.

Ford, R. and Poret, P. (1991) *Infrastructure and Private Sector Productivity*, OECD–ESD Working Paper 91, Paris.

Forrest, D., Glen, J. and Hart, D. (1987) Both sides of the track are wrong: a study of the effect of an urban railway system on the pattern of house prices, Proceedings of the UTGS 24th Annual Conference, Newcastle.

Fothergill, S., Monk, S. and Hart, D. (1987) *Property and Industrial Development*, London: Hutchinson.

Freeman, R. (1988) Immigration, trade and capital flows in the American economy, in Baker, L. and Miller, P. (eds), *The Economics of Migration*, Canberra: Australian Government Publishing Services.

Fuchs, V.R. (1985) An agenda for research on the service sector, in Inman, R.P. (ed), *Managing the Service Economy: Prospects and Problems*, Cambridge: Cambridge University Press.

Fukuchi, T. (1978) An analyse economico-politique d'un developpement régional harmonisé, *Collections de L'Insee, Serie C* 61: 227–53.

Garcia-Milà, T. and Marimon, R. (1995) Regional integration and public investment in Spain, paper presented at the 2nd Conference on Economic Integration and Regional Gaps, Cagliari.

Gillespie, A. and Green, A. (1987) The changing geography of producer service employment in Britain, *Regional Studies* 21: 397–411.

Giuliano, G. (1989) New directions for understanding transportation and land use, *Environment and Planning A* 21: 145–59.

Glass, G.V. (1976) Primary, secondary, and meta-analysis of research, *Educational Researcher* 5: 3–8.

Goodhart, C.A.E. and Smith, S. (1993), Stabilisation, in *European Economy: The Economics of Community Public Finance, Reports and Studies*, Brussels: Commission of the European Communities, Directorate-General for Economic and Financial Affairs, no. 5, .

Gramlich, E.M. (1994) Infrastructure investment: a review essay, *Journal of Economic Literature* 32: 1176–96.

Graziani, A. (1978) The Mezzogiorno in the Italian economy, *Cambridge Journal of Economics* 2: 355–72.

Greene, W. (1993) *Econometric Analysis* 2[nd] Edn, New York: Macmillan.

Grossman, G.M. and Helpman, E. (1990) Comparative advantage and long-run growth, *American Economic Review* 80: 796–815.

Grossman, G.M. and Helpman, E. (1994) Endogenous innovation in the theory of growth, *Journal of Economic Perspectives* 8: 23–44.

Gudgin, G. (1983) *Job Generation in the Service Sector*, Department of Applied Economics, University of Cambridge.

Gwilliam, K.M. (1979) Transport infrastructure investments and regional development in Bowers (ed). *Inflation, Development and Integration – Essays in Honour of A.J. Brown*, Leeds: Leeds University Press.

Hakfoort, J.R., de Haan, J. and Sturm, J.E. (1993) Investeringen in infrastructuur en economische groei, *ESB*, 670–72.

Haldane, A.G. and Hall, S.G. (1991) Sterling's relationship with the dollar and the Deutchmark *Economic Journal* 101: 436–43.

Hall, S.G., Robertson, D. and Wickens, M.R. (1992) Measuring convergence of the EC economies, *Manchester School* 60 (Supplement): 99–111.

Harberger, A. C. (1998) A vision of the growth process, *American Economic Review,* 88: 1-32.

Herzog, H.W., Schlottman, A.M and Johnson, D.L. (1986) High-technology jobs and worker mobility, *Journal of Regional Science*, 26: 145–59.

Hill, T.P. (1977) On goods and services, *Review of Income and Wealth* 23, 315–38.

Hirschman, O.A. (1958) *The Strategy of Economic Development*, New Haven: Yale University Press.

Hofer, H. and Worgotter, A. (1997) Regional trends in British manufacturing employment: tests for stationarity and co-integration, 1952–1989, *Regional Studies* 37:13–24.

Holden, K. and Thompson, J. (1992), Co-integration: an introductory survey, *British Review of Economic Issues* 14: 1–56.

Holtz-Eakin, D. (1992) Public sector capital and productivity puzzle, National *Bureau of Economic Research Working Paper* 4122.

Howells, J. (1988) *Economic, Technological and Locational Trends in European Services*, Aldershot: Avebury.

Howells, J. and Green, A.E. (1988) *Technological Innovation, Structural Change and Location in the UK Services*, Aldershot: Avebury.

Hulten, C.R. and Schwab, R.M. (1991) Public capital formation and the growth of regional manufacturing industries, *National Tax Journal* 44: 121–34.

Illeris, S. (1989) *Services and Regions in Europe*, Aldershot: Avebury.

Jimeno, J.F. and Betolila, S. (1995) Regional unemployment persistence (Spain 1976–1994), Documento de Trabajo de FEDEA 95–09.

Jin, F. (1995) Cointegration of consumption and disposable income: evidence from twelve OECD countries, *Southern Economic Journal* 62: 77–88.

Jorgenson, D. (1991) Fragile statistical foundations: the macroeconomics of public infrastructure investment, comment on Hulten and Schwab (1991) when presented at the *American Enterprise Institute Conference on Infrastructure Needs and Policy Options for the 1990s*, Washington.

Judge, E.J. (1983) Regional issues and transport infrastructure: some reflections on the effects of the Lancashire–Yorkshire motorway, in Button, K.J. and Gillingwater, D. (eds.) *Transport, Location and Spatial Policy*, Aldershot: Gower.

Kaldor, N. (1957) A model of economic growth, *Economic Journal*, 67: 591-624.

Kaldor, N. (1961) Capital accumulation and economic growth, in Lutz, F.A. and Hague, D.C. (eds), *The Theory of Capital*, New York: St Martins Press.

Kaldor, N. (1970) The case for regional policies, *Scottish Journal of Political Economy* 17: 337–47.

Kaldor, N. (1975) Economic growth and the Verdoorn Law, *Economic Journal* 85: 891–96.

Kamien, M.I. and Schwartz, N.L. (1982) *Market Structure and Innovation*, Cambridge: Cambridge University Press.

Keeble, D., Offord, J. and Walker, S. (1988) *Peripheral Regions in a Community of Twelve Member States*, Luxembourg: OOPEC.

Keeble, D., Owens, P. and Thompson, C. (1981) *The Influence of Peripheral and Central Locations on the Relative Development of Regions*, Department of Geography: University of Cambridge.

Keeler, T.E. and Ying, J.S. (1988) Measuring benefits of a large public investment: the case of the US Federal-aid Highway System, *Journal of Public Economics* 36: 69–85.

Keil, S.R. (1997) Regional trends in British manufacturing employment: tests for stationarity and co-integration, 1952–1989, *Regional Studies* 31: 13–24.

Kelijian, H.H. and Robinson, D.P. (1995) Infrastructure productivity: a razor's edge, *Papers of Regional Science* (forthcoming)

Koopmans, T.C. (1965) On the concept of optimal economic growth, in *Study Week on the Econometric Approach to Development Planning*, Pontificiae Academiae Scientiarum Scripta varia, no. 28, Chicago: Rand McNally.

Kravis, I.B., Heston, A. and Summers, R. (1982) *World Product and Income: International Comparisons of Real Gross Product*, Baltimore: Johns Hopkins University Press.

Kremer, M. (1993) Population growth and technological change: one million BC to 1990, *Quarterly Journal of Economics* 108: 681–716.

Krugman, P. R. (1995) *Development, Geography, and Economic Theory*, Cambridge, Mass: MIT Press.

Krugman, P.R. (1979) A model of innovation, technology transfer and the world distribution of income, *Journal of Political Economy* 253–66.

Krugman, P.R. (1981) Trade accumulation and uneven development, *Journal* of *Development Economics* 8: 149–61.

Krugman, P.R. (1991) History and industrial; location: the case of the manufacturing belt, *American Economic Review, Papers and Proceedings* 81: 80–3.

Krugman, P. and Venables, A. (1990) Integration and the competitiveness of peripheral industry, in Braga de Macedo, J. and Bliss, C. (eds.) *Unity with Diversity within the European Economy: The Community's Southern Frontier,* Cambridge: Cambridge University Press.

Lakshmanan, T.R. (1989) Infrastructure and economic transformation, in Andersson, A.E., Batten, D.F., Johansson, B. and Nijkamp, P. (eds), *Advances in Spatial Theory and Dynamics,* Amsterdam: North-Holland.

Langley, C.J. (1981) Highways and property values: the Washington Beltway revisited, *Transportation Research Record*, 812: 16–21.

Larre, B. and Torres, R. (1991) Is convergence a spontaneous process? The experiences of Spain, Portugal and Greece, *OECD Economic Studies* 16:169–98.

Leamer, E. (1993) The convergence hypothesis and measurement errors, in Frisch, H. and Worgotter A. (eds), *Open Economy Macroeconomics*, London: Macmillan.

Lee, K., Pesaran, M.H. and Smith, R. (1996), Growth and convergence: a multi-country empirical analysis of the Solow growth model, University of Leicester.

Leitham, S. (1993) Predicting the economic development effects of transportation projects, Proceedings of the 25th Annual Conference of the Universities Transport Research Group, Southampton.

Lengellé, M. (1980) The development of the service sector in OECD countries and its implications for the Western World, in Leveson, I. and Wheeler, T (eds), *Western Economies in Transition: Structural Change and Adjustment Policies in Industrial Countries*, Boulder: Westview Press.

Leonardi, R. (ed) (1993) *The Regions and the European Community,* London: Frank Cass.

Levine, R. and Renelt, D. (1992) A sensitivity analysis of cross-country growth regressions, *American Economic Review,* 82:942–63.

Love, J.H., Stephen, F.H., Gillanders, D.D. and Paterson, A.A. (1992) Spatial aspects of deregulation in the market for legal services, *Regional Studies* 26: 137–48.

Lucas, R.E. (1988) On the mechanics of economic development, *Journal of Monetary Economics* 22: 3–42.

Lucas, R.E. (1990) Why doesn't capital flow from the rich to poor countries? *American Economic Review* 80: 92–6.

Lynch, M. (1994) Applied economics: linking transportation policy and economic growth, paper to *Canadian Transportation Research Forum Conference*, Victoria.

Lynde, C. and Richmond, J. (1992) The role of public capital in production, *Review of Economics and Statistics* 74: 37–44.

Mackay, R.R. (1993) A Europe of the regions: a role for nonmarket forces?, *Regional Studies* 27: 419–31.

Mackie, P.J. and Simon, D. (1986) Do road projects benefit industry, *Journal of Transport Economics and Policy* 20: 377–84.

Majocchi, A and Rey, M. (1993), A special financial support scheme, in Economic and Monetary Union, *European Economy: The Economics of Community Public Finance, Reports and Studies*, Brussels: Commission of the European Communities, Directorate-General for Economic and Financial Affairs, no. 5.

Mallick, R. and Carayannis, E.G. (1994) Regional economic convergence in Mexico: an analysis by industry, *Growth and Change* 25: 325–34.

Mankiw, N.G. (1995) The growth of nations, *Brookings Papers on Economic Activity* 1: 275–310.

Mankiw, G.N., Romer, D. and Weil, D.N. (1992) The empirics of economic growth *Quarterly Journal of Economics* 107: 407–37.

Markusen, A. (1996) Interaction between regional and industrial policies, *International Regional Science Review* 19: 49–78.

Marshall, J.N. (1992) The growth of service activities and the evolution of spatial disparities, in Martin, R. and Townroe, P. (eds), *Regional Development in the 1990s: The British Isles in Transition*, London: Jesica Kingsley/Regional Studies Association.

Marshall, J.N., Alderman, N. and Thwaites, A.T. (1991) Civil service relocation and the English regions, *Regional Studies* 25: 499–510.

Martin, R. (1993) Remapping British regional policy: the end of the North-South divide? *Regional Studies* 27: 797–806.

Martin, R. and Sunley, P. (1998) Slow convergence? The new endogenous growth theory and regional development, *Economic Geography* 74: 201–27.

Mauro, L. and Podrecca, E. (1994) The case of Italian regions: converegence or dualism?, *Economic Notes by Monte dei Paschi di Siena* 24: 447–72.

McCombie, J.S.L. (1988a) A synoptic view of regional growth and unemployment: I – the neoclassical theory, *Urban Studies* 25: 267–81.

McCombie, J.S.L. (1988b) A synoptic view of regional growth and unemployment: II – the post-Keynesian theory, *Urban Studies* 25: 399–417.

McQuaid, R.W., Nelson, J.D., Leitham, S. and Esslemont, J.W. (1993) European regional policy, transport infrastructure and economic development, *Proceedings of Seminar E, PTRC 21st Annual Conference*, University of Manchester Institute of Science and Technology.

Mera, K. (1973) Regional production functions and social overhead capital: an analysis of the Japanese case, *Regional and Urban Economics* 3: 157–86.

Merriman, D. (1990) Public capital and regional output: another look at some Japanese and American data, *Regional Science and Urban Economics* 23: 436–48.

Metcalfe, J.S. (1981) Impulse and diffusion in the study of technical change, *Futures* 13: 347–59.

Mills, D.E. (1981) Ownership arrangements and congestion-prone facilities, *American Economic Review* 7: 493–502.

Milne, W.J. (1993) Income convergence across Canadian provinces: does growth theory help explain the process? mimeo.

Mintz, J.M. and Preston, R.S (eds) (1993) *Infrastructure and Competitiveness,* Ottawa: John Deutsch Institute for the Study of Economic Policy.

Molho, I. (1986) Theories of migration: a review, *Scottish Journal of Political Economy* 33: 396–419.

Molle, W.T.M. (1990a) *The Economics of European Integration (Theory, Practice, Policy)*, Aldershot: Dartmouth.

Molle, W.T.M. (1990b) Will the completion of internal market lead to regional divergence? in Siebert, H. (ed), *The Completion of the Internal Market,* Kiel: Institut für Weltwirtschaft.

Molle, W.T.M. with van Holst, B. and Smit, H. (1980) *Regional Disparity and Economic Development in the European Community,* Farnborough: Saxon House.

Moon, H.E. (1986) Interstate highway interchanges as instigators of nonmetropolitan development, *Transportation Research Record* 1125: 8–14.

Moore, B. and Rhodes, J. (1973) Evaluating the effects of British regional economic policy, *Economic Journal* 83: 87–110.

Morrill, R., Gaile, G.L. and Thrall, G.I. (1988) *Spatial Diffusion*, Beverly Hills: Sage.

Morrison, C.J. (1993) Macroeconomic relationships between public spending on infrastructure and private sector productivity in the United States, in Mintz, J..M. and Preston, R.S. (eds), *Infrastructure and Competiveness*, Ottawa: John Deutsch Institute for the Study of Economic Policy.

Munnell, A.H. (1990) Is there a shortfall in public capital investment?, *New England Economic Review* September/October: 11–32.

Munnell, AH (1992) Infrastructure investment and economic growth, *Journal of Economic Perspectives* 6: 189–98.

Myrdal, G. (1957) *Economic Theory and Underdeveloped Regions,* London: Macmillan.

Nadiri, I. and Mamuneas, T. (1996) *Contribution of Highway Capital to Industry and National Productivity Growth*, Washington: Federal Highway Adminstration Office of Policy Development.

Neven, D.J. and Gouyette, C. (1994) Regional convergence in the European Community, *CEPR* DP 914, London.

Nijkamp, P. and Poot, J. (1993) Technical progress and spatial dynamics: a theoretical reflection, in Kohno, H. and Nijkamp, P. (eds), *Potentials and Bottlenecks of Spatial Economic Development*, Berlin: Springer Verlag.

Nijkamp, P. and Poot, J. (1998) Spatial persocctives on new theories of economic growth, *Annals of Regional Science* 32: 7–38.

Noyelle, T.J. and Stanback, T.M. (1984), *The Economic Transformation of American Cities*, New Jersey: Rowman and Allanhold.

Nurske, R. (1953) *Problems of Capital Formation in Developing Countries,* Oxford: Basil Blackwell.

Ochel, W. and Wegner, M. (1987), *Service Economies in Europe: Opportunities for Growth*, London: Pinter.

Oniki, H. and Uzawa, H. (1965) Patterns of trade and investment in a dynamic model of international trade, *Review of Economic Studies* 32: 15–38.

Organisation for Economic Cooperation and Development (1989) *Employment Outlook* (July), Paris: OECD.

Oxley, L. and Greasley, D. (1995) A time-series perspective on convergence: Australia, UK and USA since 1870, *Economic Record* 71: 259–70.

Owen Smith, E. (1994) *The German Economy*, London: Routeledge.

Paci, R. and Pigliaru, F. (1995) $\beta$-convergence and/or structural change? Evidence from the Italian regions, paper presented at the 2nd Conference on Economic Integration and Regional Gaps, Cagliari.

Pearce, I.F. (1972) Some aspects of European monetary integration, paper presented at the Bournemouth Conference of the Money Study Group.

Perrson, J. (1994) Convergence in per capita income and migration across Swedish Counties 1906–90, Stockholm: Institute for International Economic Studies.

Pickett, M.W.and Perrett, K.E. (1984) The effect of the Tyne and Wear Metro on residential property values, *Transport and Road Research Laboratory Supplementary Report* SR 825, Crowthorne.

Pinnoi, N. (1994) Public infrastructure and private production: measuring relative contributions, *Journal of Economic Behaviour and Organisation* 23: 127–48.

Polese, M. (1982) Regional demand for business services and interregional service flows in a small Canadian region, *Papers of the Regional Science Association* 50: 151–63.

Poot, J. (1993) Trans-Tasman migration and economic growth in Australasia, in Carmichael, G. (ed). *Trans-Tasman Migration: Trends, Causes and Consequences*, Canberra: Australian Government Publishing Service.

Prud'homme, R. (1996) Assessing the role of infrastructrure in France by means of regionally estimated production functions, in Batten, D.F. and Karlsson, C. (eds), *Infrastructure and the Complexity of Economic Development,* Berlin: Springer-Verlag.

Quah, D. (1993) Empirical cross-section dynamics in economic growth, *European Economic Review*, 37: 426–34.

Quah, D. (1996) Empirics for economic growth and convergence, *European Economic Review* 40: 1353–76.

Ratner, J.B. (1983) Government capital, employment and the production function for US private output, *Economic Letters* 13: 213–7.

Richardson, H.W. (1973) *Regional Growth Theory,* London: Macmillan.

Richardson, H.W. (1974) Regional growth revisited, *Review of Regional Studies* 4: 1–15.

Rietveld, P. (1989) Infrastructure and regional development, *Annals of Regional Science* 23: 255–74.

Rietveld, P. (1995) Transport infrastructure and the economy, in Organisation for Economic Co-operation and Development, *Investment, Productivity and Employment*, Paris: OECD.

Rietveld, P. and Bruinsma, F. (1998) *Is Transport Infrastructure Effective? Transport Infrastructure and Accessibility: Impacts on the Space Economy*, Berlin: Springer.

Rivera-Batiz, L.A. and Romer, P.M. (1991) Economic integration and endogenous growth, *Quarterly Journal of Economics* 106: 531–56.

Rodwin, L. and Sazanami, H. (eds) (1991) *Industrial Change and Regional Economic Transformation: The Experience of Western Europe*, London: HarperCollins.

Romer, P.M. (1986) Increasing returns and long-run growth, *Journal of Political Economy* 94: 1002–37.

Romer, P.M. (1990a) Are non-convexities important for understanding growth? *American Economic Review* 80: 97–103.

Romer, P.M. (1990b) Endogenous technical change, *Journal of Political Economy* 98: S71–S102

Romer, P.M. (1994a) New goods, old theory and the welfare costs of trade restrictions, *Journal of Development Economics,* 43: 5-38.

Sala-i-Martin, X. (1994) Cross-sectional regressions and the empirics of economic growth, *European Economic Review* 38: 739–47.

Sala-i-Martin, X. (1996) Regional cohesion: evidence and theories of regional growth and convergence, *European Economic Review* 40: 1325–52.

Sala-i-Martin, X. (1997) I just ran two million regressions, *American Economic Review, Papers and Proceedings* 87: 178–83.

Sarafoglou, N., Anderson, A., Holmberg, I. and Ohlsson, O. (1994) Spatial infrastructure and productivity in Sweden, paper presented at the *34th European Congress of the Regional Science Association*. Groninggen.

Schmenner, R.W. (1982) *Making Business Location Decisions*, Englewood Cliffs: Prentice-Hall.

Scott, M. (1989) *A New View of Economic Growth*, Oxford: Basil Blackwell.

Seitz, H. (1994) Public infrastructure capital, employment and private capital formation, paper to OECD Conference on Capital Formation and Employment, Amsterdam.

Sharp, C.H. (1980) Transport and regional development with special reference to Britain, *Transport Policy and Decision Making*, 1:1–11,

Shioji, E. (1993) Regional growth in Japan, Department of Economics, University of Yale.

Simms, J.O. (1995) *Convergence, Endogenous Growth and Development in the Regions of Europe*, PhD. thesis, University of London.

Simon, H.A. (1978) Rationality as process and as product of thought, *American Economic Review* 68: 1–16.

Smith, N. (1984) *Uneven Development*, Oxford: Basil Blackwell.

Solow, R.M. (1956) A contribution to the theory of economic growth, *Quarterly Journal of Economics* 70: 65–94.

Solow, R.M. (1994) Perspectives on growth theory, *Journal of Economic Perspectives*, 8: 45-54.

Stephanedes, Y.J. (1990) Distributional effects of state highway investment on local and regional development, *Transportation Research Record*, 1274: 156

Stephanedes, Y.J. and Eagle, M.E. (1986) Time-series analysis of interactions between transportation and manufacturing and retail employment, *Transportation Research Record* 1074.

Stigler, G. (1956), *Trends in Employment in the Service Industry*, Princeton: National Bureau for Economic Research.

Sturm, J.E. and de Haan, J. (1995) Is public expenditure really productive? New evidence for the USA and the Netherlands, *Economic Modelling* 12: 60–72.

Sutherland, P. (1986) Europe and the principle of convergence, *Regional Studies* 20: 371–7.

Swan, T.W. (1956) Economic growth and capital accumulation, *Economic Record* 32: 334–61.

Swann, D. (ed.) (1992) *The Single European Market and Beyond. A Study of the Eider Implications of the Single European Act*, London: Routledge.

Talley, W. (1996) Linkages between transportation infrastructure and economic production, *Logistics and Transportation Review* 32: 145–54.

Tam, M.S. and Persky, J. (1982) Regional convergence and national inequality, *Review of Economics and Statistics*, 64:161–71.

Tatom, J.A. (1991) Public capital and private sector performance, *Federal Reserve Bank of St Louis Review* 73: 3–15.

Tatom, J.A. (1993) Paved with good intentions: the mythical national infrastructure crisis, *Policy Analysis* 196: 1–12.

Taylor J. and Lewney, R. (1993) *Regional Economic Prospects: Analysis and Forecasts to 2005*, Cambridge: Cambridge Econometrics.

Taylor, J. and Wren, C. (1997) UK regional policy: an evaluation, *Regional Studies,* 31: 835–48.

Temple, J. (1999) The new growth evidence, *Journal of Economic Literature*, 37: 112–156.

Thirlwell, A.P. (1974) Regional economic disparities and regional policy in the Common Market, *Urban Studies* 11: 1–12.

Toen-Gout, M.W. and Jongeling, M.M. (1993) Investeringen in infrastuctuur en economische groie, *ESB,* 424–7.

Verdoorn, P.J. (1949) Fattori che regolano la sviluppo della produttita del lavoro [Factors governing the growth of labour productivity], *L'Industria* 1: 3–10. English translation by Thirlwall, A.P. and Thirwall, G. in *Research in Population and Economics*, 1979.

Vickerman, R.W. (1991) Transport infrastructure in the European Community: new developments, regional implications and evaluation, in Vickerman, R.W. (ed), *Infrastructure and Regional Development*, London: Pion.

Wabe, J.S. (1986) The regional impact of de-industrialisation in the European Community, *Regional Studies* 20: 23–6.

Watterson, W.T. (1986) Estimating economic and development impacts of transit investment, *Transportation Research Record* 1046: 1–9.

White, K.J. (1978) A general computer program for econometric applications – SHAZAM, *Econometrica* 46: 239–40.

Williamson, J. (1976) The implication of European monetary integration for the peripheral areas, in Vaisey, J. (ed.) *Economic Sovereignty and Regional Policy*, Dublin: Gill and Macmillan.

Wilson, F.R., Stevens, A.M. and Holyoke, T.R. (1982) Impact of transportation on regional development, *Transportation Research Record* 851: 13–6.

Winston, C (1991) Efficient transportation infrastructure policy, *Journal of Economic Literature* 5: 113–27.

Wise, M. and Chalkley, B. (1990) Unemployment: regional policy defeated?, in Pinder D. (ed), *Western Europe: Challenge and Change*, London: Pinter.

Wrigley, N. (1985) *Categorical Data Analysis for Geographers and Environmental Scientists*, London: Longman.

Young, A.A. (1928) English political economy, *Economics* 9: 1–15.

Youngson, A.J. (1967) *Overhead Capital. A Study in Development Economics*, Edinburgh: Edinburgh University Press.

# Index